D0630140

HE HOLDS *my* HAND

HE HOLDS *my* HAND

EXPERIENCING GOD'S PRESENCE & PROTECTION

CAROL KENT

TYNDALE MOMENTUM™

The nonfiction imprint of Tyndale House Publishers, Inc.

Visit Tyndale online at www.tyndale.com.

Visit Tyndale Momentum online at www.tyndalemomentum.com.

TYNDALE, *Tyndale Momentum*, and Tyndale's quill logo are registered trademarks of Tyndale House Publishers, Inc. The Tyndale Momentum logo is a trademark of Tyndale House Publishers, Inc. Tyndale Momentum is the nonfiction imprint of Tyndale House Publishers, Inc., Carol Stream, Illinois.

He Holds My Hand: Experiencing God's Presence and Protection

Designed by Julie Chen

Edited by Bonne Steffen

For information about special discounts for bulk purchases, please contact Tyndale House Publishers at csresponse@tyndale.com, or call 1-800-323-9400.

ISBN 978-1-4964-2165-4

Printed in China

23 22 21 20 19 18 17
7 6 5 4 3 2 1

To my precious Mama,

Pauline Afman.

In every season of life,

you remind me to put my hand in His.

INTRODUCTION

Have you ever received an unexpected phone call that completely threw your world off its axis? It might have been a devastating diagnosis of cancer. Perhaps it was the shocking news of an accident that took the life of a family member and left someone else you love permanently disabled. But sometimes, unexpected calls bring magnificent surprises. You might have received good news about an upcoming wedding, or the announcement that a long-awaited baby is on the way. Or maybe you were offered a job or ministry position ideally suited to your gifts. Good or bad, in one moment in time, you knew your life would be forever changed by what you just heard. That's what happened to me.

The phone rang at 12:35 a.m., awakening my husband and me from a deep sleep. Gene picked up the receiver while I tried to figure out who was on the other end of the line. His face was horror-stricken as he looked at me and said, "Jason has just been arrested for the murder of his wife's ex-husband."

Nausea swept over me. I struggled to get out of bed and stand up, but my legs wouldn't hold my weight. I slumped to the floor and crawled my way into the bathroom. Thoughts swirled: *What is happening? Our son has never been in trouble before. He was a good student, a high-achieving graduate of the US Naval Academy. Did they pick up the wrong person? Is this a bad dream? Or a cruel joke?*

Soon after our son's graduation from the USNA, he had met a woman with two young daughters. We were all thrilled when they got married, and Jason loved being a husband and stepdad. Still, something unforeseen hovered on the horizon. The girls' biological father had been accused of abuse on multiple occasions, and these allegations had prevented him from having unsupervised visitation privileges. The abuse was never proven, but Jason firmly believed it was true.

Jason's first military assignment outside the continental United States was in Hawaii, which meant he, his wife, and his stepdaughters would be living far away from the girls' biological father. To complicate matters, the visitation restrictions for the girls' father were likely going to be lifted. If that happened, they would have six weeks of mandatory visits with their dad in the summer. Jason, fearing for the girls' safety, began to unravel mentally, emotionally, and spiritually. Then he did the unthinkable—he took matters into his own hands.

Grief consumed me, and I was deeply distraught with God. As a teenager, I had memorized Psalm 16:11, vowing to follow God wherever He led me: "Thou wilt shew me the path of life: in thy presence is fulness of joy; at thy right hand there are pleasures for evermore" (KJV). Now I was not feeling either joy or God's pleasure as I lashed out at Him. "How could You have allowed this to happen? I prayed for my son since he was in my womb. I tried to be the best mother I could be, raising my son to love and serve You! He was a loving husband and father who wanted to protect his stepdaughters from abuse. I am heartbroken. This is my only child, and You didn't stop him!"

Following seven postponements of his trial, Jason was convicted of murder and sentenced to life without the possibility of parole. (You can read the whole story in my book *When I Lay My Isaac Down*.) All the while, I wrestled with how to go on with life, how to reconcile what I knew to be true—that God is good and trustworthy—with the fact that even though He knew my son's heartfelt reason for his actions, God did not intervene and prevent this heinous crime.

In the middle of my sorrow, I turned to the place I had always gone for comfort—the Bible. For decades, I had been in Christian leadership—first as a teaching leader in Bible Study Fellowship and then as a speaker at Christian conferences—and I had seen women come to faith in God and grow closer to Him as they immersed themselves in His Word. Could I find the personal solace I needed in its pages now? In the beginning, it was hard to read, partly because I was still mad at God, and partly because my tears blurred the words. Still, I was desperate to hear His voice, and I longed for answers.

As time passed, I started to read a verse or passage and then would stop to think about what God was saying to me. In the past I had always read the Bible in a hurry because my life was busy and I didn't think I had time to ponder the Scriptures. But now, desperate to hear His voice, I intentionally paused long enough to comprehend the life-giving words He was speaking into me.

I soon discovered that the best way for me to "listen" to God's voice was to meditate on Scripture and then write out what I believed was His prayer over my life. And it comforted me. It was as if God took me by the hand, as a father would guide a child, and gently led me in the direction of unconditional love, renewed hope, and fresh faith. The more I read His Word and sought to understand what He was saying to me, the more comfort I experienced and the more my intimacy with Him was restored. Some of the prayers you'll read in this book were written during that difficult time.

Each day's selection begins with a relevant quotation, followed by a prayer, and ends with a Scripture verse or passage. I allowed myself literary freedom by creating these prayers in God's voice. However, the only part of each day's prayer that has the authority of God is the quoted and referenced verses from the Bible. Writing as if God were actually speaking is a way to hear His words of hope and blessing over you. It is with a sense of holy awe and reverence for Him that I've prayerfully written these entries. I have sought to present God's truth in each prayer, but only His words are absolute Truth. Whenever words included in the prayer are drawn directly from the Bible, they are in italics, with the complete Scripture included at the end.

My goal is not to provide all the answers to your tough questions, but to remind you that God holds your hand—in every situation. At His right hand there are eternal pleasures (Psalm 16:11), even in the middle of your darkest experience. Read this devotional as a complement to your regular Bible reading. Keep your Bible open as you read, and look for additional insights in the verses that capture your heart.

I pray that you'll experience the Bible in a more personalized way than ever before. As you read each day's Scripture, pause and listen to what you hear Him saying to you as you apply His truth to your daily life. Then try writing it out, making sure your notations are in line with God's truth and His character. He *does* hold your hand—and He won't let go.

January 1

A NEW BEGINNING

God is able to accomplish, provide, help, save, keep, subdue. . . . He is able to do what you can't. He already has a plan. . . . God's not bewildered. Go to him.

Max Lucado

It's a brand-new year, and there is much to do. As you look at all of your responsibilities and personal challenges, life may feel overwhelming and impossible. Your usual ability to engage in normal activities has been slowed due to unforeseen difficult circumstances. But I am a God who delights in giving new beginnings and restored hope. If you'd like a chance to start over this year, try praying: *God, make a fresh start in me, shape a Genesis week from the chaos of my life.* And I will listen. If you make Me your main priority and ask Me for wisdom about how to make good choices, I'll provide discernment and guidance as you move forward. You are not alone. I know your name and I cherish you. If you take My hand, I will walk with you and provide light for the journey ahead.

God, make a fresh start in me,
shape a Genesis week from the chaos of my life.

PSALM 51:10, MSG

—*January 2*—

LET GO OF WORRY

Worrying is carrying tomorrow's load with today's strength—carrying two days at once. It is moving into tomorrow ahead of time. Worrying doesn't empty tomorrow of its sorrow, it empties today of its strength.

Corrie ten Boom

You've been stressed and anxious about future events. There are work concerns and family issues, along with financial challenges. It's hard to concentrate on what you have to do today, because you already know the week ahead is filled with impossible situations—and you're not sure what you should do. You feel the weight of uncertainty, and it's too heavy for you to bear.

Instead of worrying, talk to Me. I love to respond to your requests. *Ask and it will be given to you; seek and you will find; knock and the door will be opened to you.* Worrying about what hasn't happened yet and about what might never happen is fruitless and only robs you of the strength you have today. You will find Me if you look for Me, and I will provide all you need in perfect timing. I am never late.

Ask and it will be given to you; seek and you will find; knock and the door will be opened to you. For everyone who asks receives; the one who seeks finds; and to the one who knocks, the door will be opened.

MATTHEW 7:7-8, NIV

January 3

REMEMBRANCE

Remember your own history with God. Think back on the times when God expressed his love for you. . . . Remember the love you felt for him, the joy, the tears? Remember how he touched you, embraced you, and led you?

Ken Gire

My child, you've been focusing on My past blessings in your life. When you felt My favor on your close relationships and life's work, you had a sense of deep contentment and satisfaction. But life is harder now—less predictable, and more difficult to figure out. You've had the fleeting thought that I've been distracted and that I'm not aware of your challenges. But I'm in the same place I've always been—right beside you. The fact that you can't see Me doesn't mean I've left. Even when you think I'm the most absent, I am ever present, so close that I'm aware of every breath you take.

Pause, breathe deeply, and remember our experiences together in the past. List the times when you felt comfort and peace in My company, and then list the times when you were no longer aware of My presence. Remember Moses? I appeared to him in a burning bush and told him he was standing on holy ground. Listen to My voice. Wherever I am is holy ground, including right here, where you are. Never forget that.

"Do not come any closer," the LORD warned. "Take off your sandals, for you are standing on holy ground."

EXODUS 3:5

January 4
WAITING

Waiting on God requires the willingness to bear uncertainty, to carry within oneself the unanswered question, lifting the heart to God about it whenever it intrudes upon one's thoughts.

Elisabeth Elliot

I want you to learn the benefits of perseverance. Sometimes you think I move too slowly, and your agenda seems more important than what you'll learn in the process of waiting. But hold on; be patient (Psalm 27:14). When you think I'm not responding to your prayer, I am already in the process of giving you an answer—just not the response you were looking for. I am choosing to be glorified in a different way than you anticipated.

Hope deferred makes the heart sick, but a dream fulfilled is a tree of life. While you wait for your answer to prayer, read My Word; listen to My voice through Scripture, through the wise counsel of people who spend time with Me, and through the inner impression of your heart as you seek My guidance. Your unanswered questions will draw you close to Me—and that's a good place to be.

Hope deferred makes the heart sick, but a dream fulfilled is a tree of life.

PROVERBS 13:12

January 5

STRENGTH

God uses chronic pain and weakness, along with other afflictions, as his chisel for sculpting our lives. Felt weakness deepens dependence on Christ for strength each day. The weaker we feel, the harder we lean. And the harder we lean, the stronger we grow spiritually.

J. I. Packer

You are stronger than you think because you belong to Me. On the surface, you feel weak, unable to cope, filled with apprehension, and uncertain about how to make important choices. You face decisions that won't wait until the road you're traveling has smoothed out. There's a mystery about the way I work that I long for you to understand: When you feel powerless and doubt your ability to handle simple decision making, that's when you can hang your weakness on My strength.

Pause and understand the mystery of My strength in your weakness. When you are at your lowest ebb, you're more inclined to surrender your will to Me because you know you can't survive without My help. The moment you admit, "I can't make it on my own. I'm hanging on to You, God; You're all I have," that's when My power works best on your behalf. Develop a daily habit of speaking this verse aloud: *I can do everything through Christ, who gives me strength.*

I can do everything through Christ, who gives me strength.

PHILIPPIANS 4:13

January 6

PRAISE WORKS

The climax of God's happiness is the delight He takes in the echoes of His excellence in the praises of His people.

John Piper

It's early in the year, and I challenge you to establish a new habit, beginning today. Start praising Me. You don't have to be in a quiet place or even alter the schedule of your day. When you are alone, speak out loud to Me with words of praise. I inhabit the praises of My people (Psalm 22:3, KJV). As you focus on Me, your spirits will be lifted and your heart encouraged.

Begin by speaking My names and My attributes—Abba Father, Holy One, Redeemer, Healer, Protector, Savior, Comforter, Creator, the Great I AM, the God for whom nothing is impossible, the One who is altogether lovely, your Hope, your Strength, your Fortress, He who is present everywhere, all-powerful and all-knowing, the One who is just, the One who forgives, the One who loves you. Pour out your praise to Me and be amazed at how much you become aware of My presence in your circumstances. I will be all of those things to you and much more. Change your focus to Me and allow your heart to break free from any discouragement.

Let us offer through Jesus a continual sacrifice of praise to God, proclaiming our allegiance to his name.

HEBREWS 13:15

January 7

FINDING PURPOSE

Purpose in life is not just something we do. It involves who we are and our way of being in the world. . . . Our heart is broken by what breaks God's heart, and we devote our energies to those purposes.

Jan Johnson

Take a moment to look back on your life—to a time when you found a purpose for living, a goal that made your life relevant and meaningful. There is great fulfillment when you do what I've designed you to do. You discover unexpected joy even when the work is hard, if you understand the reason why it's important. I created you to be different from every other person on the earth, and you'll find your deepest satisfaction when you use your gifts for My glory.

Lately it's been hard to rediscover your purpose because of the disheartening conditions you face. But obstacles become stepping-stones when you say yes to temporary discomfort in order to walk in the path I've designed for you. Sometimes I give you choices—but they will always be in accordance with My Word. I never go against My Word.

"For I know the plans I have for you," says the LORD.
"They are plans for good and not for disaster,
to give you a future and a hope."

JEREMIAH 29:11

January 8
ATTITUDES

We cannot change our past. . . . We cannot change the fact that people will act in a certain way. We cannot change the inevitable. The only thing we can do is play on the one string we have, and that is our attitude.

Charles Swindoll

Attitudes are the quiet judgments that shape your life. The apostle Paul wrote from a prison cell in Rome, "Whatever happens, conduct yourselves in a manner worthy of the gospel of Christ" (Philippians 1:27, NIV). Every day you have a choice—to give in to the negative voices that surround you, or to "live in such a way that you are a credit to the Message of Christ" (Philippians 1:27, MSG). Even when you encounter the toughest trials of life, you can choose to have an attitude like Paul's.

Study the life of Jesus. He is the ultimate example of how to live in a fallen world while maintaining a mind-set focused on My ultimate purpose. You've been discouraged because you can't control the negative actions of people close to you. When people wear you down, check your thoughts and ask Me for inner peace. "Fix your thoughts on what is true, and honorable, and right, and pure, and lovely, and admirable. . . . Keep putting into practice all you learned and received from me. . . . Then the God of peace will be with you" (Philippians 4:8-9). Ask for My help. Tap into My power and I will give you the strength to have a godly attitude in the midst of challenges.

Do everything without complaining and arguing.

PHILIPPIANS 2:14

— January 9 —

TALKING TO GOD

Beware in your prayers, above everything else, of limiting God,
not only by unbelief, but by fancying that you know what He can do.
Expect unexpected things "above all that we ask or think."

Andrew Murray

Prayer is simply a conversation with Me. You talk. I listen. You share your praises, concerns, joys, and sorrows, and sometimes you speak to Me through tears about your urgent needs. I respond to you through My Word, or sometimes through the wise counsel of people who spend a lot of time with Me. Sometimes I speak to you through the inner impression of your heart when you're meditating on Scripture and earnestly seeking My help or when you're eager to do My will.

The biggest barrier to your prayers is unbelief. Sometimes you pray, but you don't think I will answer or intervene in your situation. Have you forgotten that I'm the Creator of the universe and have immeasurable resources that I long to use on your behalf? Pray boldly and expect Me to respond. I may answer in a different way than you're expecting, but I know what's best for you and for those you love.

If you don't know what you're doing, pray to the Father. He loves to help. You'll get his help, and won't be condescended to when you ask for it. Ask boldly, believingly, without a second thought. People who "worry their prayers" are like wind-whipped waves.

JAMES 1:5-6, MSG

January 10

COMPASSION

Compassion asks us to go where it hurts, to enter into places of pain, to share in brokenness, fear, confusion, and anguish. Compassion challenges us to cry out with those in misery, to mourn with those who are lonely, to weep with those in tears.

Henri Nouwen

Look around and find someone who needs help even more than you do. One of the ways I help you grow is by asking you to do what My Son did. Search the Gospels and you'll find that Jesus looked compassionately on those who were in need, and in many instances, healing took place because He physically touched them. Begin by focusing on one person in need. Ask Me to help you find a creative way to perform a tangible act of kindness for that person. You may think you lack the financial resources to make a difference, but remember that money is often not the greatest need.

When you wait with someone who is longing for relational healing, or care for the child of a young parent who feels overwhelmed, or spend time with someone who's lonely, or pray with a friend who was betrayed by a spouse, you are following the example of Christ. You'll soon discover that when you show compassion to others, your own spirits will be lifted and My presence will surround you.

When he saw the crowds, he had compassion on them, because they were harassed and helpless, like sheep without a shepherd.

MATTHEW 9:36, NIV

January 11

GUIDANCE

God's guidance is almost always step-by-step; He does not show us our life's plan all at once. Sometimes our anxiousness to know the will of God comes from a desire to "peer over God's shoulder" to see what His plan is.

Jerry Bridges

My child, you have a longing to move on from where you are right now because nothing seems to be falling into place. You know I have a plan for you, but you are still filled with stress. You know that I delight in gently leading you through My Word and by the inner nudging of My Spirit, but you still long to skip the lessons I have for you in your current situation.

Relax. My guidance is never rushed, and the details will be revealed when the right time comes. I have always known "the best pathway for your life" (Psalm 32:8). Concentrate on what I have placed in front of you today. Look for signs of My presence as you encounter people, problems, everyday activities, and new opportunities. As you keep moving forward, you will find yourself making surprising progress—emotionally, mentally, physically, and spiritually. I will work out My plans for your life—I won't abandon you.

The LORD will work out his plans for my life—for your faithful love, O LORD, endures forever. Don't abandon me, for you made me.

PSALM 138:8

January 12

OVERCOME REJECTION

Affirming words from moms and dads are like light switches. Speak a word of affirmation at the right moment in a child's life and it's like lighting up a whole roomful of possibilities.

Gary Smalley

The hurts you grew up with jump into your mind at unexpected moments. During your formative years, you tried so hard to please the significant people in your life, but sometimes they didn't respond in a positive way. When you longed for encouraging words, you received rejection, criticism, harsh responses, or a wall of silence. It hurt then and it hurts now. You developed a hard shell to protect yourself from future pain, but it became a prison of your own making.

Hear My voice to you saying, "*I have loved you . . . with an everlasting love. With unfailing love I have drawn you to myself.*" Allow My love for you to teach you how to lavishly love others. Be open and encouraging to those around you. Do not allow any lingering emotional debris to prevent you from loving your own family well. Use what happened in your past as a foundation upon which you can build a different kind of future—one filled with caring personal relationships. Be the first person to build up another by saying out loud what he or she does well. Because you are loved by Me, you can overcome the rejection of those long-ago years and write a different future for your loved ones.

I have loved you, my people, with an everlasting love.
With unfailing love I have drawn you to myself.

JEREMIAH 31:3

January 13

FACING WINTER

The quickest way for anyone to reach the sun and the light of day is not to run west, chasing after the setting sun, but to head east, plunging into the darkness until one comes to the sunrise.

Gerald L. Sittser

Dear one, I know this feels like the longest winter of your life. Just when you thought there might be a shred of hope that you were entering a new season, you face yet another storm. The bleakness of winter—with no leaves on the trees, no colorful flowers in sight, harsh temperatures, and blustery storms—reflects your emotions. You're tempted to turn and run away from the demands of people who are counting on you. It's just too hard. Too intense. Too unfixable. Too unfair. I understand your longing for a better life.

Be encouraged. If you face the hard place and lean into Me, I'll teach you how to respond to the darkness and find light for your journey. Don't be afraid. You are not alone. Place your trembling hand in Mine, and together we'll face the obstacles until you see the light of day. Winter always turns into spring. I have a plan, and you will soon see My purpose unfold. Keep walking without wavering.

The LORD is my light and my
salvation—so why should I be afraid?
The LORD is my fortress, protecting me from danger,
so why should I tremble?

PSALM 27:1

January 14

HOPE

What gives me the most hope every day is God's grace; knowing that his grace is going to give me the strength for whatever I face, knowing that nothing is a surprise to God.

Rick Warren

Wake up every morning with hope in your heart. Look forward to what I will do for you today. One of the tools of the enemy is discouragement. He will look for your most vulnerable place and tell you that things are getting worse. He'll try to make you think that I've forgotten you and that you might as well give up. But hope brings a different perspective. Because you belong to Me, confidently anticipate how this experience can bring Me glory and be a catalyst for positive change in your life. Concentrate on My promises, and hope will replace discouragement (Romans 15:4). Instead of allowing negative thoughts to take over your mind, stay focused on what you know to be true about Me. My resources are available to you. I'm right beside you. I want the best for you. Your happiness is not dependent upon perfect circumstances or fluctuating emotions but comes through hope in Me (Psalm 146:5). I long for you to *overflow with confident hope through the power of the Holy Spirit.*

I pray that God, the source of hope, will fill you completely with joy and peace because you trust in him. Then you will overflow with confident hope through the power of the Holy Spirit.

ROMANS 15:13

— *January 15* —

UNSHAKABLE FAITH

Faith is deliberate confidence in the character of God
whose ways you may not understand at the time.

Oswald Chambers

Your world has been turned upside-down. Your family's life will never look like the happy, successful, trouble-free dream that you originally envisioned. Someone's bad choices have not only negatively impacted his own life, but by default—just because you care so much for him—every aspect of your own future will be different too. This turn of events feels unfair and makes no sense. You find yourself questioning My love for you and wondering if I'm busy elsewhere in the universe, totally unaware of your pain. In your darkest hour, you question your faith. It is real? Does it work? Is it worth it?

Go back to what you know to be true about Me. I am good. I am trustworthy. I have given you My Word as a guide for your decisions. I am faithful. I am available. I love you. Open the Bible and read, "Faith comes by hearing, and hearing by the word of God" (Romans 10:17, NKJV). The more you stay connected to My Word, the more you will realize that genuine *faith is confidence in what [you] hope for and assurance about what [you] do not see*. Unshakable faith is developed over time as you rehearse My goodness and My consistent presence with you during every step of your journey. Hold on.

Now faith is confidence in what we hope for and
assurance about what we do not see.

HEBREWS 11:1, NIV

January 16

VULNERABILITY

Revealing our weaknesses helps others feel connected to us. Fully understanding and unconditionally loving us shabby humans, Jesus shows up best in our weakness. He shines brightly through the cracks in our flawed armor.

Brenda Waggoner

I care about every aspect of your life. I've watched you pull away from relationships because you don't want to reveal wounds from the past. You feel too fragile to open yourself up to the possibility of being judged. Sometimes you are too afraid of rejection. You dread a look, a comment, or someone hearing your story and turning away. The potential humiliation doesn't feel worth the risk. It's easier to withdraw, to avoid social gatherings—even church—because your emotions are raw. You are isolating yourself by avoiding close, open relationships with others—even with people you used to call friends.

I have news for you. If you open up with others, people will be comfortable telling you their own imperfect stories. You will create an atmosphere of trust. Begin by being honest with Me about your sorrows, your fears, and your pain. Then be alert for the day when I bring someone into your life who desperately needs to hear what you've been through. Your vulnerability will create a safe place for that person to speak about his or her own experience.

All my longings lie open before you, Lord;
my sighing is not hidden from you.

PSALM 38:9, NIV

January 17

SILENCE

Silence is the room we create for the searching of God,
where we hear His voice and follow.

Mark Buchanan

Your life is filled with voices—some giving advice, some clamoring for attention, others possibly casting blame. Another voice comes from the enemy: "You're too weak. You will never get through this ordeal. You don't have enough resources. No one really cares about you. Just give up!" At times these voices give so many conflicting ideas that you want to scream or escape into sleep—just to flee the sound of so much input.

Stop. Be intentional about creating a quiet place where you can hear My voice. Turn off all outside sounds. Get away from the chaos around you and listen to Me. Cease striving and study My character. I maintain the same position I've always had—in sovereign control. Begin by worshiping Me. Speak My names out loud. Thank Me for what you are learning in your current situation. Read a Scripture that brings you hope. I delight in hearing your prayers. Concentrate on My power to do what looks impossible. Expect Me to work on your behalf.

Be still, and know that I am God; I will be exalted among the nations, I will be exalted in the earth.

PSALM 46:10, NIV

January 18

RELINQUISHMENT

We can hug our hurts and make a shrine out of our sorrows or we can offer them to God as a sacrifice of praise. The choice is ours.

Richard Exley

Seek to do My will above all else. Every fiber of your being wants to control the outcome in your hard places. You wish your loved one would stop being self-destructive. You long for a day when everything goes according to your well-ordered plan, but life hasn't provided that kind of security for a long time. Most of all, you wish the person closest to you would worship Me gladly without having to be reminded of how important it is to put Me in the place of highest honor. Everything feels out of your hands.

Heart sacrifices demand relinquishment. Identify someone or something precious to you. Verbalize your willingness to let go of your control over that person or situation. This is your act of worship to Me. Take a deep breath as you embrace My love while loosening your grip. Say, "Lord, I rest in the outcome, even if I'm not allowed to understand the reason for this sacrifice. I'm letting go."

This is what the LORD says: Because you have obeyed me and have not withheld even your son, your only son, I swear by my own name that I will certainly bless you.

GENESIS 22:16-17

January 19

SINGING

Every good gift that we have had from the cradle up has come from God. If a man just stops to think what he has to praise God for, he will find there is enough to keep him singing praises for a week.

D. L. Moody

Come into My presence with gladness, focusing on My gifts to you. Begin with short prayers. "Lord, my heart rejoices because You have given me life. Father, You provide shelter and food for me and for my family. You have given me friends who bless me during my struggles. You comfort me in my times of sorrow. You cover me with Your presence. You listen when I confide in You and protect me when I pray. I praise You for Your loving-kindness."

Now begin singing to Me. You can start with hymns like "Amazing Grace" or "Great Is Thy Faithfulness." I am not concerned about the quality of your singing voice but about the heart behind the song. In the midst of your personal crisis, come before Me with singing. It will transform your attitude and put you in a place of readiness to receive what I have for you. Pause for a while, and let Me sing over you through My Word. Read Scripture and hear My voice speaking to you.

Shout with joy to the LORD, all the earth! Worship the LORD with gladness. Come before him, singing with joy. Acknowledge that the LORD is God! He made us, and we are his. We are his people, the sheep of his pasture.

PSALM 100:1-3

January 20

INTERRUPTIONS

We must be ready to allow ourselves to be interrupted by God.

Dietrich Bonhoeffer

Learn to trust Me by following My call. You have an agenda that seems right, and your natural inclination is to develop a strategy that seems practical, predictable, and timely. It's easier for you to trust Me when everything makes sense and you can foresee a positive outcome. However, there are times when I will interrupt your carefully made plans and ask you to do something that makes no sense.

Always remember My great love for you and My desire to give you opportunities to minister to others along the way. Often, the most important appointment in your day will come disguised as an unwanted disruption. Some people around you need to learn from you, and I will bring others into your life to help you find renewed hope and fresh faith. Interruptions are often divine surprises that will bless your life in unexpected ways. Keep following My call, and you will be in for the adventure of a lifetime.

A little farther up the shore he saw two other brothers, James and John, sitting in a boat with their father, Zebedee, repairing their nets. And he called them to come, too. They immediately followed him, leaving the boat and their father behind.

MATTHEW 4:21-22

January 21

WISDOM

Wisdom is the right use of knowledge.

Charles Spurgeon

Do you want to discover wisdom? Turn your ears and eyes to My Word. As you travel life's journey, you will discover many people and resources that appear to be pointing you in the right direction. Sometimes there will be uneasiness in your spirit, and doubt will linger in your mind as you prepare for what is ahead. Learn to recognize these signs as the gentle leading of the Holy Spirit.

The more you store up the truth in My Word by memorizing Scripture, the more discernment you will have. If you believe you lack wisdom, "you should ask God, who gives generously to all without finding fault, and it will be given to you" (James 1:5, NIV). Ask Me for insight and understanding. Earnestly seek answers from Me. You will find My wisdom if you search for it. Come to Me first, and I will lead you to the right use of knowledge.

Wisdom is more precious than rubies, and nothing you desire can compare with her.

PROVERBS 8:11, NIV

— January 22 —

DEMONSTRATING LOVE

In the New Testament, love is more of a verb than a noun. It has more to do with acting than with feeling. The call to love is not so much a call to a certain state of feeling as it is to a quality of action.

R. C. Sproul

There is someone in your life who is hard to love. Deep in your heart you know it will please Me if you choose to love that person, but your natural inclination is to turn away, hoping your omission will not be too obvious. However, the angst you feel is causing you lack of sleep and an uncertainty about how to move forward. You're wasting too much energy on avoiding this person.

Practice a new way of responding. Even if you feel no love at first, begin by doing one loving act of service for that person. Be creative as you consider all the possibilities at your disposal. Think of My great love for you. I loved the world so much that I gave My one and only Son so you could be free from sin and enter into a personal relationship with Me. Your gesture of love will be a testimony to those who are watching that you belong to Me.

Now I am giving you a new commandment: Love each other. Just as I have loved you, you should love each other. Your love for one another will prove to the world that you are my disciples.

JOHN 13:34-35

January 23

GOD CARES

God does care. God does know what He is doing. He asks us to trust Him. He asks us to remember who we are trying to understand—even when it doesn't make sense at all.

Dee Brestin

I am the ultimate source of your help. It's been tempting to think I'm taking care of everyone except you—but that's not true. I see you. I know your needs. I know your pain. I am fully acquainted with what you are going through. Sometimes you allow anxiety to fill your mind before you think of Me. You've been finding it easier to give in to fear, stress, and quiet grumblings of the heart: *If only I had more people to come alongside and walk with me. If only I had unlimited wealth to meet my loved one's needs. If only God would demonstrate His love to me in a more tangible way. After all, He owns "the cattle on a thousand hills" (Psalm 50:10); why doesn't He rescue me?*

My help comes when you humble yourself before Me. It takes courage to admit that you need assistance. *Come to me, all of you who are weary and carry heavy burdens, and I will give you rest.* Lean on Me instead of trying to do everything yourself. Casting your worries on Me doesn't mean you don't need to do anything. It means you do what you can—and trust Me for the rest. I will take care of you.

Come to me, all of you who are weary and carry heavy burdens, and I will give you rest.

MATTHEW 11:28

January 24
SURRENDER

I saw that my hand was in another hand. That hand was pierced . . . it was Jesus' hand. I never before understood what surrender meant—our weak hand in Jesus' strong hand! His strength in our life! Surrender to the Lord Jesus is dynamic and relaxed.

Corrie ten Boom

You've been resisting a key part of the Christian life: surrender. On the surface, surrendering seems like abdicating responsibility and not following through. But the truth is that surrendering simplifies things. It's yielding to the nudge of My Spirit and allowing Me to gently lead you. You thought it was an admission of defeat and giving in to your fatigue. But the kind of surrender I want you to learn is very different from that.

Place your hand in My nail-pierced hand and allow yourself to follow Me, even though you have no idea where we're going. Realize that your timing is not My timing and be patient. Practice the mind-set of expecting a miracle without having any idea of how I will provide the answer to your prayer. Believe that I know the end from the beginning and I know how all the puzzle pieces of your life fit together. Your hand in mine—this is the beginning of surrender.

Now I will take the load from your shoulders; I will free your hands from their heavy tasks.

PSALM 81:6

— *January 25* —

ABIDE

God says that He is our dwelling place, and the Bible contains all the necessary papers, duly attested and signed. And our Lord invites us, nay more, commands us to enter in and abide there. In effect He says, "God is your dwelling place, and you must see to it that you take up your abode there. You must move in."

Hannah Whitall Smith

I long for intimate fellowship with you. When you accepted the sacrifice of Jesus Christ on the cross for you and invited Me into your life, I became your dwelling place. You have been invited to *abide in me* with all the protection, wise counsel, and safety that accompany a personal relationship. You might think a relationship like this would take a lot of effort, but that's not how I've designed it.

Abiding in Me can become a natural rhythm of your living and breathing. It is not work that engages your mind during every moment. It is a matter of entrusting yourself to My keeping, accepting My everlasting love, and believing by faith that My holy presence will protect you from the enemy—even during the many everyday moments when you need to be occupied with other things. Your heart can have rest and peace as you settle into the inner comfort of knowing that you have My constant presence.

Abide in me, and I in you. As the branch cannot bear fruit by itself, unless it abides in the vine, neither can you, unless you abide in me.

JOHN 15:4, ESV

— January 26 —

JOY

Joy is a process, a journey—often muffled, sometimes detoured; a mystery in which we participate, not a product we can grasp. It grows and regenerates as we have the courage to let go and trust the process.

Tim Hansel

Let Me help you discover the source of joy. Your life has not been easy recently, and you feel like you are on a detour that isn't going anywhere. You've tried to put a smile on your face to mask the pain inside, but it makes you feel deceitful, like you're trying to hide the truth. Your focus has been on all of the things that have gone wrong—and listing them one by one in your mind drags you even deeper into the valley of despair.

It's only possible to choose joy when you focus on its source. When you know Me, I become the foundation of your joy. When I live within you, our relationship is not a once-in-a-while experience. As you pass through pain, grief, or sorrow, you can still rejoice in Me because I will never leave you. Read My Word and you will see the word *joy* again and again. Joy is a part of the fruit of the Spirit (Galatians 5:22). Shout with joy to Me (Psalm 66:1). "Weeping may endure for a night, but joy cometh in the morning" (Psalm 30:5, KJV). As My Son approached the end of His life on earth, it was the prospect of the joy set before Him that gave Him the strength to endure the Cross (Hebrews 12:2). Just as it gave Christ strength, let My joy give you strength today.

Let all who take refuge in you rejoice; let them sing joyful praises forever. Spread your protection over them, that all who love your name may be filled with joy.

PSALM 5:11

— *January 27* —

HIS PRESENCE

Wide awake to the presence of God, I realized I had been so focused on asking why a good God allowed bad things to happen that I was missing out on the nearness of God all along. In becoming preoccupied with the *why*, I was missing the *who*.

Margaret Feinberg

I am waiting for you to practice the conscious awareness of My presence. Instead, you've been questioning why your all-powerful God would allow bad things to take place and produce heavy challenges in your life. With each doubt, you've been moving further away from experiencing the closeness we once had.

Beginning today, set a time to intentionally contemplate our relationship. Ask Me to comfort you, convict you, and lead you according to My will. Deliberately reflect on My works, My care for you in the past, and My character. An awareness of My presence will bring peace, joy, and love even when you are surrounded by troublesome distractions. Remember the words of Jacob: "Surely the LORD is in this place, and I was not aware of it" (Genesis 28:16, NIV). My presence is always with you.

You will show me the path of life; in Your presence is fullness of joy; at Your right hand are pleasures forevermore.

PSALM 16:11, NKJV

January 28

REDEMPTION

When suffering shatters the carefully kept vase that is our lives, God stoops to pick up the pieces. But he doesn't put them back together as a restoration project . . . he sifts through the rubble and selects some of the shards as raw material for another project—a mosaic that tells the story of redemption.

Ken Gire

I specialize in freeing people from bondage. You often think back to easier, less stressful times in your life and wish for a return to better days. But I want you to understand the meaning of redemption. It always involves going from something to something else. I freed you from the bondage of the law to give you freedom—a new life. The precious blood of Christ obtained your release from sin.

As you walk on the path I've established for your future, you will not be returning to the past. I am taking the hurts, the hard-fought battles, the wounds, and the kernels of your earlier faith, and I'm forming them into something brand new—a maturing faith that will be a megaphone to the world, proclaiming that I am the God of restoration and resurrection. Your testimony will be an example that will point others to Me—and help them find their own stories of redemption.

In him we have redemption through his blood,
the forgiveness of sins, in accordance with the riches
of God's grace that he lavished on us.

EPHESIANS 1:7-8, NIV

January 29

COURAGE

Courage isn't a feeling that you wait for.
Courage is doing when you don't have courage.
Courage is doing it scared.

Jill Briscoe

When you are faced with foreboding circumstances, beware of fear that comes in without warning. You can choose bravery if you ask Me for help. It's easy to look around and do what pleases people. Instead, practice Christian courage—the willingness to say and do the right thing, regardless of what anyone else thinks. Acts of valor are often painful—emotionally and mentally—especially when they involve confrontation or controversy.

A brave faith develops when you replace self-confidence with God-confidence. When you lack faith in My promises, you shrink back in fear. But when you practice God-confidence, you "take every thought captive to obey Christ" (2 Corinthians 10:5, ESV); you recognize the enemy (1 Peter 5:8); you wield the shield of faith and grip the sword of My Word (Ephesians 6:16-17). A bold reliance on Me will enable you to do more—exceedingly more—than you ever thought possible.

Be strong and courageous, all you who put your hope in the LORD!

PSALM 31:24

January 30

ONE THING

He's calling us to the Great Exchange—the one where we can never lose. As we trade the "many things" that make us anxious, He gives us the "one thing" that calms our hearts. Himself.

Joanna Weaver

Slow down. Breathe. Pause before Me. You have been bowed down with responsibilities that I never wanted you to carry. You often believe that by doing more, you are serving Me more effectively, but in reality you are worn out and uneasy. You're running on empty—driven by deadlines, schedules, appointments, and responsibilities. That makes you critical of people who don't appear to be doing their fair share of the work. It causes stress between you and Me and between you and others.

Find the balance I intend for you. Listen to My voice through reading My Word. Make Me the "one thing" you focus on first. Expect Me to speak to you about key decisions in your life. Then act on what you believe I'm asking you to do. When you take time to concentrate on My Word, you'll discover that you have plenty of time for the rest of your responsibilities.

There is only one thing worth being concerned about. Mary has discovered it, and it will not be taken away from her.

LUKE 10:42

January 31

THE COST AND THE PRIVILEGE

If you look up into His face and say, "Yes, Lord, whatever it costs," at that moment He'll flood your life with His presence and power.

Alan Redpath

There is a cost to being a follower of Jesus Christ. You may be ridiculed, laughed at, mocked, or humiliated on social media. You might lose respect from family or friends. There may even be times when you experience physical danger or harm because you choose to lift up My name and call yourself a Christian. Following Me does not exclude you from hurt or public embarrassment.

But the benefits are great. You have My presence and My power. You have access to My wisdom and direction. I am always at work, doing more than you can see. The more you trust in Me, the bolder you become in your faith. And as you move forward in confidence, the message of Jesus Christ will reach a world that desperately needs to hear it. The glorious paradox for you is that there is joy amidst the sacrifice, and spiritual riches that far outweigh the cost. The privilege is unspeakably holy.

Our hearts ache, but we always have joy.
We are poor, but we give spiritual riches to others.
We own nothing, and yet we have everything.

2 CORINTHIANS 6:10

February 1

ANGELS

Believers, look up—take courage. The angels are nearer than you think.

Billy Graham

Good and loyal angels are My agents who serve Me by doing My will. They are ministering spirits sent out "to care for people who will inherit salvation" (Hebrews 1:14). They are mighty in strength, and they carry out My specific instructions (Psalm 103:20-21). I often act independently, without the involvement of angelic beings, but sometimes I direct them in ministry to you.

Today, concentrate on how much security and safety I provide for you. My Word reminds you, *He will order his angels to protect you wherever you go.* My angels set up a circle of protection around you (Psalm 34:7). And there might come a day when you have the privilege of entertaining one of My angels. "Show hospitality to strangers, for some who have done this have entertained angels without realizing it!" (Hebrews 13:2). The closer you are to Me, the more you will understand the role of angels in My care for you.

He will order his angels to protect you wherever you go.

PSALM 91:11

— February 2 —

SEEKING GOD

We shouldn't seek answers as much as we should seek God. . . . If you seek answers you won't find them, but if you seek God, the answers will find you.

Mark Batterson

Stay calm as you await the answers to your questions. Your prayers have been desperate as you've poured out your desires before Me. You've been telling Me how you want your prayers to be answered, and you are unwilling to wait as My will unfolds in a different time frame than the one you want. You are telling Me what needs to happen—implying that your plan is better than Mine.

That's not how seeking My will works. When you earnestly seek Me, you set your mind and heart on Me, not on what I can do for you. Don't let your pride stand in the way. Humble yourself. My promise to you is that you will find Me if you seek Me. "Anyone who wants to come to him must believe that God exists and that he rewards those who sincerely seek him" (Hebrews 11:6). The answers to your questions and your prayers will come when you seek Me first.

Seek the Kingdom of God above all else, and live righteously, and he will give you everything you need.

MATTHEW 6:33

February 3

GIVE THANKS

If we ask God for a calm, thankful heart that sees all the blessings His grace imparts, He can teach us many lessons in illness that can never be learned in health.

David Jeremiah

Begin each day with thanksgiving on your lips. Physical and emotional pain distract you from concentrating on My goodness and mercy. The enemy taunts, "A good God would never allow you to suffer such pain." But Satan is defeated when you choose a heart of gratitude. Thankfulness in the middle of difficulty is a sacrifice that pleases Me.

Gratitude is the key that will turn your outlook around. Giving thanks defeats the enemy and changes your attitude from despair to hope. The recipe is in My Word: "Always be joyful. Never stop praying. Be thankful in all circumstances, for this is God's will for you who belong to Christ Jesus" (1 Thessalonians 5:16-18). Discover the power of a thankful heart.

It is good to give thanks to the LORD,
to sing praises to the Most High.
It is good to proclaim your unfailing love in the morning,
your faithfulness in the evening.

PSALM 92:1-2

February 4

HOLINESS

Holiness is about pleasing God—living in such a way that it's clear you belong to Him. Holiness is what makes you unique as a believer in Jesus Christ.

Kay Arthur

Holiness begins when you enter into a relationship with Me. I bought you with a price—the blood of Jesus Christ—and I forgave your sins. I have set you apart and moved you from the world's kingdom to My Kingdom. I don't force you to follow Me, but I delight when you choose to honor Me, obey Me, and worship Me.

Being holy is not following a list of legalistic rules and harsh guidelines. It is having a heart that turns away from darkness and focuses on living every day in the light of My truth. As you seek to live a holy life, come to Me for direction and wisdom. Think pure thoughts. Live righteously. Speak words that encourage and build up others. You are set apart. Embrace the call to live by My principles.

I am sending you to the Gentiles to open their eyes, so they may turn from darkness to light and from the power of Satan to God. Then they will receive forgiveness for their sins and be given a place among God's people, who are set apart by faith in me.

ACTS 26:17-18

— February 5 —

CONTENTMENT

Contentment should be the hallmark of the man or woman who has put his or her affairs in the hands of God.

W. Phillip Keller

Contentment comes when you are at peace with your possessions, status, and situation in life. In your own strength, achieving it is an impossible task. Your natural inclination is to allow jealousy and self-pity to take root. That brings resentment, and you're then tempted to covet the favorable life, excellent job, financial security, close-knit family, or apparent happiness of someone else.

But I'm inviting you to view your circumstances through My eyes. It's too hard to move forward without confidence in My care. When you trust that I am in sovereign control of your hardships, you can press into a safe place where there is rest, peace, and a different kind of contentment—a satisfaction not based on financial security or physical comfort, a serenity that can only be experienced when your focus is on a life beyond this one. It's a life free from physical pressures, debilitating jealousy, emotional challenges, mental anxiety, and the control of hurtful people. It's a deliberate choice to put your affairs into My hands.

I have learned how to be content with whatever I have. I know how to live on almost nothing or with everything. I have learned the secret of living in every situation, whether it is with a full stomach or empty, with plenty or little. For I can do everything through Christ, who gives me strength.

PHILIPPIANS 4:11-13

— February 6 —

FAVOR

God will not permit any troubles to come upon us, unless He has a specific plan by which great blessing can come out of the difficulty.

Peter Marshall

Look for My favor amid your difficulties. When you are in the middle of a hardship, it's easy to think nothing is going right and no one is looking out for you. Your temptation is to believe that I'm not aware of all that's gone wrong. Always remember that I'm an omnipresent God, and I am well acquainted with your sorrow.

Begin looking at your circumstances with new eyes. Search for the places where you've experienced My favor. Sometimes, favor comes in the form of unexpected acts of kindness from the people close to you. At other times, I will bless you with a passage from My Word that's so personal you will know it's intended specifically for your situation. I want you to experience double-portion blessings in the land of your suffering that are greater than you might ever have known if life had been easier. It brings Me great joy to shower My favor on you.

Joseph found favor in his eyes and became his attendant. Potiphar put him in charge of his household, and he entrusted to his care everything he owned. From the time he put him in charge of his household and of all that he owned, the LORD blessed the household of the Egyptian because of Joseph.

GENESIS 39:4-5, NIV

— *February 7* —

HIS IMAGE BEARER

You weren't an accident. You weren't mass produced. You aren't an assembly-line product. You were deliberately planned, specifically gifted, and lovingly positioned on the earth by the Master Craftsman.

Max Lucado

I created you in My likeness. It grieves Me when you put yourself down by saying you have no talent and when you act like you are without value. Sometimes your dissatisfaction isn't spoken, but you treat yourself poorly because you feel insignificant.

Change your thought pattern. Today say out loud, "God created me in His image, and I have been uniquely equipped to do His work in this world." Ask Me to reveal how you can reflect My creativity. Reflect on what you would do with your life if money, current challenges, and time were not obstacles. Consider Ephesians 2:10: "For we are God's handiwork, created in Christ Jesus to do good works, which God prepared in advance for us to do" (NIV). I have big plans for you, and I have given you everything you need to accomplish My purpose for your life.

God created human beings in his own image. In the image of God he created them; male and female he created them.

GENESIS 1:27

— February 8 —

DEFEATING FEAR

Fear is a self-imposed prison that will keep you from becoming what God intends for you to be. You *must* move against it with the weapons of faith and love.

Rick Warren

You can defeat fear if you acknowledge Me as your Protector, your Strength, your Victor, and your God. Faith and love always cast out fear. Do not allow apprehension, fright, and uncertainty to occupy your thoughts. Make room for the powerful change that faith and love will bring to your mind and heart. "There is no fear in love. But perfect love drives out fear, because fear has to do with punishment. The one who fears is not made perfect in love" (1 John 4:18, NIV).

When fear knocks at your door, it will often bring dangerous options: emotional paralysis, denial, bitterness, and escape into destructive choices. Don't let fear into your heart. Instead, use the weapons of faith and love. Whenever you experience sorrow for the things that trigger your fear, express that sadness to Me. That will lead you to a place of humbly asking for My help. By submitting yourself to My authority while embracing My love, you will begin turning fear into fresh faith, renewed hope, and purposeful action.

Do not fear, for I am with you; do not be dismayed,
for I am your God. I will strengthen you and help you;
I will uphold you with my righteous right hand.

ISAIAH 41:10, NIV

February 9

OBEDIENCE

God is God. If He is God, He is worthy of my worship and my service. I will find rest nowhere but in His will, and that will is infinitely, immeasurably, unspeakably beyond my largest notions of what He is up to.

Elisabeth Elliot

The key to knowing My will is to obey the Holy Spirit. If you are willing to trust Me, obey Me, and live a holy life, I will reveal Myself to you and make known the next steps you need to take. Some of those steps are life altering; others are day-to-day decisions that will keep you in line with My will. Yet sometimes you question why I allow certain things to happen, and you desire an easier path.

My child, you have been reluctant to trust Me with the details of your life, fearing that your own plans will be changed. But My plans for your future are infinitely better than anything you might have envisioned. I created you, I love you, and I know the purpose for which I made you. The true test of your love for Me is obedience. That's the secret to discovering My will for your life.

This is love: that we walk in obedience to his commands. As you have heard from the beginning, his command is that you walk in love.

2 JOHN 1:6, NIV

— *February 10* —

FREEDOM

Freedom is an inside job.

Sam Keen

Personal liberty is something you've been taking for granted. You make decisions about what your daily activities will be, and you move around at will. But freedom on the inside involves being at peace even during circumstances that, humanly speaking, could make you feel confined or out of control. That kind of inner contentment can be hard won, but it's worth every bit of the effort it takes. Trust Me enough to believe that there will be unexpected benefits and divine surprises along the way to attaining a God-dependent state of mind.

I sent Jesus to be the Savior of the world in order to give you liberty. The freedom He offers makes it possible to live in the middle of unresolved issues and tight spots and still experience inner peace. At times, you still try to live by a man-made list of impossible rules, but what I'm offering brings relaxation instead of stress. The apostle Paul wrote, "Now the Lord is the Spirit, and where the Spirit of the Lord is, there is liberty" (2 Corinthians 3:17, NASB). Take time to itemize the extraordinary ways you're experiencing release from anxiety on the inside.

Christ has truly set us free. Now make sure that you stay free, and don't get tied up again in slavery to the law.

GALATIANS 5:1

— *February 11* —

GRACE

Grace is getting what you don't deserve,
and *not* getting what you do deserve.

Justin Holcomb

Have you embraced the benefits of My unlimited grace? Instead of carrying around guilt for bad choices, you can experience complete forgiveness. Instead of striving for perfection or trying to be "good enough," you're set free to worship a perfect God who points you in the right direction. When you humbly confessed your sin and received salvation through My Son's sacrifice on the cross, you received My "no-strings-attached" grace. You didn't earn it. You didn't work for it. It was free. "If, by the trespass of the one man [Adam], death reigned through that one man, how much more will those who receive God's abundant provision of grace and of the gift of righteousness reign in life through the one man, Jesus Christ" (Romans 5:17, NIV).

Now it's time for you to live in the endless provision of My boundless grace and to let others know that they, too, can be free from shame, regret, and second-guessing their past decisions. Shout it from the rooftops: "God's grace covers your past. God's grace exchanges a heavy heart for a light heart. Run to Him and find what you've been looking for—a place of acceptance, complete forgiveness, and the warmest welcome you've ever received. Embrace grace!"

God saved you by his grace when you believed. And you can't take credit for this; it is a gift from God. Salvation is not a reward for the good things we have done, so none of us can boast about it.

EPHESIANS 2:8-9

— February 12 —

SOMEBODIES

One of Jesus' specialties is to make "somebodies" out of "nobodies."

Henrietta Mears

Your past does not disqualify you from being a recipient of My love. There is nothing you have ever done that will keep Me from loving you. I see your sadness over past wrong choices. I'm aware of the times you looked in the mirror and wondered if anyone could ever genuinely care for you. I know the enemy throws accusations at you, trying to make you feel unworthy of redemption and undeserving of My forgiveness. But he's a liar and an accuser. Tell him he has no power over your thoughts or your life. You belong to Me, and you are valuable to Me.

Remind yourself how much you mean to Me: I made you in My own image. I gifted you for service. I love you with an everlasting love. I comfort you when you're filled with sorrow. I gave My Son's life on the cross for you and want you to spend eternity with Me in heaven. You are somebody very special to Me!

You made all the delicate, inner parts of my body and knit me together in my mother's womb. Thank you for making me so wonderfully complex! Your workmanship is marvelous—how well I know it. . . . How precious are your thoughts about me, O God. They cannot be numbered! I can't even count them; they outnumber the grains of sand! And when I wake up, you are still with me!

PSALM 139:13-14, 17-18

February 13

EQUIPPED

Just as God gave Moses exactly what he needed to accomplish great things, he will equip us in the same way. If he calls us to slay giants, he will make us into giant slayers.

Christine Caine

I will provide everything you need to complete the tasks that lie ahead. You've seen the surrounding "mountains," and they look intimidating—physical limitations, financial challenges, relational entanglements, fear of failure, and past mistakes. You've struggled for so long that becoming a confident giant slayer seems out of the question.

Always remember that I'm on your side. You belong to Me. I cover you with My protection. When you seek Me, I equip you with My armor. It's My delight to outfit you for spiritual battle. My will, My truth, My power, and My protection are available to you at any time of the day or night. At this very moment, I am waiting for you to ask Me for wisdom to face the impossible situation that looms ahead. I never designed you to go through life alone. I will *equip you with all you need.* There is no tool more valuable than My Word to supply you with everything that's needed for personal growth and spiritual survival.

May he equip you with all you need for doing his will. May he produce in you, through the power of Jesus Christ, every good thing that is pleasing to him. All glory to him forever and ever! Amen.

HEBREWS 13:21

— *February 14* —

COSTLY LOVE

To love the Lord my God with all my soul will involve a spiritual cost. I'll have to give Him my heart, and let Him love through it whom and how He wills, even if this seems at times to break my heart.

Helen Roseveare

I know you are struggling with this reality right now—not everyone will love you. Often, the greatest hurts come because the person from whom you most long to receive affirmation, encouragement, approval, and love is the person who shuts you out, emotionally and physically. It's a severe rejection that tears your heart apart—especially when everyone around you is receiving unconditional love from their family members.

I am asking you to love that person even if your kindness, goodness, and mercy are not returned. Do your loving acts as if you are doing them to Me. Those around you may know what it costs you to serve without thanks, or to minister to the dying, or to extend kindness to the one who rejects you. The Bible says, "Love means doing what God has commanded us, and he has commanded us to love one another, just as you heard from the beginning" (2 John 1:6). Your costly love does not go unnoticed by Me.

Your love for one another will prove to the world that you are my disciples.

JOHN 13:35

— *February 15* —

ENCOURAGEMENT

Encourage one another. Many a time a word of praise or thanks or appreciation or cheer has kept a man on his feet.

William Barclay

A word of cheer lifts the heart. There are times when your mind is filled with innumerable pressures, and an unexpected word of blessing changes the course of your day. Suddenly your perspective is more hopeful. Your vision focuses on promising outcomes. Your confidence in My truth is strengthened. Your faith is renewed.

I've designed you to be an encourager. Your words can tear down or raise someone's spirits. The choice is yours. As you go through your day, look for people who need to hear words of appreciation. Let them know how they have inspired or blessed you. Honestly thank them for the way they demonstrate what it means to offer their gifts to others. Your own attitude will be uplifted as you engage in blessing them with supportive words. Build others up "according to their needs, that it may benefit those who listen" (Ephesians 4:29, NIV).

Encourage one another and build each other up,
just as in fact you are doing.

1 THESSALONIANS 5:11, NIV

— February 16 —

CONFIDENCE

Do not strive in your own strength; cast yourself at the feet of the Lord Jesus, and wait upon Him in the sure confidence that He is with you, and works in you. . . . Strive in prayer; let faith fill your heart; so will you be strong in the Lord and in the power of His might.

Andrew Murray

You can confidently rely on Me. The world wants you to be self-confident, to believe that you have what it takes to flourish in uncertain times, based entirely on your own abilities. Confidence in yourself has huge limitations, but confidence in Me gives you something solid to stand on, because you can fully depend on Me. When you have self-confidence, you believe you can do anything you set your mind to. But with God-confidence, the burden for success doesn't rest on you. As you develop confidence in Me, you'll learn how to turn fear into faith and how to exchange shyness for boldness.

Another major benefit is in your prayer life. "This is the confidence we have in approaching God: that if we ask anything according to his will, he hears us" (1 John 5:14, NIV). You can also receive the promise of My blessing. "But blessed are those who trust in the LORD and have made the LORD their hope and confidence" (Jeremiah 17:7). The main key to God-confidence is knowing that you are deeply loved by Me and that I will use My power and My wisdom on your behalf. I will give you confidence to face each day.

For I can do everything through Christ, who gives me strength.

PHILIPPIANS 4:13

February 17

HELD

Wherever you are spiritually, whatever you have been through emotionally, you are already wrapped in the Lord's embrace. Held close by nail-scarred hands. Enfolded in the arms of One who believes in you, supports you, treasures you, and loves you.

Liz Curtis Higgs

I am holding you. Don't let troubling news or unexpected obstacles throw you off course. You feel emotionally vulnerable and physically weak, but you are not alone. I am a shield around you, and I will hold your head high.

Rejoice in My Word as one who has found a great treasure (Psalm 119:162). Within the pages of the Bible, you will discover that even if your father and mother abandon you, I will hold you close (Psalm 27:10). Close your eyes and talk to Me. Take a deep breath and know that I'm wrapping you in My embrace and enfolding you in My arms. That's how precious you are to Me. I'm holding you, and I won't let go.

I cling to you; your strong right hand holds me securely.

PSALM 63:8

— February 18 —

BOLDNESS

Past boldness is no assurance of future boldness.
Boldness demands continual reliance on God's Spirit.

Andy Stanley

Supernatural spiritual boldness is a trait of those who have great faith—of those who are fully relying on My Spirit. At one time you spoke My truth with passion. You urged others to consider the claims of Christ and then challenged them to embark on adventuresome missions that would further My Kingdom work in their day-to-day lives and far beyond. But now you hesitate to share your faith. You've become more cautious and less vocal in expressing your beliefs to others. Your trials have made you withdrawn and uncertain.

Take time to evaluate what's happened between us. Your boldness has cooled because you've been relying on your own strength instead of fully depending upon Me to be the source of your faith and confidence. Boldness does not come from education or special training. It's the natural outgrowth of spending time with Me. Out of that close relationship comes a vibrant assurance that compels you to tell others about what I've done for you and what I can do for them. When your heart and Mine are knit together, you overflow with an effervescent testimony of how the gospel can transform lives.

The members of the council were amazed when they saw the boldness of Peter and John, for they could see that they were ordinary men with no special training in the Scriptures. They also recognized them as men who had been with Jesus.

ACTS 4:13

February 19

SELF-CONTROL

Feelings are indicators, not dictators. . . . They can indicate where your heart is in the moment, but that doesn't mean they have the right to dictate your behavior and boss you around. You are more than the sum total of your feelings and perfectly capable of that little gift from Jesus called self-control.

Lysa TerKeurst

It takes more than willpower to master self-control. When you face disappointing circumstances and uncooperative people, you're tempted to reward yourself with short-term indulgences that are mostly destructive. Consider your approach to life and determine where you need to exercise wise judgment.

"A person without self-control is like a city with broken-down walls" (Proverbs 25:28). Don't allow negative feelings to control your moods. Avoid choices that are damaging to your health and finances (Proverbs 21:20). Work hard to control your temper—when someone wrongs you, "it is a great virtue to ignore it" (Proverbs 19:11, GNT). Most of all, remember that I have given you "a spirit not of fear but of power and love and self-control" (2 Timothy 1:7, ESV). Biblical self-control is about being controlled by Christ.

Prepare your minds for action and exercise self-control. Put all your hope in the gracious salvation that will come to you when Jesus Christ is revealed to the world.

1 PETER 1:13

February 20

IMPERFECT PEOPLE

It's Satan's delight to tell me that once he's got me, he will keep me. But at that moment I can go back to God. And I know that if I confess my sins, God is faithful and just to forgive me.

Alan Redpath

I specialize in transforming the lives of people who have made wrong choices. When you feel like you've come to the end of your rope and the record of your past behavior suggests you're beyond redemption, look to Me. The enemy ridicules you by planting negative thoughts in your mind: *You've blown it! God could never use you! You are an embarrassment to the cause of Christ. The bad decisions that have shaped your life disqualify you from Christian service.*

Listen up! When you come to Me and ask for forgiveness and redemption, that's the moment you begin to turn weakness into strength. I have always used imperfect people to do My work. Once your sin is confessed and you realize what you've been saved from, your arrogance turns to humility. You know you can't make it on your own, and you ask for My empowerment. You follow the instructions in My Word and listen for My direction. That's when My truth shines the brightest through the story of your life. You are in the process of being transformed, becoming more and more like Me.

For by that one offering he forever made perfect those who are being made holy.

HEBREWS 10:14

February 21

GOD'S WORD

An ongoing relationship with God through His Word is essential to the Christian's consistent victory.

Beth Moore

A triumphant Christian life is only possible when you make the reading and study of My Word a significant part of your life. When you spend time with Me in this way, you'll discover the benefits of this level of intimacy. You'll know you're not alone, and you'll be reminded of My deep and abiding love for you.

The Bible will also provide you with important instruction and personal conviction. The apostle Paul wrote, "All Scripture is inspired by God and is useful to teach us what is true and to make us realize what is wrong in our lives. It corrects us when we are wrong and teaches us to do what is right" (2 Timothy 3:16). My Word will give you victory over sin; it will help you conquer fear; it will give you renewed hope as you endure personal pain. Most of all, it will guide you in the way of truth and provide answers to your tough questions.

For the word of God is alive and powerful. It is sharper than the sharpest two-edged sword, cutting between soul and spirit, between joint and marrow. It exposes our innermost thoughts and desires.

HEBREWS 4:12

— February 22 —

GETTING UNSTUCK

If you feel stuck bring your whole self to Christ, not just the problem, but you. Ask God to change your heart. Commit yourself to pray to that end. It's God's heart to give good gifts to his children.

Sheila Walsh

You belong to Me, and that means My resources are your resources. When you feel like you've reached a dead end in the middle of dealing with a contentious relationship, a health issue, a personal sin, or a heavy responsibility that erodes your ability to cope, come to Me for help. When you have no idea what to do, ask Me for guidance. You'll get My attention. Dare to ask boldly, convinced that I'm listening. Come to Me confidently, expecting an answer (James 1:5-7).

The first step to getting unstuck is to confess any sin that is getting in the way of your relationship with Me. "Search me, O God, and know my heart; test me and know my anxious thoughts. Point out anything in me that offends you, and lead me along the path of everlasting life" (Psalm 139:23-24). Once your sin is confessed, you will be able to move forward with forgiving others, turning your back on the lies of the enemy, being honest with Me about the difficulty of your journey, and pursuing balance in your life. I am right here, ready to free you so you can have a productive and joy-filled life.

For I hold you by your right hand—I, the LORD your God.
And I say to you, "Don't be afraid. I am here to help you."

ISAIAH 41:13

— February 23 —

SHINE

We are told to let our light shine, and if it does, we won't need to tell anybody it does. Lighthouses don't fire cannons to call attention to their shining—they just shine.

D. L. Moody

I am the Light of the World. After you invite Me into your life, I take great delight when you become a light-bearer to the people I put in your path. The world is filled with darkness, and as you see the results of evil behavior, it's easy to become discouraged. Keep your eyes on Me. "Put aside the deeds of darkness and put on the armor of light" (Romans 13:12, NIV).

The purpose of a lamp is to provide illumination. Let My light shine through your interactions with people and the relationships you cultivate. Be generous with your life. If you open up to others, you'll prompt them to open up to Me (Matthew 5:16, MSG). When they see My reflection in you, you can point them to the true Source of Light (John 1:9).

You're here to be light, bringing out the God-colors in the world. God is not a secret to be kept. We're going public with this, as public as a city on a hill. If I make you light-bearers, you don't think I'm going to hide you under a bucket, do you? I'm putting you on a light stand. Now that I've put you there on a hilltop, on a light stand—shine!

MATTHEW 5:14-15, MSG

February 24

WORDS MATTER

Words which do not give the light of Christ increase the darkness.

Mother Teresa

The right word at the right time can be life altering. Words are able to uplift, encourage, and provide wisdom to the hearer. But an unkind word can hurt, crush, and destroy the person who is listening. Words are powerful. What comes out of your mouth can transform the life of someone who needs faith, healing, favor, or hope—or your words can cause that person to run far away from Me.

Evaluate what comes out of your mouth. "Kind words are like honey—sweet to the soul and healthy for the body" (Proverbs 16:24). However, a warning is in order. "Do not let any unwholesome talk come out of your mouths, but only what is helpful for building others up according to their needs, that it may benefit those who listen" (Ephesians 4:29, NIV). The choice is yours—do you want to build up or to tear down?

The tongue can bring death or life; those who love to talk will reap the consequences.

PROVERBS 18:21

YOUR HEART

God is the shaper of your heart. . . . God does not display his work in abstract terms. He prefers the concrete, and this means that at the end of your life one of three things will happen to your heart: it will grow hard, it will be broken, or it will be tender. Nobody escapes.

Ravi Zacharias

I know the condition of your heart. Recent pressures have made you question why a loving God would allow you to endure hardship. Sometimes you've wondered why My people help everyone else but don't appear to see your needs. When you allow negative attitudes, judgmental thoughts, or faulty reasoning to shape the deepest part of your being, a slow, steady hardening begins to take place. At first you barely notice it. But cynicism, a critical spirit, a lack of interest in My Word, and a gradual pulling away from My people soon follow—and before long, there is distance between us.

Allow your heart to be broken by things that break My heart: injustice, sin, and the results of living in a fallen world. Ask Me to keep the inner core of your being—your thoughts, feelings, desires, and choices—focused on My truth. Allow Me to be the Sculptor of your heart.

Guard your heart above all else, for it determines the course of your life.

PROVERBS 4:23

— *February 26* —

MEEKNESS

Jesus calls us to His rest, and meekness is His method. The meek man cares not at all who is greater than he, for he has long ago decided that the esteem of the world is not worth the effort.

A. W. Tozer

Meekness is strength that surrenders to My authority. Perhaps you thought being meek has to do with a lack of confidence or being shy or reticent, but that's not what it is at all. Meekness is not weakness; it's strength harnessed. Instead of struggling to secure provisions, manage outcomes, and control the perceptions people have of you, meekness is humbly knowing you can trust Me with your life—for necessities, for reputation, for protection, and for defense. I have you covered!

It is good to "put on tender mercies, kindness, humility, meekness, longsuffering" (Colossians 3:12, NKJV). Rely on Me for justice. When people commit wrongful acts against you or your family, don't repay evil with evil (1 Peter 3:9). Don't allow worry to destroy you. Instead of manipulating people and circumstances, allow Me to provide your heart's desires (Psalm 37:4). This kind of attitude will result in peace and success as you learn to trust Me (Psalm 37:11).

Blessed are the meek, for they will inherit the earth.

MATTHEW 5:5, NIV

— *February 27* —

TRUTH

We are either in the process of resisting God's truth or in the process of being shaped and molded by His truth.

Charles Stanley

Truth is that which is consistent with My character, My will, and My mind. You've been inundated with information, advice, and opportunities, and you've wondered what to accept, what to do, and whom to trust. Some of the options seem filled with positive assurances of a better future. Others appear to promise more than is possible but include everything your heart desires. Discerning the truth is one of the most important things to learn.

I am the Source and Author of truth. My Word is truth, and Jesus said, "I am the way and the truth and the life. No one comes to the Father except through me" (John 14:6, NIV). People around you may say, "Believe whatever is true for you," but I am the God of absolute truth. Beware: All untruths are lies from the enemy. Ask Me to give you wisdom as you seek to understand and apply My principles. Truth is always consistent. Because you belong to Me, your future choices will be molded by truth as you renew your mind.

Behold, You desire truth in the inward parts, and in the hidden part You will make me to know wisdom.

PSALM 51:6, NKJV

February 28

REST

When we rest, we trust that God holds everything together.

Margaret Feinberg

When you are exhausted, look to Me. When your burdens are too heavy to carry, give them to Me. When your responsibilities are daunting and you feel like giving up, lean on Me. *I will give you rest.* I know you are weary and the accumulated duties in your life feel too overwhelming to handle. But you are carrying burdens I never intended for you to manage.

Come to Me, and I will restore to you the joy of your salvation (Psalm 51:12). Recognize who I am and worship Me with an undistracted heart. Learn to live under the shelter I provide, and you will find rest in the shadow of the Almighty. Read Psalm 91 and write out the verses that speak to you of My safe places. Spend time talking to Me about your concerns, anxieties, and desires. I want to let you "rest in green meadows" and lead you "beside peaceful streams" (Psalm 23:2). Uninterrupted time in My presence will renew your mind and heart.

Jesus said, "Come to me, all of you who are weary and carry heavy burdens, and I will give you rest."

MATTHEW 11:28

— *March 1* —

A PROCLAMATION

Giving thanks is that: making the canyon of pain into a megaphone to proclaim the ultimate goodness of God when Satan and all the world would sneer at us to recant.

Ann Voskamp

When you get up in the morning, begin with a proclamation of praise. Praise is born out of a heart that recognizes My goodness and overflows with verbal thanks. Start by reading the psalmist David's proclamations: "I will meditate on your majestic, glorious splendor and your wonderful miracles" (Psalm 145:5). List the large and small miracles you've experienced in your life. David went on: "Your awe-inspiring deeds will be on every tongue; I will proclaim your greatness. Everyone will share the story of your wonderful goodness; they will sing with joy about your righteousness" (verses 6-7). What have you heard other people say about what I've done? Now lift your voice to Me and recount My magnificent works, the stories of my goodness and favor.

David ended the psalm with these words: "I will praise the Lord, and may everyone on earth bless his holy name forever and ever" (verse 21). I know your thoughts of praise are sometimes crowded out by questions about why I have not removed all the suffering from your life. I want you to experience the unexpected joy of proclaiming My greatness and goodness while you are in the middle of personal pain. You will then discover a new strength—stomping on the enemy and letting him know you're not giving up, and that you will proclaim praises to My name until you have no more breath.

I will proclaim the name of the LORD; how glorious is our God!

DEUTERONOMY 32:3

March 2

FOLLOWING JESUS

Following Jesus isn't something you can do at night where no one notices. It's a twenty-four-hour-a-day commitment that will interfere with your life. That's not the small print—that's a guarantee.

Kyle Idleman

Following Me requires commitment. In your early days of knowing Me, you felt light and carefree. Your sins were forgiven, and you experienced the joy of your new relationship with Me. You joined Bible studies and prayer groups and pointed others to faith as you extolled the benefits of salvation by faith in Jesus Christ.

But as your faith matured, something changed. Your spiritual growth brought the conviction that followers of Jesus care about justice, even when it's unpopular. They reach out with compassion to others, even when it's messy. They sacrifice financial gain to get personally involved in furthering My mission. They hang out with homeless people, prostitutes, and criminals at the risk of their own reputations. My people have always gotten into trouble like this—you're no exception! Following Jesus is not a once-in-a-while commitment. It's keeping an open connection with Me and saying yes when I want you to feed the poor, visit the prisoners, love the unlovely, and defend the rights of those who cannot speak up for themselves. It's costly, difficult, and inconvenient—but it's worth it!

Jesus said to his disciples, "If any of you wants to be my follower, you must give up your own way, take up your cross, and follow me."

MATTHEW 16:24

— March 3 —

TIME

The most precious thing a human being has to give is time.
There is so very little of it, after all, in a life.

Edith Schaeffer

I existed before time was created. As you live on earth, you are often confused about what to do with your time, or you feel guilty because you can never get everything done. This causes stress between you and Me and between you and other people. Seek My guidance about how to use your time. Begin each morning by spending time in My Word before you plunge into the day's activities.

Ask Me what good things I have planned for you to do each day. "For we are God's masterpiece. He has created us anew in Christ Jesus, so we can do the good things he planned for us long ago" (Ephesians 2:10). There will be times when people ask you to do more than I ask you to do. Learn how to say no to them so that you can say yes to My agenda for your life. Organize your priorities and know that spending quality time with your family is a good use of the minutes in your day. Identify and eliminate unimportant activities and self-imposed obligations. When you find yourself wavering about decisions that will commit you to major tasks, seek My wisdom. You can trust My Spirit to give you either a sense of uneasiness or sweet affirmation about your time choices. I'm interested in helping you make the most of every opportunity that fits in My plan for your life.

Live life, then, with a due sense of responsibility, not as men who do not know the meaning and purpose of life but as those who do. Make the best use of your time, despite all the difficulties of these days.

EPHESIANS 5:15-16, *PHILLIPS*

— March 4 —

THE SHEPHERD

As Christians we will sooner or later discover that it is in the valleys of our lives that we find refreshment from God Himself.

W. Phillip Keller

You are My sheep, and I am your Shepherd. I have not chosen to call you *sheep* by accident. You often experience fear, and at times you are timid. Like sheep, you can be stubborn and cling to your mistakes. You require meticulous care and never-ending attention. Your natural tendency is to wander, and you need constant protection and guidance. You are often prone to getting spiritually lost in the dark valleys of your own sin.

But there is good news. I know you by name, and you respond to the gentle nudging of My rod and My staff. You are fed, comforted, and loved. I won't leave you behind when you're injured or lost. You're in a privileged position because My goodness and mercy will follow you all the days of your life (Psalm 23). Be encouraged with My Word: "He will feed his flock like a shepherd. He will carry the lambs in his arms, holding them close to his heart. He will gently lead the mother sheep with their young" (Isaiah 40:11). Speak these words aloud right now: "The Lord is my Shepherd. I have all I need."

The LORD is my shepherd; I have all that I need. . . . Even when I walk through the darkest valley, I will not be afraid, for you are close beside me. Your rod and your staff protect and comfort me.

PSALM 23:1, 4

— *March 5* —

PEACE

Expectations destroy our peace of mind.
They are future disappointments, planned out in advance.

Elizabeth George

The peace I give defies common sense and natural reasoning. It calms the mind and heart. It brings comfort in the middle of physical pain and devastating disappointments.

My peace makes no sense when chaos is all around you. It's a totally different kind of peace than the world offers. When life turns out differently from your plan, focusing on your own desires and expectations will only increase your fear. Worry takes over, and you feel uncertain, insecure, and afraid.

You have a choice. You can blame your circumstances, your family, your boss, or your bad fortune—or you can focus on Me. Jesus said, "Let not your heart be troubled" (John 14:1, KJV). You will not be able to break loose from this struggle until you take responsibility for where you are now and ask Me to bring a quiet peace to your heart. My peace will help you remain calm in wildly frightening situations. It will allow you to experience joy through pain and sing praises in the midst of ridicule. The world doesn't "get" this—but My peace overrules every struggle you will face.

I am leaving you with a gift—peace of mind and heart.
And the peace I give is a gift the world cannot give.
So don't be troubled or afraid.

JOHN 14:27

SIGHT

Sometimes the happiest ending isn't the one you keep longing for, but something you absolutely cannot see from where you are.

Shauna Niequist

Fix your eyes on Me. You have been longing to experience the carefree days of the past. Life was easier then, without the struggles that weigh you down today. At times exhaustion tempts you to give up on trusting Me. Affliction eats away at your God-confidence. When your gaze shifts away from Me, the result is fatigue, doubt, and despair. But when you focus your eyes, needs, wants, hurts, and desires on Me, your perspective changes.

It is only through Christ that you will have a clear picture of Me. Ask Me for strength as you run your personal race toward eternity with endurance, "looking unto Jesus, the author and finisher of [y]our faith, who for the joy that was set before Him endured the cross, despising the shame, and has sat down at the right hand of the throne of God" (Hebrews 12:2, NKJV). Jesus was able to go through unthinkable pain because His eyes were always on the goal—saving a lost and dying world by His sacrifice on the cross and reigning eternally in heaven with Me. You may not see a positive outcome for your situation right now, but if you keep looking at Me, your story will end with a joy that can only be explained in the supernatural dimension.

That is what the Scriptures mean when they say, "No eye has seen, no ear has heard, and no mind has imagined what God has prepared for those who love him."

1 CORINTHIANS 2:9

— *March 7* —

YOUR NAME

Quite a thought isn't it? Your name on God's hand. Your name on God's lips. Maybe you've seen your name in some special places. On an award or diploma. . . . Or maybe you've heard your name from some important people—a coach, a celebrity, a teacher. But to think that your name is on God's hand and on God's lips . . . my, could it be?

Max Lucado

I know you by name. "See, I have written your name on the palms of my hands" (Isaiah 49:16). You are that precious to Me. I care about every detail of your life. Start today by reading My Word: "Do not be afraid, for I have ransomed you. I have called you by name; you are mine. When you go through deep waters, I will be with you. When you go through rivers of difficulty, you will not drown. When you walk through the fire of oppression, you will not be burned up; the flames will not consume you" (Isaiah 43:1-2).

I see your tears. I know your thoughts. I have not forgotten your requests. When you call out My name, I am always available. "My sheep listen to my voice; I know them, and they follow me" (John 10:27). You are not a number to Me, or a symbol, or someone lost among all the other people in this world. You belong to Me, and I know your name. Because we have such an intimate relationship, *I will give you hidden treasures, riches stored in secret places, so that you may know that I am the LORD.*

I will give you hidden treasures, riches stored in secret places,
so that you may know that I am the LORD, the God of Israel,
who summons you by name.

ISAIAH 45:3, NIV

— *March 8* —

ETERNITY

Everything in Scripture points to eternity, and everything within us cries out for it. His work with us is not finished in this life.

Ray Stedman

Consider your future in heaven—no more pain, no more tears, no more wars and rumors of wars, no more abuse, no more natural disasters, no more crime, no more addiction, no more pornography, no more disease, no more death. Envision what it will be like to always be with Me, without the sadness of living in a fallen world. Look up. Choose hope. My Word reminds you of the joy that lies ahead.

That day is coming. "So we're not giving up. How could we! Even though on the outside it often looks like things are falling apart on us, on the inside, where God is making new life, not a day goes by without his unfolding grace. These hard times are small potatoes compared to the coming good times, the lavish celebration prepared for us. There's far more here than meets the eye. The things we see now are here today, gone tomorrow. But the things we can't see now will last forever" (2 Corinthians 4:16-18, MSG). When life is hard, remember that you are only passing through this world—glory is just around the corner. You're not home yet!

What a God we have! And how fortunate we are to have him, this Father of our Master Jesus! Because Jesus was raised from the dead, we've been given a brand-new life and have everything to live for, including a future in heaven—and the future starts now! God is keeping careful watch over us and the future. The Day is coming when you'll have it all—life healed and whole.

1 PETER 1:3-5, MSG

— *March 9* —

A NEW SONG

As long as God is gracious toward us, as long as he keeps showing us his power, and wowing us with his works, it is fitting that we not just sing old songs inspired by his past grace, but also that we sing new songs about his ever-streaming, never-ceasing grace.

David Mathis

Sing a fresh song of praise to Me. Meditate on what I have done to rescue you from past hurts, challenges, and pressures. You waited patiently for Me to answer your prayers, and now you have experienced new mercies. Your heart longs to respond. The psalmist said, "Sing to the LORD a new song" (Psalm 96:1, NIV). When I delivered you, I gave you a new song, a hymn to honor Me. I love all of your songs of worship, but now I want you to express your love for Me anew—with a freshness that reflects your rekindled love for Me.

You don't have to be a gifted singer to praise Me in this way. While you are at home, or driving your car, or taking a walk, sing to Me. It doesn't have to be an identifiable tune—but your words and melody will bless Me. When you sing among other people, *many will see what [I have] done and be amazed. They will put their trust in [Me]*. Through your new song and the spontaneous, heartfelt joy you express, other people will recognize the works I have done. Your act of worship will draw them to consider who I truly am.

He has given me a new song to sing, a hymn of praise to our God.
Many will see what he has done and be amazed.
They will put their trust in the LORD.

PSALM 40:3

— *March 10* —

PROMISES

God does not give us everything we want, but He does fulfill His promises . . . leading us along the best and straightest paths to Himself.

Dietrich Bonhoeffer

I always keep My promises, which are listed for you throughout My Word. These promises reveal things that I am unchangeably committed to, upon which you can totally depend. You receive them by faith, but they are conditional upon your obedience to Me. Sometimes it's hard for you to believe My promises are true; people in your life have not kept their word and this has eroded your confidence in the meaning of a promise.

Be encouraged because I am trustworthy and unchanging. Allow your heart to be lifted as you focus on a few of My absolute assurances today. I promise you forgiveness of sins (1 John 1:9), eternal life (1 John 5:11), My presence (Hebrews 13:5), My peace (Philippians 4:6-7), My joy (John 16:20), and My Spirit (Luke 24:49). My Word contains thousands of promises just waiting for you to claim. Your trust in Me will increase as you rest in the knowledge that I will meet all your needs. My promises will never be broken.

For all of God's promises have been fulfilled in Christ with a resounding "Yes!" And through Christ, our "Amen" (which means "Yes") ascends to God for his glory.

2 CORINTHIANS 1:20

March 11

BEING REAL

[God] doesn't expect us to perform for him. He loves us always—when we're disappointed or hurt or making a mess of things. Sometimes we speak to him in a language that only he can understand. What matters to him is that we are vulnerable, that we are completely ourselves.

Luci Swindoll

Show your heart to Me and to others. Stop hiding your true feelings. I don't expect you to pretend that you're not in pain, or hurt in a relationship, or disappointed that your prayers seem to go unanswered. I desire your honesty, and so do the people around you. Be truthful in your responses—and that includes the times when you're with people who aren't following Me. They will see the integrity of your responses and realize they don't have to be perfect to become Christ-followers.

Be intentional about growing your faith. Join with others in studying My Word and give voice to your questions and your doubts. When you are authentic enough to ask about your deepest concerns, you give Me room to work in your life. As you are transparent with Me while allowing the people around you to observe your spiritual journey, they will be drawn to a genuine faith—a faith that welcomes hard questions.

By the grace of God I am what I am, and his grace toward me was not in vain.

1 CORINTHIANS 15:10, ESV

March 12

SAFETY

Safety does not depend on our conception of the absence of danger. Safety is found in God's presence, in the centre of His perfect will.

T. J. Bach

I am your safe place. When the fears of an upside-down world make you feel defenseless, come to Me. The enemy wants you to believe that I am not responding to your needs and that I no longer care about safeguarding you from mental, physical, emotional, and spiritual attacks. But he is a liar and a deceiver. My concern for your well-being has not changed. I'm right here—in the same place I've always been—longing to provide you with a safe place in the center of My will. Come to Me. *Those who live in the shelter of the Most High will find rest in the shadow of the Almighty.*

The assurance of My protection is up to you. I will never force you to accept My shelter, but I am always available to provide all the security you need. When you accept My safe haven, I will cover you with My wings, like a mother hen protects her chicks. My promises will be your armor and protection. I am your refuge and strength. I will guard you at all times of the day or night (Psalm 91:4-5). You can rest in My arms, knowing that while you sleep, I am awake, watching over you.

Those who live in the shelter of the Most High will find rest in the shadow of the Almighty. This I declare about the LORD: He alone is my refuge, my place of safety; he is my God, and I trust him.

PSALM 91:1-2

— *March 13* —

WALKING

As you walk with Jesus, resting your head on His heart, you will learn to know His Word, His will, and His ways. You will want to obey Him, not out of forced compliance, but out of heartfelt connection. Your joy will abound as you remain in His love.

Sue Detweiler

The secret of walking with Me is not only the destination but also the journey. As we walk step-by-step together, our intimacy will grow, and you will learn more about how to lean into My embrace and follow My will. Sometimes in your busyness you get ahead of Me, thinking that you're saving time and getting more accomplished. Then, in frustration, you come back and admit that My pace is better. As we walk together, you rediscover your joy. You learn more about My ways, and you listen to My Word. You remember My Son's sacrifice for your transgressions and celebrate His forgiveness.

Walking isn't difficult, but it demands a choice—walking alone or walking together. When you join Me, you'll have companionship, dialogue, mutual delight, and friendship. Enjoy unbroken communion with Me as you attune yourself to the rhythm of our walking-and-talking experience. It's worth the effort.

If we walk in the light, as he is in the light,
we have fellowship with one another, and
the blood of Jesus, his Son, purifies us from all sin.

1 JOHN 1:7, NIV

— *March 14* —

TRUST

When a train goes through a tunnel and it gets dark, you don't throw away the ticket and jump off. You sit still and trust the engineer.

Corrie ten Boom

Trust Me with your life and with your future—even if you have no idea how your story will turn out. That level of trust means you believe that I love you and will look out for you. It means acknowledging that I'm all-powerful and that I want to help you and will use all of My resources on your behalf. You have a long-established habit of trusting in yourself and insisting on your independence. That pattern has caused distress, failure, and heartache.

When you face fear of the future, fear of people, fear of disasters, and fear of facing your past mistakes, let Me know. Set aside focused time each day to talk to Me and to consider what My Word says about My desire to care for you. "Look at the birds. They don't plant or harvest or store food in barns, for your heavenly Father feeds them. And aren't you far more valuable to him than they are?" (Matthew 6:26). Trust Me with your life, your loved ones, your pain, your problems, and your future. I will not let you down. You can count on Me!

Trust in the LORD with all your heart; do not depend on your own understanding. Seek his will in all you do, and he will show you which path to take.

PROVERBS 3:5-6

March 15

BROKENNESS

When things fall apart, the broken places allow all sorts of things to enter, and one of them is the presence of God.

Shauna Niequist

I am *close to the brokenhearted.* There are days when you echo Job's words: "My days are over. My hopes have disappeared. My heart's desires are broken" (Job 17:11). You feel as if the life you once enjoyed is falling apart and there's no chance of getting your joy back. But brokenness is the essential condition for My presence. It's the opposite of arrogance and pride. "The sacrifice you desire is a broken spirit. You will not reject a broken and repentant heart, O God" (Psalm 51:17).

Brokenness is your humble, obedient response to the conviction of My Spirit or My Word. It changes a critical spirit into a compassionate spirit. Sin is confessed. When brokenness shatters your will, you look to Me for help and guidance. I delight in healing the brokenhearted and in bandaging their wounds (Psalm 147:3). Brokenness is not weakness. It's coming to the end of your self-life and entering into a sweet intimacy with Me. The reward is My presence above you, under you, and around you. Bask in My closeness. I am here.

The LORD is close to the brokenhearted;
he rescues those whose spirits are crushed.

PSALM 34:18

March 16

TEMPTATION

The temptation battle is the most important battle you will ever fight.

John Ortberg

I will never lead you into sin. "Remember, when you are being tempted, do not say, 'God is tempting me.' God is never tempted to do wrong, and he never tempts anyone else" (James 1:13). Temptation is born out of your own desires, which entice you and lure you away from My will. Those desires lead to sinful actions (James 1:14-15).

I see you struggling with the pull of Satan's subtle offerings, and I know you sometimes feel weak. "Keep watch and pray, so that you will not give in to temptation. For the spirit is willing, but the body is weak" (Mark 14:38). Understand the power of Scripture to overcome temptation. Meditate on the psalmist's words: "I have hidden your word in my heart, that I might not sin against you" (Psalm 119:11). When My Word becomes an integral part of your life, you will be fortified against temptation's power. Make this a matter of prayer. Jesus told His disciples to pray that they might not fall into temptation (Luke 22:40), and you should do the same. You will experience temptations, but you can overcome them!

The temptations in your life are no different from what others experience. And God is faithful. He will not allow the temptation to be more than you can stand. When you are tempted, he will show you a way out so that you can endure.

1 CORINTHIANS 10:13

March 17

MERCY

God's mercy is so great that you may sooner drain the sea of its water, or deprive the sun of its light, or make space too narrow, than diminish the great mercy of God.

Charles Spurgeon

I am a God of mercy, and that's important news for you. It's sometimes hard for you to understand My mercy because society gravitates toward harsh criticism and an attitude of "I hope they get what they have coming to them." The human response is to want callous justice, but instead of giving you what you deserve, I offer mercy.

As you seek My wisdom, you'll learn how to react to people and circumstances in a way that honors Me. When you encounter difficult relationships, unwanted situations, and other problems, remember that My wisdom is "peace loving, gentle at all times, and willing to yield to others. It is full of mercy and the fruit of good deeds. It shows no favoritism and is always sincere" (James 3:17). Mercy isn't cheap—it cost the life of My Son, Jesus Christ, to set you free from the penalty of your sin. I long for you to respond as Peter did: "All praise to God, the Father of our Lord Jesus Christ. It is by his great mercy that we have been born again, because God raised Jesus Christ from the dead. Now we live with great expectation" (1 Peter 1:3). Because of My mercy, you can live with hope.

Let us come boldly to the throne of our gracious God. There we will receive his mercy, and we will find grace to help us when we need it most.

HEBREWS 4:16

— *March 18* —

HIS HANDS

I have held many things in my hands, and I have lost them all;
but whatever I have placed in God's hands, that I still possess.

Martin Luther

You are the work of My hands, and I will be your Provider, your Defender, your Deliverer, your Shield, and your great Reward. By My mighty hand, I brought the universe into being. "I am the one who made the earth and created people to live on it. With my hands I stretched out the heavens. All the stars are at my command" (Isaiah 45:12). When you walk through storms, remember that I can calm the seas. Even the wind and the waves obey Me. I am holding you with My almighty hands—and you need not fear.

Like a child, you sometimes let go of My hand and run ahead of Me on the path of life. But soon you find yourself lost, confused, and without direction. Come back to Me. Place your hand in Mine and enjoy the security of knowing I will not let you go. Jesus said, "I give them eternal life, and they will never perish. No one can snatch them away from me, for my Father has given them to me, and he is more powerful than anyone else. No one can snatch them from the Father's hand" (John 10:28-29). When you walk with Me and talk with Me, you can say with the psalmist, "You hold my right hand. You guide me with your counsel, leading me to a glorious destiny" (Psalm 73:23-24). Place your complete trust in Me, and I will meet your needs.

My times are in your hands; deliver me from the hands of my enemies, from those who pursue me.

PSALM 31:15, NIV

— *March 19* —

VISION

Vision leads to venture, and history is on the side of venturesome faith. The person of vision takes fresh steps of faith across gullies and chasms, not "playing safe" but neither taking foolish risks.

J. Oswald Sanders

Vision is the bridge between the past and the future. The path you've been on has clouded your ability to dream big dreams and to focus on the fact that I am the God for whom nothing is impossible. When you have no vision, you take the path of least resistance and avoid any possible discomfort. It requires sacrifice to embrace a God-sized vision and a goal to glorify Me in all you do, but that decision is well worth the effort.

You are in a strategic place at this time in history, and you have a choice—to play it safe, or to take appropriate risks as you further My Kingdom agenda. Ask Me to give you fresh faith, renewed energy, and supernatural spiritual strength for the road ahead of you. "Where there is no vision, the people perish" (Proverbs 29:18, KJV). As I carry you through your current difficulties, I will give you everything you need to point others to a better future in and with Me. You will cast vision for others in My perfect timing.

Write this. Write what you see. Write it out in big block letters so that it can be read on the run. This vision-message is a witness pointing to what's coming. It aches for the coming—it can hardly wait! And it doesn't lie. If it seems slow in coming, wait. It's on its way. It will come right on time.

HABAKKUK 2:2-3, MSG

March 20

THE RACE

Disciplined runners consistently clear their heads and focus fully on the journey ahead . . . because their passion and zeal for the goal supersedes the strain. The goal beckons them onward. Passion doesn't negate weariness; it just resolves to press beyond it.

Priscilla Shirer

Engage in the race I've set before you with full gusto! The most important requirement for success is that you keep your eyes on Jesus. Study how He did it, because He never lost sight of where He was going. He knew His race would end in an exhilarating finish with Me. Think of what He endured to get there—the shame, the Cross, the excruciating pain. But He finished well, and right now He's in the place of honor, right next to Me (Hebrews 12:1-2). "When you find yourselves flagging in your faith, go over that story again, item by item, that long litany of hostility he plowed through. *That* will shoot adrenaline into your souls!" (Hebrews 12:3, MSG).

Your Christian life is a marathon, not a sprint. Get into shape by immersing yourself in My truth. Identify and overcome the sins that trip you up. Ask friends to hold you accountable for personal and spiritual growth. Be encouraged by the people who are cheering you on! Let Me set your course and don't get distracted. Always remember that Jesus is your motivation. Keep your eyes on the goal—a forever life with Me!

I focus on this one thing: Forgetting the past and looking forward to what lies ahead, I press on to reach the end of the race and receive the heavenly prize for which God, through Christ Jesus, is calling us.

PHILIPPIANS 3:13-14

March 21

TRANSPARENCY

When we speak the truth about us,
we give others permission to do the same.

Ruth Graham

Be open with Me about your sin, and you will find forgiveness. "Whoever conceals their sins does not prosper, but the one who confesses and renounces them finds mercy" (Proverbs 28:13, NIV). An important next step is to be open with others about your struggles. The apostle James said, "Confess your sins to each other and pray for each other so that you may be healed" (James 5:16). Living a transparent life creates a safe place for others to speak about their wrong choices, deep disappointments, and doubts about faith.

This honest life also starts the best kind of spiritual movement. Others will see the results of your changed life, and they will want to be set free by the power of Jesus' blood too. Instead of being captives to sin, they can choose freedom in Christ and begin authentic and fulfilling lives. You thought transparency might bring criticism, ridicule, and derision. Instead, it brings closeness, freedom, openness, joy, mutual encouragement, and deep trust. As the testimony of your life remains open before others, it will draw them to a personal, genuine faith of their own.

Each of you must put off falsehood and speak truthfully to your neighbor, for we are all members of one body.

EPHESIANS 4:25, NIV

— *March 22* —

GOD'S WILL

Your call will become clear as your mind is transformed by the reading of Scripture and the internal work of God's Spirit. The Lord never hides His will from us. In time, as you obey the call first to follow, your destiny will unfold before you.

Charles Swindoll

Seek My guidance for your life. Beware of rushing through your life making risky, self-confident choices without consulting Me. The first step to discovering My will is to ask for My leading. Avoid selfish motives. As you remain in My Word and apply biblical truth to your life, your day-to-day decisions will fall into place. But some choices will be harder. Ask Me for mental clarity when you're faced with confusing options. I will never guide you to make choices that conflict with My Word. The closer you are to Me, the more your discernment will be sharpened.

Spend time with trustworthy people who understand My truth, and ask for their advice. Sometimes I work through other believers to give you clear direction (Proverbs 12:15). Remember that My Holy Spirit resides in you. Two of His roles are to be your Teacher and your Guide. As you seek My will, look for a sense of either uneasiness or inner peace before you make important choices. Even if your life has detours, roadblocks, and U-turns, I'll give you all the wisdom you need to move forward.

The L*ORD directs the steps of the godly.*
He delights in every detail of their lives.

PSALM 37:23

— *March 23* —

TEARS

The Christian life is not a constant high. I have my moments of deep discouragement. I have to go to God in prayer with tears in my eyes, and say, "O God, forgive me," or "Help me."

Billy Graham

Dear child, your tears are so important to Me that I keep track of each one. The psalmist said, "You keep track of all my sorrows. You have collected all my tears in your bottle. You have recorded each one in your book" (Psalm 56:8). Weeping is not a sign of weakness, and tears have many triggers—grief, joy, compassion, gratitude, loneliness, fear, and contrition. Right now, most of your tears come from sorrow, and when you are in deep anguish, you cry out for My comfort and help. I always hear your voice, and I understand your pain (Psalm 18:6). When you are sad, I'm listening, and I will save you from your troubles (Psalm 34:6).

When clouds of grief try to overtake you, ask Me for consolation and relief. Cry out to Me in your times of trouble, and I will save you from your distress (Psalm 107:19). A much better day is coming, and it won't be long before My promise is fulfilled. "He will wipe every tear from their eyes, and there will be no more death or sorrow or crying or pain. All these things are gone forever. . . . What I tell you is trustworthy and true" (Revelation 21:4-5). One day your tears will be permanently replaced with joy.

Weeping may endure for a night, but joy comes in the morning.

PSALM 30:5, NKJV

— *March 24* —

STAND

Stand firm in the Lord. . . . Stand firm and let him fight your battle.
Do not try to fight alone.

Francine Rivers

Be bold and courageous in your faith. In this world you will fall into many kinds of trials—persecution, disease, criticism, false accusations, and discouragement. Through all of these challenges, stand up for truth. Be on guard against cynicism, pessimism, and doubt. You will develop strong faith when you stand firm against harsh adversity. But don't do this in your own strength. Ask Me to fight for you. Center your heart and mind on victory as you face today's mental and spiritual battles. "Stand firm, and you will win life" (Luke 21:19, NIV).

When you face trials, remain steadfast in your commitment to Me. You are never alone because I am with you. Keep your eyes on Me, not on the fearful circumstances trying to occupy your mind. You will be blessed if you stand strong amid these temporary difficulties, and I will reward you for your courageous faith. "God blesses those who patiently endure testing and temptation. Afterward they will receive the crown of life that God has promised to those who love him" (James 1:12).

Be on guard. Stand firm in the faith. Be courageous. Be strong.

1 CORINTHIANS 16:13

March 25

KINDNESS

Let no one ever come to you without leaving better and happier.
Be the living expression of God's kindness—kindness in your face,
kindness in your eyes, kindness in your smile.

Mother Teresa

Kindness begins with caring about someone else. My kindness and love toward you were revealed when I gave you the gift of My Son—not because of the good things you've done but because of My mercy. I washed away your sins and gave you a new birth (Titus 3:4-5). Kindness is recognizing the needs of others and then taking steps to meet those needs. It's showing compassion and demonstrating understanding. Kindness is so important to Me that it's listed in My Word as something My Spirit enables you to live out (Galatians 5:22).

As you become more like Me, you'll discover that kindness is as natural as breathing. Look around and notice someone who has a need. Allow your heart to be stirred by their needs and begin to think creatively about how you can help that person. Sometimes your kindness will be shown through gracious and affirming words; in other situations you'll give your time to provide a needed service. Occasionally, your kindness will require a sacrificial gift. Sometimes it will mean being good to your enemies (Luke 6:35-36). Kindness benefits the giver and the receiver. Be tenderhearted and compassionate toward others. My merciful kindness is great toward you. Share that kindness with others.

Since God chose you to be the holy people he loves,
you must clothe yourselves with tenderhearted mercy,
kindness, humility, gentleness, and patience.

COLOSSIANS 3:12

— *March 26* —

HOSPITALITY

Hospitality . . . seeks to minister. It says, "This home is not mine. It is truly a gift from my Master. I am his servant, and I use it as he desires." Hospitality does not try to impress but to serve.

Karen Burton Mains

Welcome people into your home. If you have the spiritual gift of hospitality, you have the God-given ability to make people feel warmly received and like part of your family when they visit. But even if that's not your main gift, make your home available to those who are in need. Pursue opportunities to provide kindness and generosity to others. "When God's people are in need, be ready to help them. Always be eager to practice hospitality" (Romans 12:13).

Make showing hospitality an ongoing, continuous action and do it with a positive attitude. Check your motives and follow this pattern: "Offer hospitality to one another without grumbling" (1 Peter 4:9, NIV). Let your kindness to others be an extension of My hospitality to you. Instead of working too hard on meal preparation, enjoy the time with your guests and invite Me to be a part of the camaraderie around the table.

Cheerfully share your home with those who need a meal or a place to stay.

1 PETER 4:9

March 27

REFRESHMENT

God is most glorified in us when we are most satisfied in Him.

John Piper

Refresh yourself in My presence. Find satisfaction and contentment in your walking, talking, everyday moments with Me. I am glorified when you enjoy your time with Me. Come to Me when you are tired and when your burdens are too heavy to carry, and I will restore your body and lift the weight from your shoulders. "I will refresh the weary and satisfy the faint" (Jeremiah 31:25, NIV).

Be aware of the source of your spiritual renewal. "Times of refreshment will come from the presence of the Lord" (Acts 3:20). After you have been revitalized in your faith, make it a habit to do the same for others. One of My followers named Philemon knew how to do this, and the apostle Paul wrote these words to him: "Your love has given me much joy and comfort, my brother, for your kindness has often refreshed the hearts of God's people" (Philemon 1:7). Develop that kind of reputation, and your example will reflect My image. In the process of blessing others, you will experience a revitalized heart.

Those who refresh others will themselves be refreshed.

PROVERBS 11:25

— *March 28* —

WEAKNESS

I discovered an astonishing truth: God is attracted to weakness. He can't resist those who humbly and honestly admit how desperately they need him. Our weakness, in fact, makes room for his power.

Jim Cymbala

Acknowledging your weakness is an important step in your spiritual growth. Self-sufficiency ends in arrogance, self-centeredness, and failure. Display a humble spirit even when people put you down for your faith, or when you feel trapped due to harsh circumstances, or when difficulties weigh you down. The apostle Paul said, "That's why I take pleasure in my weaknesses, and in the insults, hardships, persecutions, and troubles that I suffer for Christ. For when I am weak, then I am strong" (2 Corinthians 12:10).

Allow your weakness and vulnerability to make room for My power. I don't need people who act high and mighty to accomplish My purposes. I intentionally use those who know how weak they are. Learn to depend on Me. My work must be done in My power. My design is to have you showcase the power of Christ by exchanging your weakness for My power, even in the middle of pain and trials. Once you learn this, your weakness becomes your greatest strength.

Each time he said, "My grace is all you need. My power works best in weakness." So now I am glad to boast about my weaknesses, so that the power of Christ can work through me.

2 CORINTHIANS 12:9

— March 29 —

LAUGHTER

For me, laughter is how we take a much-needed break from the heartache, such that when we turn to face it again, it has by some miracle grown smaller in size and intensity, if not disappeared altogether.

Liz Curtis Higgs

Cherish laughter as a gift from Me. It's one of the sounds of joy. I created you with the capacity to experience joy in sorrow as well as in good times. Laughter is not disrespectful when you're walking through the valleys of life. It gives you a sense of well-being and aids in the healing process. You will have little strength if you allow a broken spirit to rob you of a cheerful heart.

My Son, Jesus, reminded His disciples that although there was pain, sin, and chaos in the world, they would have joy if they trusted in Him and followed Him. "I have told you these things so that you will be filled with my joy. Yes, your joy will overflow!" (John 15:11). My gift of laughter can lighten your load on the pilgrimage of life. It will be a blessing to those who walk beside you, and you'll discover that it's contagious. It brings renewed hope and a fresh perspective to those who are hurting. Delight in Me, and allow your joy to erupt in laughter.

A cheerful heart is good medicine,
but a broken spirit saps a person's strength.

PROVERBS 17:22

— *March 30* —

DESIRES

It is a safe thing to trust Him to fulfill the desires which He creates.

Amy Carmichael

You have longings for significance, security, intimacy, and success. At times you expect your life to be much easier, and you believe these hidden desires should result in getting everything you want as quickly as possible. But there is a difference between personal desires and the desires I have placed in your heart. Ask for My discernment as you determine whether your longings are self-driven or God-driven. Remember what I said through My prophet Jeremiah: "My people would not listen to me. They kept doing whatever they wanted, following the stubborn desires of their evil hearts. They went backward instead of forward" (Jeremiah 7:24). You can avoid this problem by aligning your heart with My truth.

I hear your cries for help and understand your desire to be rescued. Remember that I grant the desires of those who fear Me (Psalm 145:19). Allow My Word to renew your mind and expect My Spirit to give you guidance. When your desires are in line with My will, I take deep joy in fulfilling the longings of your heart.

Take delight in the Lord,
and he will give you
the desires of your heart.

PSALM 37:4, NIV

— March 31 —

LONELINESS

Aloneness can lead to loneliness. God's preventative for loneliness is intimacy—meaningful, open, sharing relationships with one another. In Christ we have the capacity for the fulfilling sense of belonging which comes from intimate fellowship with God and with other believers.

Neil T. Anderson

Draw closer to Me. The apostle James put it this way: "Come close to God, and God will come close to you" (James 4:8). At times you feel completely alone; you don't think other people care about what you're going through, and you wonder where I am. My Son knows what it felt like to be alone. On the cross Jesus felt abandoned, and He cried out, "My God, my God, why have you forsaken me?" (Matthew 27:46, NIV). Find comfort in knowing that Jesus understands. He experienced complete abandonment. He was alone on the cross so your sin would never be a barrier between you and Me. Now you can come to Me and experience My presence whenever you're lonely.

Share your life with others. When you gather with other Christians, there is encouragement and companionship. Your shared relationship with Me gives you a basis for close communication with each other. Ask Me to give you the courage to reach out to other people. I want you to have an abundant life that is filled with close relationships with Me and with My people.

Let us not neglect our meeting together, as some people do,
but encourage one another, especially now that
the day of his return is drawing near.

HEBREWS 10:25

— *April 1* —

IMMEASURABLY MORE

Your life may be messed and your foolishness may have put you into captivity but Jesus can do the whatever it is that is immeasurably more in your life.

Louie Giglio

I can do far more than you could ever imagine in your wildest dreams. Fear has held you back because you keep rehearsing the wrong choices of your past. This leaves you stuck—never feeling good enough to receive all that I have for you. Stop denying Me the opportunity to bless you. Jesus took care of your wrongdoings when He died on the cross. If you have received Him as your Savior, you no longer have to carry the burden of your sin around like unnecessary baggage. That heavy load will weigh on your mind and keep you from concentrating on My Word. It will also rob you of feeling worthy enough to accept opportunities to serve in Christian leadership.

Instead of being a slave to your past, acknowledge that I can erase your wrong choices, bolster your inadequacy, and redeem your disgraces. As you worship Me today, say aloud, "My God is stronger than the grave, more powerful than my shame, and He will do immeasurably more in my life today."

God can do anything, you know—far more than you could ever imagine or guess or request in your wildest dreams! He does it not by pushing us around but by working within us, his Spirit deeply and gently within us.

EPHESIANS 3:20, MSG

— *April 2* —

THE ROCK

Sometimes God lets you hit rock bottom so that you will discover He is the Rock at the bottom.

Tony Evans

I am your Source of strength in times of distress and danger. When your life feels upended and you're uncertain about the path ahead, remember that I am unchangeable. You can trust Me. The psalmist said, "The LORD is my rock, my fortress, and my savior; my God is my rock, in whom I find protection. He is my shield, the power that saves me, and my place of safety" (Psalm 18:2).

When you embrace Me as your Rock, you hold firmly to the belief that I am your solid Foundation in the middle of every circumstance or trial you may face. When your heart grows faint, pray, "Lead me to the rock that is higher than I" (Psalm 61:2, NIV). Your victory and honor will come from Me alone. No enemy can reach you when I am your Refuge (Psalm 62:7). I will be your sure Hope and your Deliverer, no matter what happens to you in the future. Instead of giving in to desperation, choose My protection as your total rock-solid security.

No one is holy like the LORD! There is no one besides you; there is no Rock like our God.

1 SAMUEL 2:2

— April 3 —

BELONGING

I believe that a true sense of belonging today comes not only from knowing that we belong to God, but also from belonging to each other. . . . In Christ we have the capacity for the fulfilling sense of belonging which comes from intimate fellowship with God and with other believers.

Neil T. Anderson

I created you to experience companionship, intimacy, and meaningful relationships with Me and with others. Every time you start to feel alone and unwanted, study My truth and bask in the fact that you belong to Me! Still, I want you to do more than *believe* in Me—I want you to *belong* to a group of fellow believers who will laugh with you, weep with you, support you, encourage you, celebrate with you, and be there for you. As you spend time in each other's company and worship Me together, your hearts and minds will be united in a bond that nurtures you and builds you up. I designed you to belong!

There is a decision you need to make. You can choose loneliness or togetherness, isolation or community, withdrawal or participation. In the midst of your difficulties, you've pulled back, afraid you'll be a burden to others. These thoughts do not come from Me. Don't deprive other Christ-followers of the delight of knowing you. Reach out and take the risk. Your relationship with Me is personal, but I also fashioned you for fellowship with others. You belong to a uniquely special group!

So it is with Christ's body. We are many parts of one body, and we all belong to each other.

ROMANS 12:5

— *April 4* —

YOUR POTENTIAL

Everyone we meet is a hero waiting to happen. When Jesus saw people, He envisioned their potential. No respecter of persons, He associated with people from all walks of life.

David Jeremiah

Develop and use the gifts I've given you. Ask Me for wisdom and guidance. I have breathed My creativity and uniqueness into you. I have made you "wonderfully complex" (Psalm 139:14). Developing your potential is not about how much you can achieve alone; it's about increasing the small and large talents you have, as you surrender your life to Me every day.

When past failures threaten to devalue you, resist going down that road. I created only one "you," and no one else can do exactly what I've prepared for you to do. There are no limits on doing My Kingdom work. Instead of allowing the comments of others to make you think your life is without purpose, be fully aware of your untapped power to serve Me. Your potential will grow and be developed as you place your complete faith in Me and as you say yes to the expanding opportunities I open up for you to serve others.

For we are God's masterpiece. He has created us anew in Christ Jesus, so we can do the good things he planned for us long ago.

EPHESIANS 2:10

— *April 5* —

A LIVING LETTER

Most of the world around you doesn't read the Bible.
So . . . He gives the world a living epistle—*you*.

Kay Arthur

You are My love letter to the world. During the challenges of your current circumstances, you have demonstrated a living hope. The hope you reflect is not based on sudden riches, less pain, easier experiences, or perfect health. It's totally anchored in your unwavering faith in Jesus Christ and in your determination to stay focused on your inheritance in heaven—"an inheritance that can never perish, spoil or fade" (1 Peter 1:4, NIV). To the onlooker, your life is surprising, because you are finding joy in the midst of your trials.

As someone inscribed with My signature, you prove the genuineness of a vibrant faith. It baffles people that you give praise, honor, and glory to Me during tough times (1 Peter 1:3-7). By the way you live out your faith, observers understand the power of My love and protection. Your faithfulness speaks louder than a person using a megaphone. You are a living letter that describes authentic Christianity without words.

You show that you are a letter from Christ, the result of our ministry, written not with ink but with the Spirit of the living God, not on tablets of stone but on tablets of human hearts.

2 CORINTHIANS 3:3, NIV

— April 6 —

BALANCE

I cannot meet every need, but I can respond in obedience to the need the Spirit lays on my heart. I cannot carry every load, but I can carry the load God has for me. For his yoke, indeed, is easy, and his burden is truly light.

Joanna Weaver

One of your greatest challenges is finding balance in your life. The demands of your work are great, and many people pull at you for advice, assistance, and help with their problems. You are weary, and there is never enough time. Like the psalmist, you long for Me to lighten your load: "I am worn out waiting for your rescue, but I have put my hope in your word" (Psalm 119:81).

Study the example of My Son. In one day He did miracles, taught lessons, healed people, dealt with interruptions, and defused disputes with truth (Mark 1). It was the kind of day when most people would throw their hands in the air and say, "I can't handle this anymore!" But He did—and somehow He still maintained balance in His life. His actions early the next day give you the key to His success: "Before daybreak the next morning, Jesus got up and went out to an isolated place to pray" (Mark 1:35). He began each day by spending time alone with Me. Were there more miracles to perform? More lessons to teach? More people who begged for healing? More interruptions? Yes. There will always be more to do, and you will never have enough time. Seek My will and complete the work I give you to do (John 17:4).

Are you tired? Worn out? . . . Come to me. Get away with me and you'll recover your life. I'll show you how to take a real rest. Walk with me and work with me—watch how I do it. Learn the unforced rhythms of grace.

MATTHEW 11:28-29, MSG

— *April 7* —

QUALIFIED

The biblical model is that God deliberately chooses imperfect vessels—those who have been wounded, those with physical or emotional limitations. Then he prepares them to serve and sends them out *with their weakness still in evidence*, so that his strength can be made perfect in that weakness.

Christine Caine

Stop making excuses for not serving Me with your whole heart. If you wait until you think you're spiritual enough, or educated enough, or good enough, or attractive enough, or confident enough, or skilled enough, you'll discover there's never a time when you are adequate in your own strength. Get over it and offer Me what you have right now. I can work with people who know they need My help much more effectively than with those who think they have it all together.

Don't use your weakness as an excuse for not doing what I'm asking you to do. I love working with imperfect people. Moses couldn't speak well (Exodus 4:10). Jeremiah thought he was too young (Jeremiah 1:6). Jonah had an attitude and an obedience problem (Jonah 1–3). The disciples were afraid (Matthew 14:26). Paul had a thorn in the flesh (2 Corinthians 12:7). Are you going to keep telling Me you're inadequate, or will you allow My power to shine through your weakness? Come to Me with your limitations and apprehension, and I'll take care of the rest. Your weakness is your strongest qualification.

He gives power to the weak and strength to the powerless.

ISAIAH 40:29

April 8

WORSHIP

Worship is our response to the overtures of love
from the heart of the Father.

Richard J. Foster

You were created for the purpose of giving Me glory and honor. Your life is meant to declare My praises. "Let the godly sing for joy to the LORD; it is fitting for the pure to praise him" (Psalm 33:1). Let your worship be expressed out of sincerity, not out of obligation or to impress others. True worship is an honest exchange of pure love. You receive and experience My love for you, and then you give it back to Me—through your words, your giving, your obedience, your service to others, and your heart that asks, "How do You want me to express my love for You today?"

Use variety in the ways you worship Me—bowing your head in reverence, lifting your hands in celebration, falling prostrate before Me in passionate prayer, observing My creation and thanking Me with your eyes wide open, singing, entering into Communion, and being My hands and feet to others. Worship is not a single act—it's bringing praise to My name with a pure heart. Worshiping Me will prepare you for everything you face today.

Shout with joy to the LORD, all the earth! Worship the LORD with gladness. Come before him, singing with joy. . . . Enter his gates with thanksgiving; go into his courts with praise. Give thanks to him and praise his name.

PSALM 100:1-2, 4

April 9

THE CROSS

If we want proof of God's love for us, then we must look first at the Cross where God offered up His Son as a sacrifice for our sins. Calvary is the one objective, absolute, irrefutable proof of God's love for us.

Jerry Bridges

When you're tempted to question My love for you, look at the Cross. When you wonder if I understand your pain, read about the suffering of Jesus on the cross. When you feel you can't go on, envision wrapping up your heaviest burden and placing it at the foot of the cross—and trust Me with the results. Jesus said, "Here on earth you will have many trials and sorrows. But take heart, because I have overcome the world" (John 16:33). He did that on the cross.

The power of the Cross isn't only for the forgiveness of your sins. Yes, Jesus paid the price for your sins so you wouldn't have to, but the ongoing power of the Cross is that He died and rose again to defeat the power of sin in your life today. To the world, this is a mystery. As the apostle Paul wrote, "The preaching of the cross is, I know, nonsense to those who are involved in this dying world, but to us who are being saved from that death it is nothing less than the power of God" (1 Corinthians 1:18, *Phillips*). Because of the Cross you have life, freedom, and eternal glory.

Let us run with perseverance the race marked out for us, fixing our eyes on Jesus, the pioneer and perfecter of faith. For the joy set before him he endured the cross, scorning its shame, and sat down at the right hand of the throne of God.

HEBREWS 12:1-2, NIV

— *April 10* —

COMMUNITY

God doesn't intend for you to handle all the pain and stress in your life by yourself. We were wired for each other. We need each other.

Rick Warren

Your community includes the supportive people closest to you. Sometimes these individuals are those in your immediate and extended family. But I also want you to recognize the encouraging and helpful friends who surround you—your church family, neighbors, coworkers, and long-distance cheerleaders. I've placed these people in your life for interactive fellowship and support. When you try to carry your trials and anxiety all by yourself, you're easily discouraged. Share your concerns and needs with those you trust and give them time to speak about their challenges too.

I designed people to need each other and to provide mutual support. You love your neighbor by carrying his or her emotional, physical, mental, and spiritual loads. Some of the burdens you'll carry for one another are worry, anxiety, and sorrow. When you do that for others, your own burden won't seem as heavy. As a community of people who care for one another, keep your focus on heaven—and that will make it much easier for you to endure trials.

Carry each other's burdens,
and in this way you will fulfill the law of Christ.

GALATIANS 6:2, NIV

April 11

QUESTIONS

In all my prayers, whether I get the answers I want or not, I can count on this one fact: God can make use of whatever happens. Nothing is irredeemable.

Philip Yancey

Your hardest questions do not go unnoticed by Me. You aren't the only one who has agonized during a time of personal pain and suffering, wondering if I have turned My back on your need. My own Son, Jesus Christ, cried out on the cross, "My God, my God, why have you abandoned me?" (Matthew 27:46). I understand the depth of pain that prompted that question, and I'm aware of your anguish too. The psalmist said, "I say to God my Rock, 'Why have you forgotten me? Why must I go about mourning, oppressed by the enemy?'" (Psalm 42:9, NIV).

There are times when some of your questions are a sign of an unrepentant and unchanged heart—but when you come to Me humbly, believing I have your best interests in mind, I welcome your questions. You can speak honestly to Me about your distress, and I will listen. Come to Me in the midst of your own confusion and ask for My wisdom. I will lead you, in the right timing, to a place of peace—not always to the result you long for, but to the answer that will glorify My name.

Why am I discouraged? Why is my heart so sad? I will put my hope in God! I will praise him again—my Savior and my God!

PSALM 42:11

April 12

SIMPLICITY

Strip away all excess baggage and nonessential trappings until you have come into the stark reality of the Kingdom of God.

Richard J. Foster

Allow Me to reshuffle your priorities. Part of your stress is coming from comparing what you have with what others have, and from acquiring things that appear to help you fit in with the culture around you. That mind-set can evolve into competition, jealousy, and a never-ending desire to "fix" your life by buying something else. Instead of bringing joy, it brings agitation, discomfort, and an unsettled heart.

Simplicity begins within you—with a determination to care for the needs of others, before accumulating things that make you look impressive. Turn away from anything that distracts you from seeking the Kingdom of God first. Living a simple life gives you freedom instead of bondage. It brings balance and relief instead of anxiety and fear. I intend for you to have adequate provision, but nurture a heart attitude that says, "Lord, help me to sense Your leading to give away what I don't need and to keep my life simple enough that the things I've accumulated do not become an unnecessary burden."

Don't store up treasures here on earth. . . . Store your treasures in heaven, where moths and rust cannot destroy, and thieves do not break in and steal. Wherever your treasure is, there the desires of your heart will also be.

MATTHEW 6:19-21

— *April 13* —

TEMPTATION

Every time you defeat a temptation, you become more like Jesus!

Rick Warren

The enemy loves to tempt you to sin when you are discouraged, especially when you feel like I'm not coming through for you quickly enough. He whispers, "Allow yourself some gratification in the middle of your pain. You deserve to be happier because you've been through a lot. I'll give you a break from your disappointments and give you a chance to have mental and emotional freedom from the hard life you're living." Always remember he's a liar! The promise of temptation is that it will take away your sadness and give you pleasure, but the truth is that temptation leads to sin, which will eventually lead to guilt, sorrow, and distance from Me.

When temptations come, be encouraged with these words: "So then, since we have a great High Priest who has entered heaven, Jesus the Son of God, let us hold firmly to what we believe. This High Priest of ours understands our weaknesses, for he faced all of the same testings we do, yet he did not sin" (Hebrews 4:14-15). The best way to get away from temptation is to look to the example of Jesus and run from the lure of the enemy. You are "not fighting against flesh-and-blood enemies, but against evil rulers and authorities of the unseen world"—and it is a dark world! (Ephesians 6:12). But temptation does not have to win. You *can* make the right choice.

God is faithful. He will not allow the temptation to be more than you can stand. When you are tempted, he will show you a way out so that you can endure.

1 CORINTHIANS 10:13

April 14

OUR MANDATE

Jesus made our mission abundantly clear in meeting the needs of the forgotten, unlovely, and unpopular—"the least of these." His declaration that to serve them is to serve him is both countercultural and life-changing.

Randy Frazee

You serve Me when you meet the needs of the hungry, the poor, and the incarcerated. Look around your community and acquaint yourself with the needs of those living in poverty or behind bars. Treat these men and women with dignity and respect. They, like you, were created in My image. Study how My Son related to the weak, the helpless, and the outcasts. Care for these people as I would care for them.

Show no partiality to people based on their status in life. Take the lead, even if it isn't popular, to help others. You will not be working alone. I will open unexpected doors of opportunity for you. Keep your eyes open and serve others in the same way My Son did. He saw the pain and the hurt in the world, and He had compassion on the people He encountered. Sometimes you need to reach out to those who are in spiritual darkness. Others are in agony due to physical sickness or mental pain. And you will always find people who are hungry and homeless. Do not be afraid to visit an inmate; provide comfort and encouragement. Do the life-changing work I have asked you to do.

I was hungry, and you fed me. I was thirsty, and you gave me a drink. I was a stranger, and you invited me into your home. I was naked, and you gave me clothing. I was sick, and you cared for me. I was in prison, and you visited me.

MATTHEW 25:35-36, 40

— *April 15* —

STORMS

Sometimes the Lord rides out the storm with us and other times He calms the restless sea around us. Most of all, He calms the storm inside us in our deepest inner soul.

Lloyd John Ogilvie

When you face the storms of life, remember who I am. In your own strength you lack the resources to meet these challenges, but I will provide everything you need. One day when the disciples were crossing the lake, they were suddenly caught in a storm. Then Jesus came walking to them on the water. They didn't recognize Him and cried out in fear, "It's a ghost!" The moment Jesus climbed into the boat with them, the storm subsided (Matthew 14:22-34). On another occasion Jesus was asleep in the boat with His disciples when high waves began flooding their vessel. The disciples were absolutely terrified and awakened Him. Jesus spoke aloud: "Be still!" and there was a great calm, causing the disciples to proclaim, "Even the wind and waves obey him" (Mark 4:35-41).

Never underestimate My power to work during the stormiest times in your life. Ask for My abiding presence in the middle of your trials. When you belong to Me, you have an anchor—I will be your *lasting foundation*. I will either calm the waves or ride out the storm with you. Either way, your example of trusting Me will bring comfort to others. On the sunny days and on the stormy days, I am equally present in your life.

When the storms of life come, the wicked are whirled away, but the godly have a lasting foundation.

PROVERBS 10:25

April 16

RESURRECTION

No matter how devastating our struggles, disappointments, and troubles are, they are only temporary. No matter what happens to you, no matter the depth of tragedy or pain you face, no matter how death stalks you and your loved ones, the resurrection promises you a future of immeasurable good.

Josh McDowell

The empty tomb is there to remind you that Jesus rose from the dead. My Son's death paid for your wrongdoing and for the sins of the world. The Resurrection is your assurance of a future in heaven that will be free of death, discouragement, suffering, and pain. It is the evidence that indisputably identifies Jesus as My Son.

Right now you don't see things clearly. It feels as if you're squinting in a fog or gazing through a mist. But soon you'll see what the empty tomb ultimately means to you. The apostle Paul said, "We'll see it all then, see it all as clearly as God sees us, knowing him directly just as he knows us!" (1 Corinthians 13:12, MSG). He lists three things you need to do as you get ready for the ultimate resurrection: "Trust steadily in God, hope unswervingly, love extravagantly" (1 Corinthians 13:13, MSG). Hold on. You're not home yet.

I am the resurrection and the life. Anyone who believes in me will live, even after dying.

JOHN 11:25

— April 1…

HOLD M…

You'll get through this. It won't be painless. It …
will use this mess for good. In the meantime, do …
But don't despair either. With God's help you w…

Max Lucado

Let Me take you by the hand and give you guidance and support for what is ahead of you. No matter where you're going or whom you'll meet, I will be right beside you—giving you strength for every decision, every encounter, every trial, and every need. I will not leave you to handle harsh circumstances or underserved criticism on your own. The important prerequisite is that you keep your hand in Mine and listen to My voice.

When you face unexpected obstacles, I am with you. When life is complicated and people you love are wreaking havoc in your life, I am there. Release false shame. Let go of guilt. You have carried these burdens long enough. Allow the sweet innocence of your first love for Me to return. Relax in My presence. Hear Me say to you softly, "There is nothing that will stop My unconditional love for you. You are precious to Me. I will hold you close."

If I ride the wings of the morning, if I dwell by the farthest oceans, even there your hand will guide me, and your strength will support me.

PSALM 139:9–10

SHOWERS OF BLESSING

Whenever you get a blessing from God, give it back to Him as a love gift. . . . If you hoard a thing for yourself, it will turn into spiritual dry rot. . . . God will never let you hold a spiritual thing for yourself, it has to be given back to Him that He may make it a blessing to others.

Oswald Chambers

The key to receiving My blessing is to listen to My voice and follow My leading. When you spend time with Me daily, your discernment will be refined and you will become sensitive to My divine nudging. As you walk in obedience, you will be drawn deeper into an intimate working relationship with Me. And when you are blessed, you will want to pass those blessings on to others.

My blessings come to you in the natural realm and in the spiritual realm. You desire a more comfortable life—better health, less tension, more financial stability, and a closer relationship with Me. Here are the directions for receiving My blessing: "Seek the Kingdom of God above all else, and live righteously, and he will give you everything you need" (Matthew 6:33). As you seek Me, live in obedience, and receive My favor, ask Me to lead you to others you can bless. You are My ambassador of blessing—pass it on!

I will bless my people and their homes around my holy hill.
And in the proper season I will send the showers they need.
There will be showers of blessing.

EZEKIEL 34:26

— April 19 —

WONDER

God is not merely at your fingertips but within your grasp. Live each day like a child digging through a treasure chest, rifling for the next discovery. Open your arms and your eyes to the God who stands in plain sight and works miracles in your midst.

Margaret Feinberg

Be aware of My presence each day. Look for My assignments and blessings in your life. There is so much I want to share with you. Ask Me to give you eyes that see opportunities to do My work in this world. Invite Me to work through you as you recognize fears, hardships, and needs. As you join Me in touching lives and doing Kingdom work, you will be amazed at what can be accomplished.

Stop and ponder the wonder of creation. Consider the beauty of the oceans and the mountains. They are the work of My hands. I am the Creator and the Sustainer of life. I hung the sun and the moon in place. I created you in My own image—and I have a significant plan for your life. Ask Me to guide you each step of the way, and lean on Me for direction. If you follow My leading, you will stand in awe as you see what we can accomplish together—your hand in Mine all the way. Press into the comfort of knowing that we are a team and I won't leave you stranded.

O LORD my God, you have performed many wonders for us. Your plans for us are too numerous to list. You have no equal. If I tried to recite all your wonderful deeds, I would never come to the end of them.

PSALM 40:5

April 20

SAY YES

Whatever the particular call is, the particular sacrifice God asks you to make . . . will you rise up and say, in your heart, "Yes, Lord, I accept it; I submit, I yield? I pledge myself to walk in that path, and to follow that Voice, and to trust Thee with the consequences."

Catherine Booth

I am looking for people who are willing to risk everything to follow My call. Sometimes what I lead you to do makes no sense at the moment, but later you see how My plan unfolds. Are you willing to sacrifice your comfort, reputation, security, and hopes for a pain-free life so you can follow Me with your whole heart? If your answer is yes, I promise you will be in for an adventure full of both joy and sorrow. It will be a life of serving others and of finding deep and lasting fulfillment in a way that makes no sense to people who cling to predictability and a carefully made agenda for their own lives.

The journey will not always be easy. My disciples have a long history of leaving the comfortable lives they once knew and of following Me, often without knowing My plan ahead of time. When you choose to trust Me in this way, our relationship will grow. Your response to the leading of the Holy Spirit will become second nature. You will understand your calling and purpose, and you will never want to return to an ordinary life.

For my part, I wholeheartedly followed the LORD my God.

JOSHUA 14:8

— April 21 —

STORIES

Your story includes your life before encountering Christ, the actual encounter, and your subsequent response. . . . Your faith story includes your life experience and the ways in which God has been woven into its fibers.

Nish Weiseth

Your story has the power to draw someone to Christ. Maybe you think your story is too imperfect, too ordinary, too embarrassing, too bizarre, or too uninteresting to be worth telling. That's exactly why I want you to share your life journey with others—to let them know that no matter where they've been, what they've done, or what's been done to them, I can transform, redeem, and use lives that are fully committed to Me. Many people you encounter will not read a Bible or step inside a church, so I'm asking you to share your life with them in a conversational way. They need to hear what it's like to be set free from the past into a hope-filled future.

People relax when they listen to a story, and that gives My Spirit time to work in their lives, gently calling them to follow My teachings, to leave the past behind, and to consider the life and work of My Son. You'll discover that conversation flows more easily after they hear about the roadblocks, choices, challenges, and opportunities you've had along the way. Be honest about your struggles and respond to their questions. Then, in the right timing, tell them the story of Jesus and what He offers them—forgiveness, healing, a fresh start, and a heavenly future.

[Jesus] taught by using stories, many stories.

MARK 4:2, MSG

April 22

CAPTIVE THOUGHTS

What repeatedly enters your mind and occupies your mind, eventually shapes your mind, and will ultimately express itself in what you do and who you become.

John Ortberg

Your inner life determines the kind of person you become. I created you with the ability to choose what your mind dwells on. The way you think controls what your priorities are and the actions you take every day. My Word says, "For as he thinks in his heart, so is he" (Proverbs 23:7, NKJV). I can see when you are struggling inside.

To develop a mind that pleases Me, set your thoughts on things above and keep them focused there (Colossians 3:2). The key to resisting temptation is to decide ahead of time what you will and won't do. Take control of your wayward thoughts every time they head in a sinful direction. Practice the habit of capturing rebellious thoughts and focus on obeying Me (2 Corinthians 10:5). Renew your mind with Scripture—not as a "once in a while" option, but as an ongoing habit of transforming your thought patterns. Don't be conformed to the world's way of responding—confront your sinful thoughts and turn them over to Me. It isn't easy to respond this way, but you can gain self-control and honor Me with a pure mind. Strive to round up and corral wrong notions, conforming each one to My truth.

Those who live according to the flesh have their minds set on what the flesh desires; but those who live in accordance with the Spirit have their minds set on what the Spirit desires. The mind governed by the flesh is death, but the mind governed by the Spirit is life and peace.

ROMANS 8:5-6, NIV

— *April 23* —

IN HIS HAND

God loves you intensely, wants to heal your wounds, and beckons you to safety in the shadow of his hand.

Judith Couchman

You are irresistible to Me. When life is hard and you feel beaten up by the unkind words of others and the circumstances that plague your days with uncertainty, I want to place you in My hand. There you will find quiet rest, sweet comfort, and My personal protection. You will be barricaded from the guilt that steals the precious time you need for recovery and renewal. The shadow of My hand is a place of refuge and safety.

Allow these words to comfort you: "He is a shield for all who look to him for protection" (Psalm 18:30). If you are seeking respite from the emotional, mental, and spiritual pressures you've been facing, let Me use My hand as your covering. Your hardship can change you for the better, transforming the ways you process trials and minister to the needs of others. Your body requires sleep and nourishment—take care of yourself and allow Me to strengthen you before you stretch yourself to the breaking point. Accept this time of healing as a gift from My hand.

I have put my words in your mouth and hidden you safely in my hand.

ISAIAH 51:16

April 24

FIRE TIME

It takes time to come to the fire, it takes effort to keep the fire burning, it takes a willingness to become quiet enough to hear what God might be saying, and it takes courage to snuff out competing sounds and demands that attempt to shorten or neutralize the effect of the fire time.

Gail MacDonald

What is the condition of your faith-fire? When you were a brand-new Christian, your first sparks were just beginning to flicker. After you developed more history with Me, your faith became a raging bonfire. Now, due to suffering amid the harsh realities of life, you may feel like your once-vibrant faith is turning into an ash heap. If you're discouraged, look for the ember in the middle of the fire that is still red-hot on the inside. All it needs is more fuel and fresh wind.

Dig into My Word, even when it feels inconvenient. Come into My presence and talk to Me often. As you "come to the fire," remember that you need to add the fuel of Scripture and invite the wind of the Holy Spirit. The apostle Paul inspired young Timothy to carry on the legacy of his family's faith, saying, "That precious memory triggers another: your honest faith—and what a rich faith it is, handed down from your grandmother Lois to your mother Eunice, and now to you!" (2 Timothy 1:5, MSG). Allow Me to stir up a faith-fire within you that not only encourages you with the warmth of My presence, but also spreads like wildfire to others.

Don't burn out; keep yourselves fueled and aflame. Be alert servants of the Master, cheerfully expectant. Don't quit in hard times.

ROMANS 12:11-12, MSG

— *April 25* —

SEASONS

Everything has seasons, and we have to be able to recognize when something's time has passed and be able to move into the next season. Everything that is alive requires pruning as well, which is a great metaphor for endings.

Henry Cloud

Learn to recognize the season of life you are in and to accept change, even if it's uncomfortable for a while. There is a progression in life from the challenge of winter to the first breath of spring, to the growth of summer, to the harvesting of fall. Sometimes you want to stay where you are indefinitely, and at other times you want to move prematurely to a different season. When you face uncertainties, remember My faithfulness to you in the past (Lamentations 3:22).

During the season of planting, it may look like nothing positive is happening in your life. It's a time of watering and nurturing, long before the bountiful harvest can be seen. But in time, you will experience the fruit of your righteousness. The most difficult challenge for you may be the season of pruning. "He cuts off every branch of mine that doesn't produce fruit, and he prunes the branches that do bear fruit so they will produce even more" (John 15:2). Pruning is necessary so more fruit can be produced. Every season is a gift from Me. Don't get tired of doing what's right. At just the right time, you'll reap a harvest of blessing, if you don't give up (Galatians 6:9).

For everything there is a season, a time for every activity under heaven. A time to be born and a time to die. A time to plant and a time to harvest.

ECCLESIASTES 3:1-2

April 26

DISCIPLINE

Discipline is the wholehearted yes to the call of God. . . .
I put myself gladly, fully, and forever at His disposal,
and to whatever He says my answer is yes.

Elisabeth Elliot

Discipline is a word that sometimes makes you uncomfortable. You think of it as chastisement for wrongdoing and equate it with harsh rebuke. Today I'm asking you to look at another aspect of discipline. As you commit your life to My purpose and plan, be intentional about sacrificing everything it takes to serve Me in the most effective way. That kind of spiritual discipline means setting aside time every day to read My Word, and then meditating on how you can live a pure life and show My love to others.

As you make this discipline a regular part of your routine, there will be a natural rhythm to the way you read, listen, and respond to My truth. Add further discipline by doing physical exercise each day. That will clear your mind and give you more energy to focus on your daily responsibilities and on serving others. You will begin looking forward to the new doors I'm opening for you because you have become My trusted servant. In the beginning, personal discipline is hard—but the long-term benefits are worth it!

All athletes are disciplined in their training. They do it to win a prize that will fade away, but we do it for an eternal prize.

1 CORINTHIANS 9:25

— *April 27* —

HEART'S DESIRE

May God so fill us today with the heart of Christ that we may glow with the divine fire of holy desire.

A. B. Simpson

My promise to give you the desires of your heart is often misunderstood. You have quoted this verse, *Take delight in the LORD, and he will give you your heart's desires*, and then made a list of what you want. By talking to Me through prayer, you've demanded things that you think will make you happy—but you've forgotten about the conditions for the fulfillment of that promise.

Reread that verse in context: "Trust in the LORD and do good; dwell in the land and enjoy safe pasture. Take delight in the LORD, and he will give you the desires of your heart. Commit your way to the LORD; trust in him and he will do this: He will make your righteous reward shine like the dawn, your vindication like the noonday sun. Be still before the LORD and wait patiently for him" (Psalm 37:3-7, NIV). The conditions for getting your heart's desires are to trust in Me, to do good, to delight in Me, and to commit your way to Me. Then the Holy Spirit will align your desires with My desires. If you do this, you will have a heart on fire with holy desires—and I will delight in giving you all you want.

Take delight in the LORD, and he will give you your heart's desires.

PSALM 37:4

— *April 28* —

COMFORTING OTHERS

I believe we go through what we go through,
to help others go through what we went through.

Kathe Wunnenberg

Be ready to comfort others in the middle of their suffering. You may feel too weak to reach out to someone else—but that's the very thing that qualifies you. Suffering often isolates people. They're embarrassed to always be the needy, hurting ones. Be aware of the pain of others and reach out to them in caring, creative ways. Offer tangible help with their physical needs. Wait with them on an answer to prayer. Weep with them when they go through heart-wrenching loss. The gift of your presence is often more comforting than words.

My plan is that your suffering will not be wasted. Give to others the same hope and comfort you've received from Me. By comforting others in the middle of your own weakness, you prove My strength to hold and sustain you during difficult seasons. Let Me redeem your suffering. Take your eyes off your own pain and turn them toward Me for strength. Then bless others with the same comfort I give to you.

He comforts us in all our troubles so that we can comfort others.
When they are troubled, we will be able to give them
the same comfort God has given us.

2 CORINTHIANS 1:4

— April 29 —

SIGNIFICANCE

We have two alternatives: We can base our self-worth on our success and ability to please others, or we can base our self-worth on the love, forgiveness and acceptance of Christ.

Robert S. McGee

You were created with a desire for fulfillment. My plans for you are far greater than you could ever imagine. As you mature in your faith, you'll discover the work I have for you to do—work that will make your heart sing. It will be in perfect alignment with the gifts I placed within you. Your self-worth should not be based on the accolades of others, how much education you have, or your personal accomplishments. Base your worth on My love and acceptance of you—just the way you are!

Step out in faith and grab hold of the opportunities I place before you. The enemy tries to make you believe his lies: "You're not good enough. You could never do *that*. You will be an embarrassment to your family. You're a failure." But he's a deceiver. You're a winner, not a loser. I created you to declare My praises and to do My work. You are forgiven, accepted, and deeply loved! Help others find their significance in Me too—by stepping out of darkness and into My glorious light.

You are a chosen people, a royal priesthood, a holy nation, God's special possession, that you may declare the praises of him who called you out of darkness into his wonderful light.

1 PETER 2:9, NIV

— *April 30* —

LIVING WATER

Christ is not a reservoir but a spring. . . . If we do not perpetually draw the fresh supply from the living Fountain, we will either grow stagnant or empty. It is, therefore, not so much a perpetual fullness as a perpetual filling.

A. B. Simpson

Evaluate your walk with Me. Since you became a follower of Christ, have you experienced rivers of living water flowing from your heart? When life is challenging, your faith-stream may feel more like a trickle than a river. Perhaps you thought the waters from the Living Fountain were for other people and not for you. Take a look at John 7:37 and read it slowly: "Anyone who is thirsty may come to me!" *Anyone!* That includes *you.*

Water is an essential element for life, and the living water offered by Christ was offered to you the day you said yes to Jesus. But living water does more than sustain your own own soul. My beloved Son said, "Anyone who believes in me may come and drink! For the Scriptures declare, 'Rivers of living water will flow from his heart'" (John 7:38). That means that as you allow yourself to be purified and refreshed by My Spirit, you will in turn refresh others—in abundance! Continue to draw your own fresh supply of water from the Living Fountain, keep announcing the Good News of the gospel, and lead people to the Source of living water. Ask them "Is anyone thirsty?" and invite them to "come and drink" (Isaiah 55:1).

But those who drink the water I give will never be thirsty again.
It becomes a fresh, bubbling spring within them,
giving them eternal life.

JOHN 4:14

— May 1 —

REFINER'S FIRE

Our Refiner . . . will take what is impure and make it pure. He will take what is dull and make it beautiful. He'll take what is of potential value and reveal the actual value. He will transform us into treasure.

Kay Arthur

The furnace of affliction is never fired up to destroy you; it's meant to refine you. Those who follow Me can attest that there is no painless path to heaven (1 Peter 4:12). When your trials seem too heavy to bear, trust in My unchanging, purifying love. This intense time seems endless, but it will not last forever—only for a little while. Trust My goodness and know that after you pass through the flames, you will arrive at a place of indescribable joy.

In the Refiner's fire, impurities rise to the top. Sin is confessed and forgiven. You develop a heart that is totally dependent upon Me. I reveal attitudes and behaviors that need to change. The process is never enjoyable. It scorches. It feels unwarranted. It tempts you to turn your back on Me. But remember that "the testing of your faith produces perseverance. Let perseverance finish its work so that you may be mature and complete, not lacking anything" (James 1:3-4, NIV). Allow Me to do My refining work in you.

In all this you greatly rejoice, though now for a little while you may have had to suffer grief in all kinds of trials. These have come so that the proven genuineness of your faith—of greater worth than gold, which perishes even though refined by fire—may result in praise, glory and honor when Jesus Christ is revealed.

1 PETER 1:6-7, NIV

— *May 2* —

PLANTED

Sometimes when you're in a dark place you think you've been buried, but you've actually been planted.

Christine Caine

Build a root system so strong that when the hurricanes of life come, you will remain firmly planted in truth. Dark clouds hover over your head and make you question where I am. Sometimes you feel forgotten and alone. But if your life is grounded in My Word, you will reflect the beauty and nature of Christ in the middle of the storms. Roots anchor a tree to the soil, providing stability and a firm base. When your roots go deep, supplying you with spiritual food and drink for a healthy life, you will display strong branches, leaves, and fruit.

Paul prayed this for the Ephesians: "I ask him to strengthen you by his Spirit—not a brute strength but a glorious inner strength—that Christ will live in you as you open the door and invite him in. And I ask him that with both feet planted firmly on love, you'll be able to take in with all followers of Jesus the extravagant dimensions of Christ's love. Reach out and experience the breadth! Test its length! Plumb the depths! Rise to the heights! Live full lives, full in the fullness of God" (Ephesians 3:16-19, MSG). That is what I want for you—a thriving life enriched by My truth and love.

They are like trees planted along a riverbank, with roots that reach deep into the water. Such trees are not bothered by the heat or worried by long months of drought. Their leaves stay green, and they never stop producing fruit.

JEREMIAH 17:8

— *May 3* —

SOMETHING GREATER

You have to decide in life for whom or what you're going to live. You're either going to live a self-centered, miserly life or you're going to live for something greater than yourself—the kingdom of God.

Rick Warren

Catch the vision of living for something that will outlast your life. You have a choice—living to bring pleasure to yourself, or living for something greater than yourself. If you choose to live for the Kingdom of God, your life will be filled with opportunities to follow a Spirit-driven calling. Look at people around you. What is the biggest need you see? Ask yourself what Jesus would do if He saw that need, and then use your resources, your influence, and your passion to do something that produces positive change that glorifies Me. Make it a daily habit to personally respond to this question: "What can I do today to further the Kingdom of God?"

The more Christlike you become, the more your outer life will express the character and teachings of Jesus. As your life is transformed, you will live for something greater than yourself. Invite Me to be at work within you, accomplishing what you cannot do on your own. As you live for a bigger purpose, you'll experience a more fulfilling, deeper joy than you've ever known before.

He must become greater and greater,
and I must become less and less.

JOHN 3:30

— *May 4* —

YOUR FATHER

When your earthly father fails you, your heavenly Father finds you.

Jenna Lucado

Do not be surprised when people fail you. It especially hurts when the pain of rejection is inflicted by a parent—by someone you thought would always give you the benefit of the doubt, cheer for you, encourage you, and nurture you. This pain is often multiplied when you see other families expressing sincere love and appreciation for each other. The antidote to this kind of hurt is to realize how much I love you and that I am a *father to the fatherless.* I know exactly what you need even before you ask (Matthew 6:8).

When you accepted My Son as your Savior, you became My child—and I've invited you to participate in the special connection that only a father and his children enjoy. Call Me your Abba Father because I'm your loving Father who desires the best for you. The relationship you've entered into with Me is personal. It's adventurously expectant. Greet Me with a childlike "What's next, Papa?" My Spirit touches your spirit and confirms who you really are. You will receive what I have planned for you—comfort and advice in this world, and in the future, an inheritance beyond description! (paraphrased from Romans 8:15-17, MSG). That's because we're in the same family!

Sing praises to God and to his name! . . . His name is the LORD—rejoice in his presence! Father to the fatherless, defender of widows—this is God, whose dwelling is holy.

PSALM 68:4-5

May 5

OPEN HANDS

Hold everything in your hands lightly,
otherwise it hurts when God pries your fingers open.

Corrie ten Boom

You've been asking for My blessing, but you still want to hold on to secret sins, unhealthy relationships, the memory of wrong choices, and the security of predictable circumstances. I'm asking you to let go. Surrender to Me, confess and turn your back on sin, and go in a new direction. Quit spending time in relationships that drag you down or offer unwholesome enticements. When you yield your will to the mind of Christ, you refuse to entertain thoughts about past sinful choices and instead concentrate on right living—now and in the future. Rather than worrying about little things, trust Me with your safety and well-being.

Opening your hands and heart requires complete faith in Me—without knowing ahead of time what the future will look like. It's a quiet confidence that embraces My plan for your life and believes that I will take care of you and your loved ones. I long to have you trust Me enough to let go.

Let God work his will in you. . . . Say a quiet yes *to God and he'll be there in no time. Quit dabbling in sin. Purify your inner life. . . . Get serious, really serious. Get down on your knees before the Master; it's the only way you'll get on your feet.*

JAMES 4:7-10, MSG

— *May 6* —

ONE WAY

Too many people are trying to worship God apart from Jesus Christ. . . . There is only one way to come into God's presence, and that is through Jesus Christ. Yes, you can worship without Jesus, but you're not worshiping the God of the Bible.

A. W. Tozer

There is only one way for you to have a relationship with Me, and that is through My Son—believing in His sacrifice on the cross and His resurrection. He is the Way, the Truth, and the Life. When pressures increase, the enemy tries to make you question the foundation of your faith, suggesting that there are many ways to connect with Me that are more tolerant and inclusive. But the enemy lies. "There is salvation in no one else! God has given no other name under heaven by which we must be saved" (Acts 4:12).

Be firm in your convictions and speak to everyone you know about this truth! Other religions urge you to believe in some other person, in another philosophy, or in following a different path to find Me. Paul said, "If Christ has not been raised, then all our preaching is useless, and your faith is useless. . . . And if Christ has not been raised, . . . you are still guilty of your sins" (1 Corinthians 15:14, 17). Establish this truth in your heart—Jesus is the *only* Way to come into My presence. He is your sure Foundation!

Jesus told him, "I am the way, the truth, and the life. No one can come to the Father except through me."

JOHN 14:6

May 7

ANGER

Here's a question every angry man and woman needs to consider: How long are you going to allow people you don't even like—people who are no longer in your life, maybe even people who aren't even alive anymore—to control your life? How long?

Andy Stanley

Anger is a powerful emotion that can become a controlling passion. It usually stems from feelings of injustice, unmet needs, jealousy, strife, or abuse. Sometimes you're so angry that you forget why you aren't speaking to someone. These feelings can hold you captive for a short time period or for a lifetime. Sometimes you mask your indignation with the silent treatment. At other times uncontrolled rage spews from your mouth. Hurtful words and actions are aimed at the object of your wrath.

Ask for My help with restraining your anger. Practice self-control. "Sensible people control their temper; they earn respect by overlooking wrongs" (Proverbs 19:11). Seek wise counsel. Identify the root cause of your anger and deal with it in a biblical way. It is very difficult to change the way you respond to this intense emotion, so don't give up trying when you take a step backward. You have a choice—you can allow people you don't even like to control you, or you can change your life for the better. Begin praying for the people who have hurt you or abused you. Forgive them and look for a way to bless them. I will take care of the rest.

"In your anger do not sin": Do not let the sun go down while you are still angry.

EPHESIANS 4:26, NIV

May 8

THE NEXT GENERATION

The greatest legacy one can pass on to one's children and grandchildren is not money or other material things accumulated in one's life, but rather a legacy of character and faith.

Billy Graham

You are being watched by the younger people who are close to you—your children, grandchildren, nieces, and nephews. They are observing the spiritual disciplines of your life. Do they see you reading the Bible? Do they hear you praying for your own needs and for them? Have they seen you reach out to someone who's hurting, even when you are in the middle of your own hard circumstances? Do they hear praise on your lips, or do they hear complaints, criticism, and grumbling?

Be intentional about verbalizing what you know about My power and My creation. When you are awestruck by My works, talk out loud about praiseworthy things, powerful things, and the wonders I've done. Teach the children about My mighty deeds that are recorded in the Bible. Let them participate in praying for your needs, and then rejoice together when I answer your prayers. Teach them My statutes and speak of My promises. Put Me first in your daily decisions and demonstrate what it means to trust Me in every area of your life. Share your own story of how your personal faith has helped you endure with hope in difficult times. As you explain what I have done for you, the children in your life will learn to trust Me and to keep My commands.

We will tell the next generation the praiseworthy deeds of the LORD, his power, and the wonders he has done.

PSALM 78:4, NIV

— *May 9* —

NEVER ALONE

God has promised that whatever you face, you are not alone. He knows your pain. He loves you. And He will bring you through the fire.

Sheila Walsh

Life is filled with separations—children leave home, friends move far away, spouses make bad choices, disease and death rob you of loved ones, and sometimes you make decisions that distance you from Me. But you are not alone. I promise to be with you wherever you go (Joshua 1:9).

On days when you feel lonely, look to Me. I care about your loneliness. When I created Adam in the Garden of Eden, I recognized his need to connect with another human being, so I created Eve. "It is not good for the man to be alone" (Genesis 2:18). I designed you to need relationships. It is My deepest desire for you to walk through life with Me. I will carry your burdens and comfort you during times of loss. I will listen to your cries for help and give you rest when you're weary. Your friendship with Me lays the groundwork upon which you can build relationships with others. Rather than seeking isolation, open up to those around you. It is not good for you to do life alone.

Never will I leave you; never will I forsake you.

HEBREWS 13:5, NIV

May 10

HUMILITY

God talks to those who are humble enough to listen
to wise advice, willing to relinquish their plans for His,
able to wait and not move ahead of Him impulsively.

Becky Tirabassi

I have gifted you with many things to enable you to do My work. When you exercise your gifts and lead people to faith, hope, and trust, it brings you deep fulfillment and joy. Often, they respond with overwhelming praise and thanks to you. Remember: The key to ongoing success is to use your gifts with humility. Humility is not denying the strength and abilities you have; it is admitting to yourself and to others that the power comes *through* you and not *from* you. "Do you want to be counted wise, to build a reputation for wisdom? Here's what you do: Live well, live wisely, live humbly. It's the way you live, not the way you talk, that counts" (James 3:13, MSG).

The key to My blessing is to humble yourself, turn from sin, pray, and seek My face. If you leave arrogance behind and come into My presence without acting pretentious, I will give you wisdom. If you humble yourself before Me, at the right time I will lift you up in honor (1 Peter 5:6). The benefits are great. "True humility and fear of the LORD lead to riches, honor, and long life" (Proverbs 22:4).

If my people, who are called by my name, will humble themselves and pray and seek my face and turn from their wicked ways, then I will hear from heaven, and I will forgive their sin and will heal their land.

2 CHRONICLES 7:14, NIV

— *May 11* —

A NEW THING

At some point, most of us will encounter a challenging situation that permanently alters the rest of our life. Will you withdraw and focus only on your personal pain, or will you recognize that God is doing a new thing and make choices based on His unshakable truth?

Carol Kent

Life is filled with unexpected upheavals. At some point, nearly everyone experiences the gut-wrenching reality of something happening in life that will forever change the future, so stay alert. "Here on earth you will have many trials and sorrows. But take heart, because I have overcome the world" (John 16:33).

When this happens, do not rehearse what you enjoyed about the past and despair about your life now. Take time to see what I am birthing out of the pain. During this season of suffering, you have matured in your faith. You've studied My Word to find answers. You've ministered to others who are struggling. There is a deepening spiritual maturity in you that will bless the lives of others. I don't want you to live in the past—instead, look to the future. Life will not be the same. It will be different and beautiful in a new way. I will open doors for you and provide spiritual nourishment along the way. Embrace this emerging opportunity and recognize My plan going forward.

I am about to do something new. See, I have already begun!
Do you not see it? I will make a pathway through the wilderness.
I will create rivers in the dry wasteland.

ISAIAH 43:19

May 12

MY HELPER

O God, our help in ages past, our hope for years to come, our shelter from the stormy blast, and our eternal home.

Isaac Watts

I have heard your cries for help, and I am here—ready to give you comfort, shelter, and assistance. Like the psalmist, you have prayed, "Hear me, LORD, and have mercy on me. Help me, O LORD" (Psalm 30:10). Your prayers are precious to Me. During the tests and trials of your life, you can lift your hands to Me, or you can wring your hands with anxiety, stress, and fear. The choice is yours.

My promises reveal that I am reaching out to you with My strong hand to grasp your trembling one. Say this verse aloud: "Behold, God is my helper; the Lord is the upholder of my life" (Psalm 54:4, ESV). Envision Me upholding your life. Remember My willingness to help you. I offer you forgiveness of sins (1 John 1:9), peace of mind (Philippians 4:7), freedom from fear (Isaiah 12:2), rest (Matthew 11:28), deliverance from distress and trouble (Psalm 107:13), and eternal life (John 3:36). I'm offering you help for every one of your needs. Reach out and accept the provisions I've made available, and you'll discover a never-ending supply of support for today and every day.

So we can say with confidence, "The LORD is my helper, so I will have no fear. What can mere people do to me?"

HEBREWS 13:6

— *May 13* —

OPENHANDED

I invite you to send your treasures on to heaven, where they will safely await you. When you do, you'll feel the freedom, experience the joy, and sense the smile of God. When you give, you'll feel His pleasure.

Randy Alcorn

Open your hands and be generous in your giving. Your gifts to My Kingdom work are an act of worship (1 Corinthians 16:2). You sometimes wonder if you'll have enough money to take care of yourself and your family, and you've hesitated to give because your gift might seem too small. Give in accordance with your means (2 Corinthians 8:12). I never ask you to contribute more than you have or to give beyond your means. Those who have more should give more.

I can't resist people who give cheerfully. "You must each decide in your heart how much to give. And don't give reluctantly or in response to pressure. 'For God loves a person who gives cheerfully'" (2 Corinthians 9:7). When you give, don't do it to impress people; do it secretly, and I will reward you (Matthew 6:3-4). When you give to others even when you have personal needs, I see your heart of generosity and your focus on living for things that will outlast your life. "Wherever your treasure is, there the desires of your heart will also be" (Luke 12:34).

Don't store up treasures here on earth, where moths eat them and rust destroys them, and where thieves break in and steal. Store your treasures in heaven, where moths and rust cannot destroy, and thieves do not break in and steal.

MATTHEW 6:19-20

— *May 14* —

SHELTER

That little bird has chosen his shelter. Above it are the stars and the deep heaven of worlds. Yet he is rocking himself to sleep without caring for tomorrow's lodging, calmly clinging to his little twig, and leaving God to think for him.

Martin Luther

When you feel unprotected and uncared for, observe the birds of the air. "They don't plant or harvest or store food in barns, for your heavenly Father feeds them. And aren't you far more valuable to him than they are?" (Matthew 6:26). Let Me be your safe haven during the storms of life. When you need a shelter, I will provide a sanctuary for you. Take refuge in My arms. I will give you everything you need.

If you live under My protection, you can trade anxiety for peace and rest. When your enemies come after you, I will be your Defense. Make Me your Rock of refuge. Pray with the psalmist: "But my eyes are upon You, O God the Lord; In You I take refuge; Do not leave my soul destitute. . . . Let the wicked fall into their own nets, while I escape safely" (Psalm 141:8, 10, NKJV). Enfold yourself in the sturdy shelter of My almighty wings and know that I will keep you secure.

For in the day of trouble he will keep me safe in his dwelling;
he will hide me in the shelter of his sacred tent
and set me high upon a rock.

PSALM 27:5, NIV

— *May 15* —

PRAISE POWER

When I find myself getting weary from life's pressures,
I put on praise music and begin to thank the Lord.

Thelma Wells

There is power in praise. It will get your focus off your life's pressures and back on Me. Instead of centering your thoughts on the struggles of life, you'll be drawn close to Me because I inhabit the praises of My people (Psalm 22:3, KJV). Your praise-filled lips invite My presence. Do you know how special you are? "You are a chosen people, a royal priesthood, a holy nation, God's special possession, that you may declare the praises of him who called you out of darkness into his wonderful light" (1 Peter 2:9, NIV).

Praise pushes back the enemy and makes room for My blessing in your life. Glorify Me right where you are this moment. Your spirit will be refreshed, and you'll be renewed in My presence. When your heart is aching, listen to worship music and begin singing your praise. Allow Me to lift your head. Pray these words: "Because your love is better than life, my lips will glorify you. I will praise you as long as I live, and in your name I will lift up my hands" (Psalm 63:3-4, NIV). Praise paves the way for My power to be displayed. Miracles happen—and often the greatest miracle is in your heart.

Praise the LORD! Praise God in his sanctuary; praise him in his mighty heaven! Praise him for his mighty works; praise his unequaled greatness! . . . Let everything that breathes sing praises to the LORD! Praise the LORD!

PSALM 150:1-2, 6

May 16

KEEP MOVING

When God says go forward, don't even think about standing still.

Beth Moore

You are on the path of My choosing. The best way for you to gain momentum in your life is to keep moving in the direction of My will. Allow Me to open doors for you in life and in ministry. I know best how you can use your gifts and resources for the maximum Kingdom result as you go forward. Remember: "The LORD directs the steps of the godly. He delights in every detail of their lives. Though they stumble, they will never fall, for the LORD holds them by the hand" (Psalm 37:23-24).

When you fall down, I will lift you up and give you another chance to make right choices. Don't allow your failings to make you stand still. I have big plans for you. Keep looking to Me for clarity, wisdom, and direction. I delight in grasping your hand in Mine and in guiding you as your desires and thoughts are conformed to the likeness of Jesus Christ. Listen for My voice. It will be revealed to you as you read My Word, when you pray and seek My counsel, and as you listen to input from Christians who have a mature faith. When My Spirit nudges you to take action, respond with conviction. "Whatever your hand finds to do, do it with all your might" (Ecclesiastes 9:10, NIV).

Whether you turn to the right or to the left, your ears will hear a voice behind you, saying, "This is the way; walk in it."

ISAIAH 30:21, NIV

— *May 17* —

FRAGRANCE

There should be a fragrance of grace that permeates the air around us as we live victoriously in Christ. What a privilege and an honor to give off a sweet savor to God and the world as Christ lives in us, through us, and for us.

Darrell Creswell

Your life of sacrifice is a sweet perfume to Me. Live out your days in a way that glorifies Me, and your example will permeate the atmosphere with a pleasant fragrance. You may think no one notices your behavior, attitudes, and way of living, but people are watching. Your actions have a lingering effect on those around you. "Live a life filled with love, following the example of Christ. He loved us and offered himself as a sacrifice for us, a pleasing aroma to God" (Ephesians 5:2).

As you live victoriously in Christ in the middle of heavy challenges and multiple hardships, your life gives hope to others. People will begin directing others to talk to you when they need answers. Always be ready to respond to their questions and speak openly about biblical principles. Treat others with respect even when they scoff at your faith or try to argue about My existence. Continue to share the gospel and stand against sin. Your godly conduct will reveal My character, and their curiosity will keep them listening. In time, some will say yes to Jesus.

But thanks be to God, who in Christ always leads us in triumphal procession, and through us spreads the fragrance of the knowledge of him everywhere.

2 CORINTHIANS 2:14, ESV

— *May 18* —

COMMUNION

Whenever we receive Communion, we must do so in humility and brokenness before God. We must rejoice and be grateful and thankful for our salvation.

Michael Youssef

You are in My family. Meet regularly with other believers who know and love Me, and together enter into the Lord's Supper. It's a time to stop and remember what Jesus did for you. Sometimes you neglect gathering at the table because you feel unworthy or because you have unconfessed sin in your life. But you don't have to be perfect before you gather for Communion. Come as you are and spend time in My presence. Ask the Holy Spirit to reveal anything that isn't pleasing to Me. Repent of those sins and then partake of the bread and the wine.

Look back and remember My love for you and consider what Jesus accomplished for you on the cross. In an unrushed state of mind, think about what Scripture says—to do this *until he comes again*. Then look ahead and focus on your conquering King—Jesus will come back. Rejoice and celebrate as you participate in Communion, just as the early church demonstrated. Come in honesty. Come with reverence. Leave with joy!

On the night when he was betrayed, the Lord Jesus took some bread and gave thanks to God for it. Then he broke it in pieces and said, "This is my body, which is given for you. . . ." In the same way, he took the cup of wine after supper, saying, "This cup is the new covenant between God and his people—an agreement confirmed with my blood. Do this in remembrance of me as often as you drink it."

1 CORINTHIANS 11:23-25

May 19

HEAVEN

My hope is that this life is not all there is. This life is like preparation for what is coming next, and what is coming next is something so glorious that the Bible says minds can't conceive it, eye has never seen, your imagination could never even enter into all that God is preparing for those who love him.

Anne Graham Lotz

Set your eyes on heaven. One day you will live with Me forever in a redeemed place. Jesus said, "My Father's house has many rooms; if that were not so, would I have told you that I am going there to prepare a place for you? And if I go and prepare a place for you, I will come back and take you to be with me that you also may be where I am" (John 14:2-3, NIV). In this grand and glorious home, there is great joy and pleasures abound (Psalm 16:11). That means that no matter what burden you are carrying now, in heaven you will experience relief from your current human condition. Close your eyes, take a deep breath, and envision what your life will be like when the cares of this world no longer bind you. You will be in My presence experiencing extraordinary beauty, complete peace, and everlasting joy.

The condition for this kind of a future is that you accept the offering of Jesus on the cross for your sin. Love Me with your whole heart and trust Me with the challenges you face now. All of your trials will come to an end, and you will see Me face-to-face in all of My glory. You will be home—at last!

No eye has seen, no ear has heard, and no mind has imagined what God has prepared for those who love him.

1 CORINTHIANS 2:9

— *May 20* —

MIND MATTERS

The secret of living a life of excellence is merely a matter of thinking thoughts of excellence. Really, it's a matter of programming our minds with the kind of information that will set us free.

Charles Swindoll

What occupies your mind? What's the first thing you think about in the morning and the last thing you reflect on at night? My Word says, "For as he thinks in his heart, so is he" (Proverbs 23:7, NKJV). Practice the habit of focusing on things that are honest, just, pure, lovely, and worthy of praise. Nourish a godly mind by meditating on biblical truth. Make a commitment to Me: "I will study your commandments and reflect on your ways" (Psalm 119:15). As you read the Scriptures, make a list of My promises. Intentionally fill your mind with thoughts that are excellent.

When you establish the daily exercise of transformed thinking, the people around you will notice a change in the way you think and live. It takes discipline, along with a heart that's intent on purity. "Meditate on these things; give yourself entirely to them, that your progress may be evident to all" (1 Timothy 4:15, NKJV). Altered thinking doesn't happen without My help. Ask Me to give you the courage, willpower, and resolution to follow through with pure thoughts.

And now, dear brothers and sisters, one final thing. Fix your thoughts on what is true, and honorable, and right, and pure, and lovely, and admirable. Think about things that are excellent and worthy of praise.

PHILIPPIANS 4:8

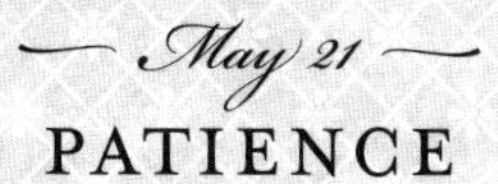

PATIENCE

Patience is the ability to idle your motor when you feel like stripping your gears.

Barbara Johnson

I want you to develop patience. This is not easy, and it doesn't feel natural. You long for answers to questions, resolutions in relationship difficulties, fewer hardships, and peace and serenity in day-to-day living. Your personal attempt to fix things has failed again, and you're discouraged. When you feel under pressure, remember that you are chosen and loved. I've provided the fruit of the Spirit to help you. "The Holy Spirit produces this kind of fruit in our lives: love, joy, peace, patience, kindness, goodness, faithfulness, gentleness, and self-control" (Galatians 5:22-23).

You're trying so hard to figure everything out. Stop long enough to take a breath and ask Me to clothe you with perseverance and staying power. As time unfolds, you'll see that I am responding to your needs in a very different way than you were expecting. Wait with hope and know that it brings Me joy to meet your needs in My perfect timing.

We also pray that you will be strengthened with all his glorious power so you will have all the endurance and patience you need. May you be filled with joy.

COLOSSIANS 1:11

— *May 22* —

RESTORATION

The work of restoration cannot begin until a problem is fully faced.

Dan B. Allender

I hear your cry for restoration. There was a time when your relationship with Me brought gladness. You lingered in My presence. You delighted in expressing your love for Me and in speaking words of hope to others. But now you have allowed your mind to return to former days, and you're encumbered with thoughts of past abuse or hurts. That response has created distance between us. I haven't moved, but you keep trying to soothe yourself with too much work, perfectionism, or escape into addictive patterns. I have heard your prayer: "Restore to me the joy of your salvation" (Psalm 51:12, ESV).

The first step to restoration is to face your problem. What sin needs to be confessed? What abuse have you kept locked up inside, burdening you with false guilt? Ask Me to hold a magnifying glass to your heart and reveal what is placing a wedge between us. When you have identified the problem as sin, come to Me in repentance, and I will forgive you and make you whole again. Reject guilt over the wrongs done to you. I want you to be in spiritual alignment with Me so you can boldly proclaim, "He restores my soul. He leads me in paths of righteousness for his name's sake" (Psalm 23:3, ESV). I will *restore you and make you strong, firm and steadfast.* Welcome back!

The God of all grace, who called you to his eternal glory in Christ, after you have suffered a little while, will himself restore you and make you strong, firm and steadfast.

1 PETER 5:10, NIV

— *May 23* —

SEEKING COUNSEL

Prayer lays hold of God's plan and becomes the link between His will and its accomplishment on earth. Amazing things happen, and we are given the privilege of being the channels of the Holy Spirit's prayer.

Elisabeth Elliot

Practice the daily habit of talking to Me. You have been dismissing prayer because it seems mysterious and you're not sure how it works. But I have designed prayer as the mechanism that leads you to strength and victory in your life. Prayer allows you to partner with Me in the fulfillment of My will. You can personally contact Me any time of the day or night. Through prayer the power of heaven comes down to earth.

Prayers don't need to be long and eloquent. Talk to Me as a friend. Express your praise and thanks. Then present your requests. Ask Me to be involved in your daily living and in your urgent needs. Voice your concerns as the psalmist did: "Listen to my prayer for mercy as I cry out to you for help" (Psalm 28:2). When you pray, you invite Me to come into the middle of your problems and work on your behalf. "The prayer of a person living right with God is something powerful to be reckoned with" (James 5:16, MSG). Talk to Me about anything and know that I'm listening to your every word.

You faithfully answer our prayers with awesome deeds,
O God our savior. You are the hope of everyone on earth.

PSALM 65:5

— *May 24* —

THE ADVENTURE

We like to control the map of our life and know everything well in advance. But faith is content just knowing that God's promise cannot fail. This, in fact, is the excitement of walking with God.

Jim Cymbala

You like a predictable life, but I have a better plan for your future. As you learn the rhythm of walking beside Me, you'll get more comfortable with the detours along the way. Sometimes the unexpected stops in your path will bring indescribable joy. At other times the sudden turns will feel devastating and unwanted. Allow Me to be your constant Companion on the journey of life during the best and worst of times. When you're afraid, reach out and let Me hold your hand as we navigate the twists and turns in the road.

There will be times when you think you can't go any farther, but pressing on will eventually bring you to quiet streams and still waters. You'll discover that when I'm at your side, obstacles become stepping-stones and mountains are conquered as you keep putting one foot in front of the other. One day you will awaken to the excitement of this faith-walk, and you'll develop the habit of anticipating how I will make a way in the midst of impossible challenges. This will build your faith-muscle, and you will begin enjoying the adventure of life. Let Me be your GPS as you learn to embrace the thrill of walking in supernatural strength above your circumstances.

The LORD directs the steps of the godly.
He delights in every detail of their lives.

PSALM 37:23

— *May 25* —

CHOICES

Choices can change our lives profoundly. The choice to mend a broken relationship, to say "yes" to a difficult assignment, to lay aside some important work to play with a child, to visit some forgotten person—these small choices may affect many lives eternally.

Gloria Gaither

The most important choice you ever made was to become a follower of Jesus Christ. Now that you are a believer, I give you choices every day about how you can live out your faith. Each day is busy and filled with activity that captures your attention and demands your time. Some of the people around you clamor for help, even though they are capable of moving forward on their own. Others never ask for assistance, and you must be alert to their needs. Allow wisdom to guide you, and then be decisive with the intentional use of your time.

Some questions you can ask yourself are: Who would appreciate a visit from me? How can I bring a smile to a child's face? Do I owe anyone an apology? Is there an action I need to take that will further the Kingdom of God? Whom can I bless with my words? When you make choices—even small ones—that bless others, you will experience unexpected joy that permeates your being and overflows into the lives of others. With practice, you will begin making good choices on a daily basis.

Wisdom will enter your heart, and knowledge will fill you with joy. Wise choices will watch over you. Understanding will keep you safe.

PROVERBS 2:10-11

— *May 26* —

RAIN OF GRACE

When we lay the soil of our hard lives open to the rain of grace and let joy penetrate our cracked and dry places, let joy soak into our broken skin and deep crevices, life grows.

Ann Voskamp

Lift up your face and look at Me. "Let me see your face; let me hear your voice. For your voice is pleasant, and your face is lovely" (Song of Songs 2:14). I love to spend time with you. Throughout the day, watch for My unexpected blessings, opportunities, and interruptions. Dare to pray, "Lord, rain Your grace on me." Expect to be surprised by My personal involvement in small and large things. Learn to delight in the beauty of a flower, the majesty of a tree, the notes of a songbird, and the utter magnificence of a newborn baby.

I'm raining grace all around you, so much so that you may not be able to recognize or appreciate all of it at once. Beware of becoming numb to the glory of My creation or to the innumerable splashes of joy all around you. Sometimes you think mercy is only My forgiveness for your big mistakes. However, My mercy is everywhere—it's in the air you breathe; it's in the kindness of a friend; it's in the comfort you found in a sermon; and it's in the death and resurrection of My Son. Look up again. Envision grace, like rain, falling on you—soaking you with the awareness of My goodness, My forgiveness, My delight in you, and My joy in spending time with you. Linger in My presence before rushing into your day.

Because of God's tender mercy, the morning light from heaven is about to break upon us.

LUKE 1:78

— *May 27* —

LEGACY

Yes, your family history has some sad chapters.
But your history doesn't have to be your future.
The generational garbage can stop here and now.

Max Lucado

What will you pass on to future generations? If you had a godly heritage, you want to give the same thing to your children and your children's children. But your background may have been filled with ungodliness, neglect, cruelty, violence, addictions, or scarring from verbal abuse, and you may wonder if it will ever be possible for you to pass a blessing on to your family members.

You can allow the pain of the past to hold you in bondage, or you can make a choice that the past will not dictate your future. In the name of Jesus Christ and His shed blood on Calvary, tell the enemy he is through messing with your family. Begin each day by reading My Word. Talk to your children about what it means. Live a life immersed in love, truth, and hope, and give your children the security of knowing that I am their Comforter and Protector. Reject fear. Embrace hope. Live as a child of the Most High God and pass that confidence and legacy of faith on to your entire family.

Write these commandments that I've given you today on your hearts. Get them inside of you and then get them inside your children. . . . Talk about them from the time you get up in the morning to when you fall into bed at night.

DEUTERONOMY 6:6–7, MSG

May 28

RECURRENCE

Are you experiencing a sacred echo? A moment where God speaks the same message again and again to your heart.

Margaret Feinberg

Look for My repeated themes in Scripture. There are certain things I want to remind you of on a regular basis because they are important. One of those themes is how much I love you. "I have loved you with an everlasting love; I have drawn you with unfailing kindness" (Jeremiah 31:3, NIV). There is nothing you can do that will stop My unquenchable love for you. I created you in My image. I gave you the gift of My Son, who died on the cross so that you could be forgiven of your sins and have everlasting life. "For God so loved the world that he gave his one and only Son, that whoever believes in him shall not perish but have eternal life" (John 3:16, NIV).

You have been distracted and agitated, wondering if the life of faith will ever measure up to your expectations. Life has thrown you a curveball, and it's been hard to get back on your feet. Spend some free moments today concentrating on My multidimensional love for you. Everything around you may look like it's falling apart, but "love never fails" (1 Corinthians 13:8, NIV). Hear My tender whisper in your ear: "I love you."

All glory to him who loves us and has freed us from our sins by shedding his blood for us.

REVELATION 1:5

May 29

THE DEEP PLACE

Go to the deep place, and sit on the steps of your soul and talk to the Lord; then come back to the shallow places of life and tell those you meet what God said to encourage you, which may then serve to encourage them.

Jill Briscoe

Linger over My Word and listen for My instruction. Ask Me to take you deeper into an ever-increasing knowledge of My truth. Talk to Me about what you're learning as you grow in wisdom and insight. Experience My love as it washes over you and be comforted by My nearness. I will take you deeper still until your life is lost in Jesus. In that place of total surrender, you will discover My will and My peace. Going deeper has a cost, and others may be critical of your desire to separate from the cares of this world for a while. But the end result of your commitment is worth it—the spiritual fruitfulness, the increased wisdom, and the intimacy you have with Me.

I know you are afraid of what might be ahead of you, so place your hand in My firm grip. When you return to the shallower places of life, take what you have learned and bless the lives of people I place in your path. Teach them how to come to the deep place and find renewal, refreshment, and understanding in My presence. Pray that My glorious, unlimited resources will empower them with inner strength through My Spirit (Ephesians 3:16).

Come close to God, and God will come close to you.

JAMES 4:8

May 30
BECOMING

Like someone peeling an onion, the Lord reveals one layer of sin in my life at a time. He gently exposes my failings, my prejudice, and my pride. Then He invites me to repent . . . to move toward becoming what I was meant to be.

Joanna Weaver

Ask Me to help you become more like Christ. Study His life, attitudes, and behavior. What needs to change in your life so you can be transformed into His likeness? Is there jealousy, anger, pride, or a bad habit that needs to go? When you recognize sin, are you willing to call it what it is and ask for My forgiveness? As My Spirit continues to work in your life, you'll be transformed from the inside out.

There's a cost to being a Christ-follower. My disciples ran into all kinds of trouble for doing the right things—and you will too. Don't be surprised when you're criticized, wrongfully accused, or ridiculed. Instead of fostering bitterness and hurt feelings, put on the mind of Christ. Forgive quickly and continue to set your heart on what I require: "to do what is right, to love mercy, and to walk humbly with your God" (Micah 6:8). This doesn't happen overnight. As you make a habit of right living, you will become what you were meant to be.

If any of you wants to be my follower, you must give up your own way, take up your cross daily, and follow me. If you try to hang on to your life, you will lose it. But if you give up your life for my sake, you will save it.

LUKE 9:23-24

— *May 31* —

SERVANTHOOD

Being a servant of God is different from being a servant of a human master. A servant of a human master works *for* his master. God, however, works *through* His servants.

Henry T. Blackaby

Authentic servanthood is expressed by sacrificial living. It is a lifestyle of thinking of others before thinking of yourself. It means acting with humility, not arrogance and self-sufficiency. It asks the question "How can I *serve*?" not "How can I *be served*?" It requires a temperament that is peace loving, not argumentative. "A servant of the Lord must not quarrel but must be kind to everyone, be able to teach, and be patient with difficult people" (2 Timothy 2:24).

Avoid comparing your service with others. Servanthood is about *your* sacrifice, not about what someone else is doing. Serve with a glad heart and keep your own faith-fire ignited by staying close to Me. When someone is in need, show generous hospitality. Be alert to the hurts of fellow believers and seek My leading about how to creatively bring hope and comfort to My people. Don't seek applause for what you're doing. Paul said, "We don't go around preaching about ourselves. We preach that Jesus Christ is Lord, and we ourselves are your servants for Jesus' sake" (2 Corinthians 4:5). I will honor and reward those who faithfully serve Me.

Whoever wants to be a leader among you must be your servant.

MATTHEW 20:26

June 1

THIRSTY

Those who follow Jesus grow hungry and thirsty on the way.

Dietrich Bonhoeffer

When you invited Jesus into your life, you longed for more wisdom and deeper truths. You spent hours with Me. Spiritual thirst came naturally when your faith was new. Your sins had just been forgiven, and your hunger for more knowledge was a compelling factor in the way you spent your time. You read in My Word that I satisfy the thirsty and fill the hungry with good things (Psalm 107:9). When you set your heart on following Jesus, your desire for a closer, more intimate, and totally committed relationship became a driving force in your life. The more you got to know Him, the thirstier you were for His teaching, His example, and His presence.

Time has passed, and pain has eroded your once-vibrant passion for more of My truth. I have a banquet of spiritual food and drink available to you, but you've been distracted by current pressures and have pulled away from the tender intimacy we once knew. You were created for fellowship with Me. Ask Me to reveal what's wrong. "Search me, O God, and know my heart; test me and know my anxious thoughts" (Psalm 139:23). If you pray in this way, I will reveal what needs to change. When you repent of wrong thinking and wrongdoing, your hunger and thirst for Me will return. The banquet table is ready for you. Come thirsty!

O God, you are my God; I earnestly search for you. My soul thirsts for you; my whole body longs for you in this parched and weary land where there is no water.

PSALM 63:1

— June 2 —

UNFULFILLED DREAMS

Perhaps disappointed dreams are our best opportunities to transfer hope to its rightful place. Heaven is where our biggest dreams belong. Realizing that can help us make it through the here and now without placing a burden on the present that it was never meant to bear.

Paula Rinehart

You had big dreams for how your life would unfold, but there have been some disappointments along the way. Many of your hopes for the future seem unreachable, and your dreams have submitted to the reality of the here and now. Discouragement has set in, and there are days when you feel like giving up. But you've been misplacing your hopes and dreams. This earth will never resemble heaven. If you understand that your best dreams will be fulfilled in another place, you can get through the tough stuff of this life more easily. It's a matter of focus. "Set your mind on the things above, not on the things that are on earth" (Colossians 3:2, NASB).

To transfer your unfulfilled dreams to a firm future reality, remember that heaven provides mansion accommodations (John 14:2, NKJV); it's a place of rest for the afflicted and troubled (2 Thessalonians 1:7); it provides eternal life (Matthew 25:46); and it's a Kingdom that cannot be shaken (Hebrews 12:28). Those descriptions will fill your heart with hope! When unfulfilled dreams distract you, remain faithful and keep your eye on the prize—a life with Me forever and ever. It won't be long until you get there. Hold on!

I have fought the good fight, I have finished the race, and I have remained faithful. And now the prize awaits me. . . . And the prize is not just for me but for all who eagerly look forward to his appearing.

2 TIMOTHY 4:7-8

June 3

SECOND CHANCES

We have a God of the second chance. He not only restores us but recycles our failures, using them for his purposes. . . . Failure can be the best preparation for this kind of success, if we submit ourselves to its lessons while we wait for another chance.

Elisa Morgan

You've been reluctant to come into My presence. You've been running in the opposite direction of what you already know is My desired path for your life. It hurts Me when you snub My advice and push through your days without My direction. You say you love Me, but you've been holding back because you think the cost of following Me with abandon might be uncomfortable or even frightening. In front of other believers, you say all the right things about your commitment to Me, but I see your hard heart and feel your resistance to My Spirit.

When you run away from Me, the enemy can convince you that you can never have a do-over. He wants you to think you've gone too far, that you've resisted My will for so long you don't deserve another chance to offer your abilities, resources, or influence for My Kingdom purposes. But he's wrong—again! Just as I gave Jonah another opportunity to go to Nineveh, I will give you a second chance. Come to Me with a repentant heart and listen to My instructions. Then move forward in obedience. This will bring unexpected joy and meaning to your life.

The LORD spoke to Jonah a second time: "Get up and go to the great city of Nineveh, and deliver the message I have given you."

JONAH 3:1-2

June 4

MY DEFENDER

To me, it has been a source of great comfort and strength in the day of battle, just to remember that the secret of steadfastness, and indeed, of victory, is the recognition that "the Lord is at hand."

Duncan Campbell

The secret to winning a spiritual battle is to allow Me to be your Defender. The enemy challenges you when you are physically exhausted and emotionally exasperated, and he finds your most vulnerable places. He wants you to believe that you're too weak to fight, too tired to resist temptation, too defeated to care, and too discouraged to ask anyone else for help. That's the way he works—wearing you down and taunting, "You're a failure. Just quit trying. God loves other people more than you, or you wouldn't be in this situation."

Stop giving in to the enemy of your soul. Quit trying to defend yourself. Allow Me to be your Strength and your Rescuer. Trust in My unfailing love for you and give Me the opportunity to fight your battles. If you do this, I will provide a way for you to look down in triumph on your enemies (Psalm 59:9-10). Call upon Me, and I will come to your aid. Pray, "The Lord is my rock and my fortress and my deliverer; my God, my strength, in whom I will trust; my shield and the horn of my salvation, my stronghold" (Psalm 18:2, NKJV). Remain in Me, and I will be your Champion.

When the enemy comes in like a flood, the Spirit of the Lord will lift up a standard against him.

ISAIAH 59:19, NKJV

June 5

INTEGRITY

You teach a little by what you say. You teach most by what you are.

Henrietta Mears

Live righteously even when you think no one is watching. You hold Me in the place of highest honor when your life exhibits a moral code, ethics, and values based on My precepts. Don't be wishy-washy. Keep your word and follow through with your promises. Be honest in your dealings with others and let truthfulness be evidence of your character. When you demonstrate a Christlike attitude, you become a magnet for people who are longing for straightforward answers to their tough questions. Word gets around that you are someone who can be trusted.

Duplicity and dishonesty are so prevalent in society that your display of integrity announces to the world that your faith is real. People find hypocrisy disgusting, and they have no respect for someone who says one thing and then does another. "Be careful to live properly among your unbelieving neighbors" (1 Peter 2:12). When you say you are a follower of Christ, let your life, your speech, and your kindness to others reflect what you say you believe. Continue to walk in constant awareness of Me, and people will be drawn to your faith, even without words.

He is a shield to those who walk with integrity. He guards the paths of the just and protects those who are faithful to him.

PROVERBS 2:7-8

June 6

CHERISHED

You are left alone with Jesus. Quietly, he comes close. He reaches out and lifts your chin up with his hand. He smiles and wipes away the tears that stain your cheeks. His touch takes your breath away. He makes you feel cherished. . . . Slowly, he helps you to your feet.

Betsy Lee

Sometimes you will be alone, but that doesn't mean you have to be lonely. Learn to enjoy solitude so you can fully enjoy My presence. You've been rushing here and there and keeping yourself busy so you won't have time to concentrate on the sadness in your life. But the harder and more perfectly you work, the more you feel unfulfilled and incomplete. Sometimes you expect other people to fill the hole inside your heart, but no one else can ever give you the completeness and satisfaction that come only from Me.

Slow down long enough to let Me be your Comforter, your Healer, and your Lover. Consider these words from the psalmist: "For his unfailing love toward those who fear him is as great as the height of the heavens above the earth" (Psalm 103:11). Bask in My unfailing love and realize it knows no end. I cherish you, and our times together bring Me great joy. Linger in My company and find yourself totally embraced by the One who loves you most. I want to quiet your heart and feel you relax in the safety of My embrace.

The LORD your God in your midst, The Mighty One, will save; He will rejoice over you with gladness, He will quiet you with His love, He will rejoice over you with singing.

ZEPHANIAH 3:17, NKJV

June 7

CHOSEN

Have you ever longed to be chosen because you were really wanted . . . you were really desired? Child of God, the Lord chose you "before the creation of the world." He chose you because He wanted you, not because of your strength, scholarship, or skill.

June Hunt

Dear one, sometimes you get hung up over whether I chose you or you chose Me. But today, I want you to concentrate on what it means to be chosen. You are My child, My beloved, My delight, and My joy. When you know you are chosen, it confirms to your heart that you are wanted, included, and deeply loved. Imagine Me saying, "I pick you! You're on My team. We were meant to be together."

The truth of the matter is that I *did* choose you, and you chose to follow Me. You were chosen "before the foundation of the world" (Ephesians 1:4, ESV), and you walked through a door that said, "Whosoever will, let him come." What a wonder! Our relationship is special, unique, and close. I will give you guidance in your life, but I will never force your hand. Obedience is your part. I have given you everything you need to find My plan, decipher My will, and walk in wisdom. Do not fear the future. I will triumph over every enemy of your soul, and you will reign with Me—you, My chosen one. For I am "Lord of all lords and King of all kings" and you "are called and chosen and faithful" (Revelation 17:14).

You didn't choose me. I chose you. I appointed you to go and produce lasting fruit, so that the Father will give you whatever you ask for, using my name.

JOHN 15:16

— *June 8* —

DIRECTION

Your abilities are the map to God's will for your life. It points the direction. When you know what you're good at, then you can know what God wants you to do with your life.

Rick Warren

My design for your life includes seasons. Some seasons require intensity, hard work, study, discipline, and targeted focus. At other times, My Spirit will lead you to take a breath, slow down, and intentionally engage in rest. It's important that you stay close to Me, listen to My voice, and discern My will during the rhythms of life. Sometimes your insecurity leads you to hold back when I want you to be confident and courageous.

When I open a door, start walking. As you move forward, depend on Me to either affirm the direction you're going or give you a sense of uneasiness. When the Holy Spirit gives you a passion for a cause, a project, a mission, or a specific assignment, engage others of like mind to join you in the adventure. When obstacles get in the way, remember this: "Don't sit around on your hands! No more dragging your feet! Clear the path for long-distance runners so no one will trip and fall, so no one will step in a hole and sprain an ankle. Help each other out. And run for it!" (Hebrews 12:12-13, MSG).

Whatever your hand finds to do, do it with all your might.

ECCLESIASTES 9:10, NIV

June 9

KNOWING GOD

Let us occupy ourselves entirely in knowing God. The more we know Him, the more we will desire to know Him. . . . The more we know God, the more we will truly love Him. And we will learn to love Him equally in times of distress or in times of great joy.

Brother Lawrence

You are sometimes tempted to pick out a Scripture verse and claim it as your own because it seems to promise a happy ending. When you are in times of crisis, hardship, or distress, it's comforting to say that everything works together for good for those who love Me (Romans 8:28), but you sometimes forget to consider the conditions. Read the verse that comes next: "For those God foreknew he also predestined to be conformed to the image of his Son" (Romans 8:29, NIV). Suffering was part of the process for the Lord Jesus Christ, and it will be part of life for those who love Me.

All of the hurtful things that are happening to you are reminders that there is evil in the world. But I will turn those things to good. What "good" is coming out of your struggle? You are becoming more like Jesus. Your love for Me is maturing, and you are experiencing the joy of knowing that My love for you is consistent on the good days and on the bad days. You are no longer expecting perfection and completion in this world—your eyes are fixed on heaven and the life that is to come. As you get to know My character, your love for Me is the same in times of pain or joy.

We know that God causes everything to work together for the good of those who love God and are called according to his purpose for them.

ROMANS 8:28

June 10

A HAPPY HEART

We can find lasting and settled happiness by saying yes to the God who created and redeems us and by embracing a biblical worldview. When we look at the world and our daily lives through the lens of redemption, reasons for happiness abound.

Randy Alcorn

I want you to have a happy heart—not only on days when everything is going according to your plan, but on the difficult days too! This heart response is a deliberate decision to choose joy, delight, and gladness based on what you know to be true about My character. False happiness is pretending everything is fine. Authentic happiness is embracing the peace, contentment, and inner satisfaction of walking with Me and looking for bursts of joy in everyday life.

When you walk in My truth and follow My principles, your heart will delight in My presence. The psalmist learned the secret: "Make me walk along the path of your commands, for that is where my happiness is found" (Psalm 119:35). You may go through loss of health, family members, financial security, and reputation, but continue to lean on Me. Look for the specific places where I am providing for your physical needs and for your personal encouragement. Find joy in the little things and you'll soon discover reasons for the happiness that surrounds you right now. Allow yourself to laugh out loud and take pleasure in the joyful sound coming out of your mouth. Cultivate the spirit of celebration in your heart by making room for laughter. Deliberately seek it out.

For the despondent, every day brings trouble;
for the happy heart, life is a continual feast.

PROVERBS 15:15

June 11

STICKY TRUTH

Joseph filled the barns in the time of plenty to be prepared for the time of famine. . . . Gather the riches of God's promises which can strengthen you in the time when there will be no freedom. Nobody can take away from you those texts from the Bible which you have learned by heart.

Corrie ten Boom

You fear the future because of wars, rumors of wars, natural disasters, family strife, alluring temptations that beckon those you love, disintegrating health, and discord among My people. Sometimes these concerns occupy your mind and produce an ongoing anxiety that makes you afraid of what will come next. The good news is that you don't have to dwell on things that drag you down. Begin a regular practice of committing Scripture to memory—verses that will prepare you for those challenges.

No one can take My Word away from you if you memorize it! Renew your mind with My promises so you can be fortified against any trouble that will come your way. Rehearse them aloud each day; announce to the enemy that he dare not tread on your turf because you and your loved ones belong to Me. The Scripture that is seared into your heart will not only give you strength for tomorrow's problems; it will give you confidence to face everything that comes across your path today. In the worst-case scenario—if you lose everything—the Word of God etched in your heart will still be securely in place, providing everything you need to make the next right choice.

I shall delight in Your statutes; I shall not forget Your word.

PSALM 119:16, NASB

June 12

STARS

Have you ever stood in the night wind and looked up at a blanket of stars? The blazing brightness of the heavens so captures you that words can hardly express the ache in your heart. . . . One day you will put on glory like that. It will be yours for ever and ever.

Joni Eareckson Tada

The glory of My earthly creation is a little taste of the splendor that awaits you in eternity. The heavens are spectacular in their contrast of darkness and light. The darker the night, the more the moon and stars sparkle with brightness, glittering in the night as if to say, "You can shine in darkness too!"

Right now the heaviness in your heart is making it hard for you to believe that My light is visible through your pain. But you have put your faith and trust in Me, and because you've stood strong in the middle of your trials, the bright light of My presence is reflected through your face and your actions. Your faithful testimony has not gone unnoticed. It has been a guiding light, leading others to find sure footing along their own difficult and poorly illuminated paths. They see Me and reach for My hand when they feel afraid, because you have pointed them to the light of My presence.

Those who are wise shall shine like the brightness of the sky, and those who lead many to righteousness, like the stars forever and ever.

DANIEL 12:3, NRSV

June 13

BEAUTY FOR ASHES

Of one thing I am perfectly sure:
God's story never ends with "ashes."

Elisabeth Elliot

Exchange the ashes of a burned-out dream for the beauty of a life restored by Me. Ashes represent complete ruin and total devastation, and you may feel that describes your life. Some people think following Jesus will mean an untroubled, problem-free existence. But that is not what I've promised. "In this world you will have trouble. But take heart! I have overcome the world" (John 16:33, NIV).

Look for the ways I'm turning ashes into beauty. Sometimes it's through the kindness of a stranger, or through the joy of a restored relationship with a friend or family member, or by the way My Holy Spirit reveals the meaning of a Scripture you've read, bringing renewed comfort and peace to your heart. Be aware of My favor through improved health, financial blessings, or wide-open doors for ministering to others. When these things happen, recognize My hand at work in your life. I'm turning your despair into festive praise.

The time of the LORD's favor has come. . . . He will give a crown of beauty for ashes, a joyous blessing instead of mourning, festive praise instead of despair.

ISAIAH 61:2-3

MESSY PEOPLE

We are the ones who throw stones. We are quick to judge without knowledge. . . . We label the messy people and gossip about the sinners and shake our heads in disgust. . . . And it couldn't possibly be what Jesus had in mind when He said, "Go and teach them about Me."

Angela Thomas

Have you ever felt like one of the messy people? Your life is chaotic, your family members are flawed, your own past is questionable, and your faith wavers. You've looked around and had the fleeting thought that I have "favorites" because those people appear to have loving families, financial security, perfect church attendance, encouraging friends, and stable health. Listen up! I love messy people who are not arrogant, self-absorbed, judgmental, and condescending. They admit they need help, and I can't resist lavishing love and grace on them. I'm attracted to these people!

Once you've experienced this kind of unconditional acceptance, share it with everyone you meet. Don't act shocked when you see people sin. Revel in My complete forgiveness yourself and pass the good news on to others. You may feel weak, but I am strong. There is no failure that can't be covered by the blood of Christ.

The Samaritan woman, taken aback, asked, "How come you, a Jew, are asking me, a Samaritan woman, for a drink?" (Jews in those days wouldn't be caught dead talking to Samaritans.) Jesus answered, "If you knew the generosity of God and who I am, you would be asking me *for a drink, and I would give you fresh, living water."*

JOHN 4:9–10, MSG

—*June 15*—

SPIRITUAL SECRETS

A spiritual secret is to learn contentment with the things God doesn't explain to us.

Amy Carmichael

Your life has unfolded in a different way than you imagined. It's harder, more complicated, and more confusing due to unexpected challenges. At times you feel frustrated and discontent. You've been seeking specific answers, and your heart longs for resolution. Much like the psalmist, you question, "O Lord, why do you stand so far away? Why do you hide when I am in trouble?" (Psalm 10:1).

Take heart. In this world your understanding is imperfect and distorted. As you grow in your faith, spiritual maturity and wisdom will allow you to see yourself, your problems, and others with clarity. Practice contentment in all situations as you develop the habit of trusting Me without fully understanding why you are going through tough times. Learn this spiritual secret from My apostle Paul: "I have learned how to be content with whatever I have" (Philippians 4:11).

Now we see things imperfectly, like puzzling reflections in a mirror, but then we will see everything with perfect clarity. All that I know now is partial and incomplete, but then I will know everything completely, just as God now knows me completely.

1 CORINTHIANS 13:12

June 16

FAMILY

The same Jesus Who turned water into wine can transform your home, your life, your family, and your future. He is still in the miracle-working business, and His business is the business of transformation.

Adrian Rogers

Your family can bring you great joy and intense sorrow. Think back to the beginning of time and envision the first family. Adam and Eve faced a heartbreaking crisis when Cain killed his brother Abel. When you study the Scriptures, you'll discover marital problems, sibling rivalry, infertility challenges, jealousy, bitterness, cheating, and anger. You'll also discover families that loved Me with pure hearts. Noah lived during a time when sin prevailed, but I found him blameless, and I saved him and his family from destruction during the great Flood.

Your family is precious to Me too. Do everything possible to live in peace with each other. I see your desire for unity in the midst of disagreements and injured feelings. Remember to think before you speak; your words can either stir up family strife or bring understanding and calm. Worship Me together. Study and memorize Scripture as a family. Encourage one another and speak of your love for each other. True transformation in your family will come as My Word is lived out in day-to-day practice.

My child, listen to me and do as I say, and you will have a long, good life. I will teach you wisdom's ways and lead you in straight paths. When you walk, you won't be held back; when you run, you won't stumble. Take hold of my instructions; don't let them go. Guard them, for they are the key to life.

PROVERBS 4:10-13

— *June 17* —

FEAR NOT

We encounter the merchants of fear at every turn. Choose what voice you will listen to. It will determine whether you step out of the boat and take the risks of faith that God has for you, or whether you stay crippled and immobilised in the boat overwhelmed by the wind and waves.

Christine Caine

What are you afraid of? How long have you allowed fear to control your mind and the activities of your day? When will you choose to accept My help and defeat this crippling emotion? Fear can paralyze you and destroy your effectiveness. Stop allowing fear to rule your mind. Make this the day that you apply My Word to your life. I will help you to confront your fears, and I'll be with you before, during, and after you make this choice. When you're afraid of people, think of what Moses said on My behalf: "Be strong and courageous! Do not be afraid and do not panic before them. For the LORD your God will personally go ahead of you. He will neither fail you nor abandon you" (Deuteronomy 31:6).

As I was with Joshua, I will be with you. "This is my command—be strong and courageous! Do not be afraid or discouraged. For the LORD your God is with you wherever you go" (Joshua 1:9). As you practice being aware of My presence in your life every day, you will develop the habit of turning fear into faith. I am with you. I will strengthen you and help you. I will hold you up with My victorious right hand (Isaiah 41:10).

The LORD is my light and my salvation—
so why should I be afraid? The LORD is my fortress,
protecting me from danger, so why should I tremble?

PSALM 27:1

June 18

UNIQUELY YOU

A life of obedience is not a life of following a list of do's and don'ts, but it is allowing God to be original in our lives.

Vonette Bright

You are one of a kind! Take time today to declare what My Word says about you. You are My righteousness in Christ (2 Corinthians 5:21). You are My beloved. I formed you in your mother's womb (Psalm 139:13). I cherish you and love you dearly. I have gifted you to do works that will exalt My name. The apostle Paul said, "We are God's masterpiece. He has created us anew in Christ Jesus, so we can do the good things he planned for us long ago" (Ephesians 2:10). You are precious and valuable to Me.

Don't compare yourself with others. Don't live by a list of rules someone else has set for you. Run the race *I* have set for you, rather than being distracted by someone else's pace and progress. Remember that your weaknesses can become strengths if you allow Me to work in your life. Beware of allowing criticism to cripple you. Often, people will put you down to lift themselves up. You are already complete in Me, so hold your head high and walk in God-confidence. I have work for you to do that is different from anyone else's. I'm counting on you to accomplish My purpose for your life.

Thank you for making me so wonderfully complex!
Your workmanship is marvelous—how well I know it.

PSALM 139:14

June 19

SMALL THINGS

There are thousands willing to do great things
for one willing to do a small thing.

George MacDonald

There's a verse in Zechariah that asks an important question: "Who has despised the day of small things?" (4:10, NKJV). I sense your frustration over all the pressures of life that have been thrust upon you. It feels like you aren't accomplishing any of your big goals. Stop and think of the small things mentioned in My Word that made a big difference in people's lives—a little boy's lunch, a cup of cold water, coins given by a widow, and a babe in a Bethlehem manger.

When you do small acts of kindness in My name, I am glorified. I've noticed your faithfulness in caring for a loved one who needs assistance. I've seen your genuine concern for hurting people. I've watched you give to a worthy cause. These acts of generosity and compassion have not gone unnoticed. "If you are faithful in little things, you will be faithful in large ones" (Luke 16:10). One day you will understand that the little things are actually the big things when they are done in My name. Do not despise the day of small things. I see you. I know your heart. Your attitude brings Me joy.

*Truly I tell you, anyone who gives you a cup
of water in my name because you belong to the
Messiah will certainly not lose their reward.*

MARK 9:41, NIV

— June 20 —

EXPERIENCE FORGIVENESS

Remember: God can heal the deepest wounds and restore the most messed-up lives.

Margaret Feinberg

The enemy is a deceiver. He wants you to think the bad choices you've made in the past will diminish My love and concern for you. But he's wrong. I created you in My image, and you are important to Me. I watched as My Son died on the cross for every sinful decision you've made. There is nothing you can ever do that will make Me turn My back on you or withhold My grace from you.

Turn your face toward Me, confess your sins, receive My forgiveness, and walk in a new direction. I have big plans for your life, and if you're willing to follow Me, I'll use the ugliness of your past as a showcase for My glory. Don't wait to experience My forgiveness, thinking you have to earn My approval first. I'm here now, ready to listen to you and eager to set you free from the burden of your past.

If we confess our sins to him, he is faithful and just to forgive us our sins and to cleanse us from all wickedness.

1 JOHN 1:9

June 21

WELCOME BACK

When you stray from His presence, He longs for you to come back. He weeps that you are missing out on His love, protection, and provision. He throws His arms open, runs toward you, gathers you up, and welcomes you home.

Charles Stanley

It's time for a soul check: How are you doing in your relationship with Me? Sometimes I sense that you're embarrassed to come into My presence because you think you've messed up and you feel unworthy. At other times your life has been so busy with work, life, and the demands of others that you haven't spent any time talking to Me or reading My Word. It feels like there's distance between us. I miss your closeness and long for you to come back.

If sin is separating you from Me, will you acknowledge your wrongdoing and ask for My forgiveness? I promise that your confession will be accepted and you will have complete and unconditional forgiveness. Return to My love, My protection, and My fellowship. I specialize in new beginnings, and all heaven takes notice. "There is joy in the presence of God's angels when even one sinner repents" (Luke 15:10). Find fresh delight in My presence, and come back to My embrace.

He also brought me up out of a horrible pit, out of the miry clay, and set my feet upon a rock, and established my steps.

PSALM 40:2, NKJV

June 22

UNCHANGEABLE

If the Lord be with us, we have no cause of fear. His eye is upon us, his arm over us, his ear open to our prayer; his grace sufficient, his promise unchangeable.

John Newton

"For I am the LORD, I do not change" (Malachi 3:6, NKJV). That's My promise to you! You've been disillusioned because people you once had faith in have proven to be untrustworthy. That will not happen in your relationship with Me. I will never love you less than I love you today. I watch over you and listen to you when you call upon My name. I gave you gifts to use for My Kingdom purposes. I have given you grace to make it through the rough patches of life, and I will never leave you or walk away from you. My promises will always be kept.

Think about what it means to have an unchangeable God in your life. I'm here for the long haul. I'll be here for you throughout your life on this earth, and I'll rejoice with you one day in heaven. Some of your friends are "here today, gone tomorrow"; they're people who don't follow through with their commitments. But you can count on Me. Leave your fears behind and be confident, knowing you have a changeless God who delivers on what He says He will do. That will give you the security to rest in My arms.

God is not a man, so he does not lie. He is not human, so he does not change his mind. Has he ever spoken and failed to act? Has he ever promised and not carried it through?

NUMBERS 23:19

June 23

ORDINARY PEOPLE

Don't assume you have to be extraordinary to be used by God. You don't have to have exceptional gifts, talents, abilities, or connections. God specializes in using ordinary people whose limitations and weaknesses make them ideal showcases for His greatness and glory.

Nancy DeMoss Wolgemuth

I use ordinary people to carry out My extraordinary plan. One day the angel Gabriel told a teenage girl named Mary that she would give birth to the Son of God. She wondered how this could be, since she was a virgin. Gabriel responded, "Nothing will be impossible with God" (Luke 1:37, NASB). There are times when you feel too unqualified, too weak, or too average to do My work. The enemy jeers, "You're nobody special. You aren't educated enough. You don't have enough experience. There are other people who are much more qualified." Tell him to leave immediately! I have already equipped you with everything you need to carry out My plans.

Throughout the Scriptures you will discover that I often use unlikely people to do improbable things for eternal purposes. Study the lives of Moses, David, the apostle Paul, and Mary, the mother of Jesus. They were human beings who were sometimes reluctant, rebellious, arrogant, or shy—until they followed Me with total abandon. They were ordinary people who gave Me their potential. My power shows up best when you offer Me your greatest weakness and then exchange it for My strength.

I can do everything through Christ, who gives me strength.

PHILIPPIANS 4:13

June 24

COMPELLED TO TELL

When we experience his grace, we're compelled to tell others so they may praise the Lord with us. In doing so, their faith is bolstered, knowing that God is real, God is powerful, God is sovereign, and God is moving.

Liz Curtis Higgs

This is who I am—"the God of compassion and mercy! I am slow to anger and filled with unfailing love and faithfulness. I lavish unfailing love to a thousand generations. I forgive iniquity, rebellion, and sin" (Exodus 34:6-7). Drench yourself in My grace and experience the joy of lavish love and forgiven sins! Your faith will be shored up as you celebrate the freedom and delight of being embraced by grace.

When you immerse yourself in the richness of our relationship, you can't help but tell others about it. Your powerful testimony is a megaphone to a world full of broken people. Tell them that grace is undeserved favor, unmerited love—and that it's absolutely free! Proclaim this message everywhere you go. Your joyful countenance and transformed life will announce to others that I am real, that I am powerful, and that they can experience My grace too!

God, in his grace, freely makes us right in his sight. He did this though Christ Jesus when he freed us from the penalty for our sins.

ROMANS 3:24

June 25

GENEROUS GOD

We serve a generous God. He delights in giving us opportunities beyond our capabilities. He has promised to equip us, and remain with us through each bend in the road.

David Jeremiah

Your life has taken many turns, and the journey you travel now has brought you face-to-face with a trying bend in the road. Take time to remember My faithfulness. You have been saved by grace, and that's My gift to you. Now it's time for you to enter into the benefits of being My child. I take delight in giving you opportunities that far exceed what you think you can do. When you do My work in this world, I'll supply all your needs. That way you can look back and say, "It was in God's power that this work was accomplished," and "It was by the mercy of God that this impossible situation was resolved."

The secret to experiencing My generosity is this: "Remain in me, and I will remain in you. For a branch cannot produce fruit if it is severed from the vine, and you cannot be fruitful unless you remain in me" (John 15:4). The closer you are to Me, the more you will have the supernatural strength, wisdom, and power to handle whatever problems come your way. And when you make mistakes, know that I have infinite mercy and My love for you is great. I will equip you for every unexpected turn life takes. I will be with you, and I will give you all the courage you need to make it to your final destination.

You know the generous grace of our Lord Jesus Christ. Though he was rich, yet for your sakes he became poor, so that by his poverty he could make you rich.

2 CORINTHIANS 8:9

June 26

MIRACLES

When God is involved, anything can happen.

Charles Swindoll

You have read in My Word about many miracles where I initiated a divine operation that transcended natural law. The psalmist records, "When he spoke, the world began! It appeared at his command" (Psalm 33:9). You are well aware of My power, and you have prayed for a miracle to transform your current difficulty into an easier, more comfortable situation. You've read accounts of Jesus turning water into wine, feeding huge crowds with a little boy's lunch, calming the raging seas, and raising Lazarus from the dead—and you wonder why I have not yet spoken a word or lifted a hand for you.

Sometimes you may see dramatic answers to prayer that are indeed miraculous. But more often, the greater miracle will be in your heart as you develop a steadfast faith in the midst of adversity, focusing on the joy that awaits you in heaven. I want to mature your character so you will be grounded in Christ. Will you continue to trust Me, without being able to see what My higher purpose is in your suffering? Put your faith in Me. I will not let you down.

At present you trust him without being able to see him, and even now he brings you a joy that words cannot express and which has in it a hint of the glories of Heaven; and all the time you are receiving the result of your faith in him—the salvation of your own souls.

1 PETER 1:9, *PHILLIPS*

—June 27—

CLEAN

Our Savior kneels down and gazes upon the darkest acts of our lives. . . . He reaches out in kindness and says, "I can clean that if you want." And from the basin of his grace, he scoops a palm full of mercy and washes away our sin.

Max Lucado

Sometimes you don't come to Me because you feel undeserving to be in My presence. The memory of a past sin or a frustrating bad habit haunts your mind. There are days when you try to minimize the devastation your sin has caused, and at other times you're paralyzed by regret.

If you need forgiveness for bitterness, anger, moral failure, or anything else that is separating you from Me, come as you are. As you experience a personal awareness of sin, there will be a time of grieving your wrong choices. Then do what David did—he confessed his transgressions, repented of his sin, and went in a new direction. I will cleanse you, forgive you, and give you grace for a new beginning. Ask Me to examine your life and to reveal anything that displeases Me. Then honestly admit your sin and ask for mercy—and I will forgive you and make you clean again.

Purify me from my sins, and I will be clean;
wash me, and I will be whiter than snow.

PSALM 51:7

June 28

HEARING GOD'S VOICE

If you want to hear God's voice clearly and you are uncertain, then remain in His presence until He changes that uncertainty.

Corrie ten Boom

You have decisions to make, and there is unrest in your heart. You are anxiously longing for answers, and you don't know what to do. Begin by seeking Me, as David did. "You, God, are my God, earnestly I seek you; I thirst for you, my whole being longs for you" (Psalm 63:1, NIV). Then go to My Word. The primary way I speak to you is through the Bible. As you study, look for My direction through teachings and stories that are relevant to your situation. Ask Me to help you understand and apply what you're reading.

The most important key to hearing My voice is to listen after you read My Word. Turn off all outside noise, and I will help you discern My voice from all the other voices that clamor for your attention. Hearing My voice requires a quiet heart—stillness on the inside in the middle of commotion on the outside. Practice patience. Humbly wait for My answers, and eventually your nagging doubt will be replaced with vibrant faith. You will experience peace and understanding in My presence. And when answers come, act in obedience.

My sheep hear My voice, and I know them, and they follow Me.

JOHN 10:27, NASB

—*June 29*—

CONNECTED

Life is simply better when we are with others, and worse when we are isolated. God designed us to be connected, and life breaks down when we are not.

John Townsend

I didn't create you to be independent and self-sufficient. You were made to live in humble, worshipful, accountable dependency upon Me and in close relationship with other members of the body of Christ. Your independence has caused you to internalize your struggles, instead of sharing your heart and needs with others. This has created loneliness and separation from people who would gladly cover you with prayer and offer help. I did not design you to do life alone.

I want you to set an example for people to follow by opening your heart with other believers. Care for each other, comfort one another, build each other up, do good to each other, be kind to each other, forgive one another, show hospitality to each other, and pray for each other's needs. When you respond in this way, you know you are not alone. You are encouraged in tangible ways by fellow Christians who walk with you on a difficult path, and your heart is lifted by their faith. Reach out and accept My provision for you through the blessing of being connected to others who love Me.

Love each other with genuine affection, and take delight in honoring each other.

ROMANS 12:10

June 30

WRESTLING

The point of wrestling with God is to give you an opportunity to cling to him. God wants you to hang on to him no matter what—and the result will be blessing. . . . In that divine wrestling match, you may feel wounded, but you will also receive a blessing you couldn't have received any other way.

Jennifer Rothschild

My child, you've been wrestling with Me night and day for a long time. Through tears, you've begged Me for answers. You know I'm the Author of peace, not confusion, and that I hear your cries. You've pleaded with Me for resolution and understanding. You keep seeking My face as you implore Me to intervene on behalf of your loved one. You won't let go until I bless you—and that's something I can't resist.

Jacob wrestled with Me one night, and during that struggle I threw his hip out of joint. He walked with a limp after that, but he finally reached a place of peace and blessing. From then on he walked in God-confidence. His faith was no longer only the faith of his father and his grandfather—it was his own. When you cling to Me in the middle of your struggle, totally committed to not letting go until you get My blessing, your faith will be cemented. You may feel wounded, but you will know you've been touched by Me.

Jacob said, "I'm not letting you go 'til you bless me."
The man said, "What's your name?" He answered, "Jacob."
The man said, "But no longer. Your name is no longer Jacob.
From now on it's Israel (God-Wrestler);
you've wrestled with God and you've come through."

GENESIS 32:26-28, MSG

—*July 1*—
GOODNESS

God is good whether or not His choices seem right to us, whether or not we feel it, whether or not it seems true, and whether or not He gives us everything that we want.

Nancy DeMoss Wolgemuth

Goodness is one of My attributes, but in the middle of your struggles you sometimes question how good I've been to you. Today I want you to taste and see that I am good (Psalm 34:8). My love for you is great, and I want to immerse you in My goodness. Join the psalmist and say, "You are good and do only good; teach me your decrees" (Psalm 119:68). Just as parents want goodness for their children, I desire only goodness for you. That's why I gave you the gift of My perfect, holy Son, Jesus, so you could join My family and live with Me forever in heaven.

Look around and name some of My good gifts to you today. Know that they are freely given from My hand. "Whatever is good and perfect is a gift coming down to us from God our Father. . . . He never changes or casts a shifting shadow" (James 1:17). Allow that truth to give you encouragement and security. You can depend upon My steady supply of goodness.

How great is the goodness you have stored up for those who fear you. You lavish it on those who come to you for protection, blessing them before the watching world.

PSALM 31:19

— July 2 —

ROYALTY

You and I are children of the King, the Creator of the universe!
No matter what family we're born into—or not born into—
it isn't possible to have a better lineage than that!

Ramona Cramer Tucker

When you accepted the Lord Jesus Christ as your Savior, you became a child of the King. You now have the privilege and the responsibility of representing Me in every area of your life. Because you're not in your heavenly home yet, it's sometimes hard for you to believe that you're royalty, but that doesn't change your lineage! You are My child, and along with Jesus Christ, you are an heir of My glory.

The benefits of being royalty are great. You are the apple of My eye. You are beloved and blessed. You will share in Jesus' inheritance. "[I have] enabled you to share in the inheritance that belongs to [My] people, who live in the light" (Colossians 1:12). Embrace your identity as royalty and use your gift of influence to tell others about the incredible turnaround I orchestrated in your life. You are now part of My family. No matter what your earthly family background is, when you put your faith in Jesus, you became part of My family!

You are the ones chosen by God, chosen for the high calling of priestly work, chosen to be a holy people, God's instruments to do his work and speak out for him, to tell others of the night-and-day difference he made for you—from nothing to something, from rejected to accepted.

1 PETER 2:9-10, MSG

— July 3 —

THIS IS THE DAY

God wants you to trust him one day at a time: "Give us this day our daily bread." Not for next week. Not for next year. Not for next month. Just one day at a time.

Rick Warren

This is the day I have made! Take a deep breath and revel in the joy of waking up to the sunrise and to all of the possibilities I have provided for you on this day. If you keep your eyes open, you'll discover unexpected gifts and new opportunities to grow in our relationship. Invite Me to participate in every part of your day. Choose peace by spending time with Me before attacking the challenges in front of you. Choose joy and pass it on to others through a smile, a touch, or a word of hope. Choose life, instead of curling up in a ball and refusing to participate in this day.

Instead of expecting bad things to happen, anticipate positive results as you live and move in My will throughout your day. Let thankfulness become as natural as breathing. Determine to have a grateful heart, remembering that in a fallen world sorrow and grief are intertwined with great delights and joy-filled experiences. When you remember that this day is a gift from Me, you'll be able to thank Me for the good things and the hard places. Develop the habit of expressing gratitude to Me as you experience both the highs and the lows. Live one day at a time and thank Me for the provision of today. Tomorrow is not here yet—and I will be with you then, just as I am today. Say aloud, "This is the day the Lord made. I am choosing joy!"

This is the day the LORD has made. We will rejoice and be glad in it.

PSALM 118:24

— July 4 —

RESTORATION

When God restores, he restores beyond our dreams. I'm learning not to be surprised at the amazing things he does, just very thankful. I now look forward to the future with excitement and enthusiasm. By faith, you can, too!

Virelle Kidder

Let Me completely restore you—no matter what you've done or what you've been through. No matter how big of a mess you're in, I can bring you back to a place of peace, honor, joy, and blessing. There are times when you feel like a failure, and you come to Me saying, "I've blown it again." You're not alone. Abraham failed. Samson failed. David failed. "GOD was not at all pleased with what David had done" (2 Samuel 11:27, MSG). Solomon failed, and Jonah failed too. The list goes on and on, and Scripture notes the sobering evidence of each person's wrong choices. But I am the One who restores and reclaims those who have willfully disobeyed My will.

If you need to be restored today, here's your action plan. Come to Me and honestly admit what you have done; confess your wrongdoing. Change your course and go in a new direction. Be accountable to someone you trust who loves Me, someone who will help you stay connected to My Word. Now live confidently, free of your past, empowered to face the future.

Instead of shame and dishonor, you will enjoy a double share of honor. You will possess a double portion of prosperity in your land, and everlasting joy will be yours.

ISAIAH 61:7

July 5

CHARACTER

God values Christian character, which shines in positive, outward conduct. Fashion your heart after Jesus'!

Elizabeth George

Your character is the strength of your moral fiber. When you follow the example of My Son, you will develop Christlikeness in your thoughts, desires, disposition, intentions, and actions. Your character will influence your choices. When Daniel was in captivity, he consistently made choices that honored Me, resulting in unquestionable integrity. "Daniel was determined not to defile himself" (Daniel 1:8).

My purpose is to develop good character in you. You feel you've been in a fiery furnace of affliction. The enemy wants you to give up. Remember what Daniel's three friends said when King Nebuchadnezzar threatened to throw them into a roaring furnace if they would not bow down to his idol: "If you throw us in the fire, the God we serve can rescue us. . . . But even if he doesn't, it wouldn't make a bit of difference. . . . We still wouldn't serve your gods" (Daniel 3:16-18, MSG). Even though you face challenging obstacles, if you continue to be a person who is above reproach, self-controlled, peacemaking, honest, mature, and respectable, your character will shine with the light of My Son, setting an excellent example for others.

May you always be filled with the fruit of your salvation—the righteous character produced in your life by Jesus Christ—for this will bring much glory and praise to God.

PHILIPPIANS 1:11

July 6

ONE DAY AT A TIME

I'm glad God doesn't announce upfront what we'll be doing in the future—it could be overwhelming. But knowing God himself holds the past, present, and future should put our minds at ease.

Ramona Cramer Tucker

I give you strength for one day at a time, but you've been upset about what might happen in the future. Be assured that I will be doing the same thing tomorrow that I did yesterday and today—watching over you and those you love! Worry paralyzes you and makes you too upset to accomplish anything. You have enough to deal with today without trying to handle the challenges of tomorrow as well.

When you push one day into the future, you give up the joy I have for you today. What you're worrying about may never happen, but you forfeit precious time with Me and with those closest to you. You're trying to control what you should place in My hands. Use the resources I've given you right now to handle today's needs, and everything else will fall into its proper place. I promise to take care of you.

That is why I tell you not to worry about everyday life—whether you have enough food and drink, or enough clothes to wear. Isn't life more than food, and your body more than clothing? Look at the birds. They don't plant or harvest or store food in barns, for your heavenly Father feeds them. And aren't you far more valuable to him than they are?

MATTHEW 6:25-26

SOAR

God created us with an overwhelming desire to soar. . . . He designed us to be tremendously productive and to "mount up with wings like eagles," realistically dreaming of what He can do with our potential.

Carol Kent

Instead of looking at your limitations, consider your strengths. I've equipped you to face the headwinds of life and to survive the gales you've encountered. Be at peace and rest in My embrace, knowing I'm capable of holding you up on stormy days. When you come humbly before Me, I will lift you up (James 4:10). You need the strength of My Spirit and the comfort of My love to know you can rise above any problem.

Hardships are never pleasant, but I have a plan to use what you've learned to help others. I created eagles with an extraordinary ability to see objects far away, and I'll give you sharp vision and keen insight to know whom you should reach out to with the spiritual lessons you've learned along the way. I will supply all the strength you need to turn your suffering into a platform for My glory. Keep soaring!

Those who hope in the LORD will renew their strength. They will soar on wings like eagles; they will run and not grow weary, they will walk and not be faint.

ISAIAH 40:31, NIV

July 8

GOSSIP

We should ask ourselves three questions before we speak:
Is it true? Is it kind? Does it glorify Christ?

Billy Graham

When you speak unkind, untrue, or unnecessary words about others, it displeases Me. Gossip is especially hurtful when it is wrapped in a prayer request. You have known the sting of words that wound, so you understand the pain they inflict. Gossip may be true, partially true, or completely false, but it always includes personal information that portrays someone in a bad light. Gossip unjustly colors how others are perceived, causing deep hurt to their hearts and their reputations.

Guard your mind and your mouth when you speak about others. "A troublemaker plants seeds of strife; gossip separates the best of friends" (Proverbs 16:28). Treat people the way you want to be treated. Beware of listening to gossip. Turn the conversation to uplifting and edifying speech. Be known as someone who keeps a confidence and speaks words of praise about others. When you develop this habit, you will be known as someone who brings people together and can always be trusted.

A gossip goes around telling secrets, but those who are trustworthy can keep a confidence.

PROVERBS 11:13

— July 9 —

DIVINE APPOINTMENTS

Jesus . . . wants us to see that the neighbor next door or the people sitting next to us on a plane or in a classroom are not interruptions to our schedule; they are there by divine appointment.

Rebecca Pippert

Keep your vision sharp so you can recognize My divine appointments today. I often redirect your schedule or path to arrange a special moment with someone who is expressing interest in Me. These opportunities often seem like interruptions—an unexpected knock at your door, a phone call, or an urgent text message or e-mail. This pause in your day can come from a complete stranger, or it can come from a neighbor, relative, or coworker. In each case I've already been softening their hearts, and I've selected you to be My ambassador of truth. Your role is to whet their appetites to learn more about Me. Sometimes these people are ready to follow Jesus, and you will have the privilege of leading them to a personal relationship with My Son. Or they may need your listening ear and encouragement.

It's easy for you to become irritated when these opportunities distract you from your carefully made plans and keep you from your usual productivity. But they are your most important appointments of the day. You could easily miss them if you aren't listening to My Spirit and responding to My holy nudges to initiate a conversation. Learn to anticipate these divine encounters. As you engage in My Kingdom work, you will find great fulfillment and abiding joy.

The LORD directs the steps of the godly.
He delights in every detail of their lives.

PSALM 37:23

July 10

SHATTERED DREAMS

Shattered dreams are never random. They are always . . . a chapter in a larger story. . . . [The Holy Spirit] uses the pain of shattered dreams to help us discover our desire for God. . . . They are ordained opportunities for the Spirit first to awaken then to satisfy our highest dream.

Larry Crabb

Broken dreams often bring feelings of hopelessness. But they are more than endings—they are important opportunities for new beginnings. You often ask Me why I've allowed something to happen, but instead I want you to ask Me what I am teaching you through this experience. Sadness and anger can make room for peace and joy. When your dreams are broken, you have an opportunity to build character, patience, and endurance. You also long for My presence. Allow your shattered dreams to draw you close to Me.

Consider the crucifixion and resurrection of My Son, Jesus. New beginnings come after death. Right now the death of your dream has brought hurt, pain, and grief, but if you ask Me for help, I will give you a new dream. Take time to grieve what you've lost, pursue healing, and then get ready for what I'm preparing you to do next. Throughout this process, I am changing you into someone more like Jesus.

We can rejoice, too, when we run into problems and trials, for we know that they help us develop endurance. And endurance develops strength of character, and character strengthens our confident hope of salvation.

ROMANS 5:3-4

— July 11 —

LAYERS

Forgiveness isn't always a onetime thing. There are layers of it that need to be recognized. . . . Sometimes we think we have forgiven, but we don't realize how many layers there are. And if we don't deal with each layer, hardness of heart can set in.

Stormie Omartian

What is the state of your heart? Practicing forgiveness is important to you and to the person you need to forgive. Refusing to forgive places you in a self-imposed bondage to the past. Ask Me to search your heart. Are you holding grudges? Are you avoiding someone because of what she's said about you or done to you? When someone has asked you for forgiveness, have you said, "I forgive you," but later realized you're still harboring bitterness and anger?

Be aware of the layers of hurt that caused the initial problem. Harsh words are often hard to forget, and the memory of evil deeds may be deeply embedded in your heart. The apostle Paul said, "Get rid of all bitterness, rage, anger, harsh words, and slander, as well as all types of evil behavior. Instead, be kind to each other, tenderhearted, forgiving one another, just as God through Christ has forgiven you" (Ephesians 4:31-32). Allow Me to heal your heart and that of the offender. This may take some time. Let Me peel back the layers of your pain and breathe My healing into your soul through Scripture and through the peace you will find in My presence.

Peter came to him and asked, "Lord, how often should I forgive someone who sins against me? Seven times?" "No, not seven times," Jesus replied, "but seventy times seven!"

MATTHEW 18:21-22

July 12

NEARNESS

So when we sing, "Draw me nearer, nearer, nearer, blessed Lord," we are not thinking of the nearness of place, but of the nearness of relationship. It is for increasing degrees of awareness that we pray, for a more perfect consciousness of the divine Presence.

A. W. Tozer

Draw near to Me. Come close. Be still in My presence. Enjoy our time together. Take pleasure in spending time with Me. Instead of diving into the busyness of your day, linger in My presence and talk to Me. I love the sound of your voice, and the light in your eyes brings Me pleasure. You may need to rise earlier for us to spend these precious moments together, but it will be worth your extra effort. Everything about your day will go more smoothly if you spend time with Me before making decisions, zigzagging in and out of meetings, or rushing to your next appointment.

I want you to approach Me with assurance so you can receive mercy and grace during your time of need (Hebrews 4:16, NIV). I reward those who search for Me. When you seek Me, you will always find Me. The nearer you are to Me, the more you will become like Me. Your choices, attitude, behavior, speech, compassion, and giving will be a reflection of My heart, and your actions an extension of My will. Come even closer, My child.

Let us draw near to God with a sincere heart and with the full assurance that faith brings.

HEBREWS 10:22, NIV

— *July 13* —

SOVEREIGN GOD

This truth is hard to grasp, but you can stake your life on it: even when everything seems a mess, you can press your face into the mane of the Lion of Judah and trust Him. Our God is sovereign.

Sheila Walsh

Be comforted with these words: I am in control. Nothing happens in the universe outside of My authority and influence. I have no limitations. Review these truths: I created all things in the heavens and the earth, visible and invisible, and I hold them together (Colossians 1:16). There is no limit to My knowledge—past, present, and future (Romans 11:33). Nothing is too hard for Me (Jeremiah 32:17). I have power and authority over nations, rulers, angels, and demons (Psalm 103:19). I am immortal—the beginning and the end (Revelation 21:6).

I rule in love, and I want the best for you. Nothing can come into your life that I don't allow. Take comfort in knowing that I'm in charge of your life. Don't be afraid. Don't give up. Don't despair. I am on your side. I will be your Deliverer, your Protector, your Shield, and your Strong Tower (Psalm 144:2). If you trust Me, I will direct you through your circumstances.

The LORD has established His throne in the heavens,
and His sovereignty rules over all.

PSALM 103:19, NASB

— *July 14* —

GRATITUDE

God is in control, and therefore in *everything* I can give thanks—not because of the situation but because of the One who directs and rules over it.

Kay Arthur

It takes courage to give thanks when you get devastating news and when bad things are happening. King Jehoshaphat was devoted to Me. When he was told a vast army made up of three different enemies was on its way to Jerusalem, he feared for the kingdom of Judah. However, this faithful ruler's first response was to ask Me for guidance and to proclaim a fast in his kingdom. People came from all the cities of Judah to pray, and the king prayed powerfully, "O GOD, God of our ancestors, are you not God in heaven above and ruler of all kingdoms below? You hold all power and might in your fist—no one stands a chance against you!" (2 Chronicles 20:6, MSG).

Jahaziel, a priest, gave these prophetic words: "You won't have to lift a hand in this battle; just stand firm . . . and watch GOD's saving work for you take shape" (2 Chronicles 20:17, MSG). To honor God, Jehoshaphat appointed a choir to march ahead of the troops singing, "Give thanks to the LORD; his faithful love endures forever" (2 Chronicles 20:21). As the choir sang, I caused these three armies coming against Judah to fight each other. When Jehoshaphat's soldiers arrived at the lookout point over the Valley of Beracah, the soldiers of the other armies had already killed each other. Do you believe that I can handle your situation too? Begin by giving thanks and then leave the results up to Me.

Be thankful in all circumstances, for this is God's will for you who belong to Christ Jesus.

1 THESSALONIANS 5:18

— July 15 —

THE TAPESTRY

We will stand amazed to see the topside of the tapestry
and how God beautifully embroidered each circumstance
into a pattern for our good and His glory.

Joni Eareckson Tada

Don't be surprised when you encounter momentary troubles in this world. Your life will be woven with dark and light threads. From your earthly viewpoint, the underside of the tapestry may look like an odd mixture of mismatched colors, random textures, countless knots, tangled threads, and loose ends. To you, there is no order or visible image. You wonder what the "big picture" is, when, in fact, I'm weaving the events of your life into a meaningful pattern.

Look at My Word and notice how often the words *suffering* and *glory* are paired in Scripture. Peter said, "But rejoice inasmuch as you participate in the *suffering*s of Christ, so that you may be overjoyed when his *glory* is revealed" (1 Peter 4:13, NIV, emphasis added). When I give you glimpses of what I'm weaving into the fabric of your life, be encouraged. No thread of experience is wasted, and nothing happens by accident. Your suffering is only temporary, but you will enjoy My glory forever. When you get to heaven and see the finished tapestry, you'll understand.

For our light and momentary troubles are achieving for us
an eternal glory that far outweighs them all.

2 CORINTHIANS 4:17, NIV

July 16

MEMORIES

Create a trophy room in your heart. Each time you experience a victory, place a memory on the shelf. Before you face a challenge, take a quick tour of God's accomplishments.

Max Lucado

I want you to know you can face the future by remembering what I've done in the past. Memorials are important because they remind you of spiritual lessons learned, missions accomplished, and times when you experienced personal and spiritual triumphs. Record the prayers I've answered, the financial needs that have been met, and the blessings you've received. You can list these things in a journal or store them in your heart. Talk about these experiences with your children and your grandchildren. Remind them of My faithfulness.

Whenever you find your faith flagging, go over the reminders of what I've already done and repeat Philippians 4:19 aloud: "This same God who takes care of me will supply all your needs from his glorious riches, which have been given to us in Christ Jesus." Tell the stories of how I've met your needs, and keep a clear memory of My faithfulness. This practice will remind you to focus on hope.

We will use these stones to build a memorial. In the future your children will ask you, "What do these stones mean?" Then you can tell them, "They remind us that the Jordan River stopped flowing when the Ark of the LORD's Covenant went across." These stones will stand as a memorial among the people of Israel forever.

JOSHUA 4:6-7

July 17

MORE TO COME

When you see that sunset or that panoramic view of God's finest expressed in nature, and the beauty just takes your breath away, remember it is just a glimpse of the real thing that awaits you in heaven.

Greg Laurie

Take time to enjoy My creation. You've been so busy recently that it's been hard to watch a sunset or walk through a flower garden, taking in the wide array of colors on the earth and in the sky. Consider the design of a butterfly's wing and the intense hues of the planets. Marvel at the majesty of the mountains and the vastness of the galaxies. I created the heavens and the earth for you. "Through [Christ] God created everything in the heavenly realms and on earth. He made the things we can see and the things we can't see" (Colossians 1:16).

Whatever you are experiencing during this stage of your journey, allow the beauty of My creation to be a preview of the breathtaking glory that I have prepared for you in heaven. "I saw a new heaven and a new earth, for the old heaven and the old earth had disappeared. And the sea was also gone. And I saw the holy city, the new Jerusalem, coming down from God out of heaven like a bride beautifully dressed for her husband. . . . And the one sitting on the throne said, 'Look, I am making everything new!' And then he said to me, 'Write this down, for what I tell you is trustworthy and true'" (Revelation 21:1-2, 5).

The heavens proclaim the glory of God.
The skies display his craftsmanship.

PSALM 19:1

July 18

MEANING

Solomon talks of having everything, but finally concludes that the only thing of value is having God in your life. He alone gives meaning to life.

Mary Ann Mayo

Beware of searching for meaning by focusing only on your own goals and desires. No matter what height of success you achieve, that approach can lead to discouragement and disillusionment. Think about King Solomon, who was considered the wisest man who ever lived. He amassed great power and wealth, but he indulged in lusts that pulled him away from Me. Eventually he concluded, "'Everything is meaningless . . . completely meaningless!' What do people get for all their hard work under the sun?" (Ecclesiastes 1:2-3).

My Word is the manual for living a meaningful life. Start with discovering your purpose: "'You must love the Lord your God with all your heart, all your soul, all your strength, and all your mind.' And, 'Love your neighbor as yourself'" (Luke 10:27). This purpose will lead to meaning. When you put Me first and seek My will, you will discover the mission I have for your life—one that will bless others, bring you fulfillment, and glorify My name.

Praise the Lord! For all who fear God and trust in him are blessed beyond expression. Yes, happy is the man who delights in doing his commands.

PSALM 112:1, TLB

July 19

CELEBRATION

Celebration, at its core, is the practice of choosing to be truly present in the moments in our lives.

Shauna Niequist

Today I want you to focus on celebration. Sometimes enjoying the happy things in life feels awkward, especially when you know people who are struggling—but I am the Creator of joy. Look around and identify the good things in your life. You won't find perfection until you are at home in heaven with Me, but if you keep your eyes open, you'll find plenty of reasons to smile and sing right now.

You can start by celebrating the relationship you have with My Son—an intimate, secure, never-ending commitment to each other that brings comfort, protection, healing, love, and even laughter to your life. Take a moment to express your delight to Me as you once again recognize the benefits of this union. Notice the provisions I've made available to you. Then think about the people I've placed around you. They bring encouragement, companionship, and spiritual camaraderie. Open your mouth and speak out loud about your blessings. You can tell Me about them or rejoice with someone on your path today. Celebration lifts your spirit and puts your focus on glorifying Me. Enjoy this day. I made it for you!

GOD rules: there's *something to shout over! On the double, mainlands and islands—celebrate!*

PSALM 97:1, MSG

July 20

HIS SECRETS

As Christians, we have direct access to the secret things of God. That's right—God wants to share His secrets with us! Can you imagine this? Just picture God bowing near, cupping His hand, and whispering His secrets into your ear.

Lori D'Augostine

You have experienced difficult days, and you often wonder if there is any purpose in your suffering. I long to open your eyes to things you have not yet seen. There are hidden treasures in the middle of your pain—secret riches. I want you to explore these gifts you might never have received apart from this season of brokenness.

The key to receiving My riches is to act in faith. Dare to look for My blessings in your season of anguish. As you walk by faith, not by sight, you will experience a deeper intimacy with Me because I am close to the brokenhearted (Psalm 34:18). In times of sorrow, your relationships with others will be without pretense, and you'll discover a different kind of joy. This joy is not based on being trouble-free. It's the quiet certainty that I am still in control, I am on your side, and I am working on your behalf. Those who have a pain-free life don't understand this—that *I will give you treasures hidden in the darkness*. When you receive these riches reserved for you, then you will know that *I am the one who calls you by name*.

And I will give you treasures hidden in the darkness—secret riches. I will do this so you may know that I am the LORD, the God of Israel, the one who calls you by name.

ISAIAH 45:3

July 21

DON'T GIVE UP

Have you felt like giving up lately? . . . Let's stop thinking about the vastness of the journey. Let's recognize that when things seem out of control, God is always in control.

Rachel Wojo

I will transform your splintered life into something that will give life to others. There are times when you wonder how you'll make it through the next month, week, or hour, but I am using your trials to build your strength. The apostle Paul understood this principle. He said, "I was given the gift of a handicap to keep me in constant touch with my limitations. Satan's angel did his best to get me down; what he in fact did was push me to my knees" (2 Corinthians 12:7, MSG). When your trials propel you into My presence, the enemy can't win.

Today I want you to focus on My names and attributes and consider the strength at your disposal. I am your Shield—I'll provide protection from the enemy. I am your El-Shaddai—your all-sufficient Supporter. I am your Strong Tower—a place of refuge when you're afraid. My power will defend you and equip you with the resources you need. The enemy expects you to throw up your hands in surrender, but he is powerless against the strength I am pouring into you. Your endurance in the face of suffering redeems your sorrow and gives hope to a watching world.

So we're not giving up. How could we! Even though on the outside it often looks like things are falling apart on us, on the inside, where God is making new life, not a day goes by without his unfolding grace.

2 CORINTHIANS 4:16, MSG

July 22

LONG-SUFFERING

This hard place in which you perhaps find yourself is the very place in which God is giving you opportunity to look only to Him, to spend time in prayer, and to learn long-suffering . . . to learn the depths of the love that Christ Himself has poured out on all of us.

Elisabeth Elliot

Practice the fruit of the Spirit—become a long-suffering person. Every time you exhibit endurance in the middle of your hard place, you please Me. Patience is difficult when you are waiting for a positive outcome, a more favorable financial situation, or better health, or for children to follow Me or a spouse to return to Me. Your suffering seems to last forever. But remember that long-suffering is the opposite of despair. It's waiting with hope.

Paul was encouraged by the long-suffering Thessalonians when he wrote: "We are always thankful as we pray for you all, for we never forget that your faith has meant solid achievement, your love has meant hard work, and the hope that you have in our Lord Jesus Christ means sheer dogged endurance in the life that you live before God" (1 Thessalonians 1:2-3, *Phillips*). I am watching as you demonstrate perseverance in the face of great challenges. Your deep love for Me is evidenced by your trust in the middle of adversity. In due time you will be rewarded.

Walk worthy of the Lord, fully pleasing Him, being fruitful in every good work and increasing in the knowledge of God; strengthened with all might, according to His glorious power for all patience and longsuffering with joy.

COLOSSIANS 1:10-11, NKJV

July 23

MORAL EXCELLENCE

A person with integrity knows what is important to God and consistently lives in light of what is important to Him. It involves more than living our values; it involves subscribing to God's values and with His help learning to conform our conduct to those values.

Steven C. Riser

You honor Me when you stand out as a person of moral excellence. In the past you've been tempted to create a list of taboos to avoid—overt sins like lying, cheating, adultery, stealing, and gossiping. But I'm asking you to stop living by what you *don't* do and to start living by what you *know* I want you to do. Seek personal integrity by pursuing My will in every area of your life. This quest for Christlikeness begins in your mind and influences your attitudes, priorities, values, goals, choices, and devotion.

The apostle Peter gives good advice. "Make every effort to respond to God's promises. Supplement your faith with a generous provision of moral excellence, and moral excellence with knowledge, and knowledge with self-control, and self-control with patient endurance, and patient endurance with godliness" (2 Peter 1:5-6). Ask Me to convict you when your thoughts drift away from purity. Respond immediately by confessing your sin, and fill your mind with wholesome thinking that honors Me. This practice will soon become second nature.

Instead, let the Spirit renew your thoughts and attitudes. Put on your new nature, created to be like God—truly righteous and holy.

EPHESIANS 4:23-24

— *July 24* —

SCARS

Wherever God leads, I pray that you will not be ashamed of your scars but reveal the truth of God's healing, redeeming, restoring power in your life. Your scars are beautiful to God.

Sharon Jaynes

Your life has had unexpected sorrow. When you heal from personal pain, past abuse, ongoing health challenges, children in rebellion, the results of your own sin, or any other devastating suffering, your wounds eventually turn into scars. Those scars remind you of what the journey cost you and how you can use your experiences to help others. Sometimes you carry emotional scars, and other times they are physical. If your suffering comes at the hands of fellow Christians or family members, the wounds are especially painful. The scar that is left marks a time when your life changed forever—and it is a reminder of what you learned.

After the Resurrection, when My Son appeared to His disciples, they didn't know who He was until they saw His scars. Jesus said to Thomas, "Put your finger here; see my hands. Reach out your hand and put it into my side. Stop doubting and believe" (John 20:27, NIV). The apostle Paul said, "I bear on my body the scars that show I belong to Jesus" (Galatians 6:17). Like Paul, allow your scars to be a powerful testimony to your relationship with Me. Satan wants your scars to immobilize you. I want your scars to point people to Me.

He personally carried our sins in his body on the cross
so that we can be dead to sin and live for what is right.
By his wounds you are healed.

1 PETER 2:24

July 25

UNAFRAID

If God is good and loving (and He is), and if God is all-powerful (and He is), and if God has a purpose and a plan that includes His children (and He does), and if we are His children (as I hope you are), then there is no reason to fear anything.

David Jeremiah

Fear is a natural response to living in a cursed world filled with imperfect, self-centered, and thoughtless people, but I want you to live without fear. Imagine what your life would be like if you lived unafraid—not afraid of people, suffering, failure, global turmoil, or the future. Envision My peace covering you as I provide a place of safety, confidence, and protection.

When you put your trust in Me, you have a sure hope, a firm foundation, and an eternal home. Meditate on these words: "Do not be afraid or discouraged, for the Lord will personally go ahead of you. He will be with you; he will neither fail you nor abandon you" (Deuteronomy 31:8). Guard your heart against panic or fear. When I hold your hand, you don't need to be fainthearted and you do not need to tremble. You and I are on a first-name basis, and we are intimately connected. I will not leave you without protection. Cling to these words: "Don't be afraid. Just stand still and watch the Lord rescue you today" (Exodus 14:13).

God has not given us a spirit of fear and timidity, but of power, love, and self-discipline.

2 TIMOTHY 1:7

— *July 26* —

GLORY

The deepest longing of the human heart is to know and enjoy the glory of God. We were made for this.

John Piper

My glory is displayed through My character and divine nature. It is the manifestation of all that I am—it's My splendor, brightness, excellence, grace, and majesty. My Son radiates My glory and expresses My character (Hebrews 1:3), and I want you to do the same. When you have confessed your sin and bear the fruit of a Spirit-filled life, you make Me visible to the world.

You bring Me glory when you enjoy My presence—spending time walking and talking with Me, asking for My wisdom, seeking biblical resolutions to your problems, and being My hands and feet to people in need. Others see My glory through you because your life reflects My character. Actively proclaim My truth and lead people to faith in Christ. "And as God's grace reaches more and more people, there will be great thanksgiving, and God will receive more and more glory" (2 Corinthians 4:15). When you glorify My name, your momentary worry and discouragement will be replaced with supernatural joy.

Who will not fear you, Lord, and glorify your name? For you alone are holy. All nations will come and worship before you, for your righteous deeds have been revealed.

REVELATION 15:4

July 27

BLESSED

Have you heard God's blessing in your inmost being?
Are the words *"You are my beloved child, in whom I delight"*
an endless source of joy and strength? Have you sensed,
through the Holy Spirit, God speaking them to you?

Tim Keller

Although there may be moments when you question this, I want you to know you are blessed beyond measure. Feel the pleasure of My favor pouring over you. Enjoy being fully satisfied no matter what your circumstances are. When an experience draws you closer to My Son, you are blessed. When something happens that causes you to let go of earthly goods and temporary happiness in order to cling to the eternal, you are blessed. When you suffer pain and loss, and those experiences drive you deeper into My Word, you are blessed. If you long for My presence in the middle of darkness and uncertainty, I will look into your face and give you peace.

Follow Me and you will be on the right road going in the right direction—on target for experiencing My blessings of protection, favor, and peace. You are My beloved one. I will be your endless Source of joy and strength.

Blessed are those who trust in the LORD and have made the LORD their hope and confidence.

JEREMIAH 17:7

—July 28—

JARS OF CLAY

A clay pot sitting in the sun will always be a clay pot. It has to go through the white heat of the furnace to become porcelain.

Mildred Witte Struven

You've been trying hard to be strong, but I want you to embrace the fact that you are made of breakable material. You are a human being; you get tired, make mistakes, get sick, and fret over what's happening in your circle of family and friends and in the world at large. Crises happen, children rebel, employers demand, friends disappoint, Christians criticize, cancer cripples, and bodies grow old. You are a clay pot, and you feel vulnerable.

Clay pots often look attractive on the outside, but they can easily crack or shatter. They are more delicate than they appear. Concentrate on the treasure inside your clay pot. When you come to faith in Me, I fill you with unimaginable strength. "The LORD is the everlasting God, the Creator of all the earth. He never grows weak or weary. No one can measure the depths of his understanding" (Isaiah 40:28). As you point people to the Source of your power, you are directing them to the Master Potter. I long to do for them what I've done for you. Keep walking confidently in My strength.

We have this treasure in jars of clay to show that this all-surpassing power is from God and not from us.

2 CORINTHIANS 4:7, NIV

— July 29 —
IMPORTANT MOMENTS

What I mean by living in the moment is fully engaging in the moment. Not just the casual 'hello' to someone or the polite, yet superficial, conversation that we are tempted to have. . . . Not living in the moment is equivalent to throwing away a precious gift without unwrapping it.

Lori Salierno

There are people all around you whom I want to touch through you. Many are hurting, hopeless, and lonely. They long for a kind word, a warm glance, a helping hand, or a living example of faith in action. Sometimes they reach out to you because they've observed your faith-filled response to a difficult experience and they desire insights that will keep them moving forward. At other times, strangers will come across your path, knock on your door, or encounter you in a public place. They need help, and they're looking for hope.

Learn from the example of My Son. Jesus looked at people with eyes of compassion. His touch brought healing, encouragement, and faith. Word got around that He took time to listen and recognize the deep needs of people who came to Him, and He did something to help them. I want you to have a reputation like that. You might be the only person who ever listened to the heartache of a discouraged mother. You might be the one person who prayed out loud for a stranger who trusted you with a serious concern. Don't miss these opportunities because you're too busy or distracted. They are important moments. Look for them today.

Just then a woman who had suffered for twelve years with constant bleeding came up behind him. She touched the fringe of his robe, for she thought, "If I can just touch his robe, I will be healed."

MATTHEW 9:20-21

July 30

DISCOURAGEMENT

Discouragement neutralizes optimism, assassinates hope, and erases courage. Perhaps no other human emotion is so commonly experienced and yet so infrequently exposed.

Dennis Rainey

My child, for far too long you have been burdened with the weight of discouragement. This may be caused by exhaustion, failure, fear, or never-ending frustration. Discouragement doesn't mean you're sinning, but you might be trying to find a solution in the wrong way. First, sit down and rest. Tell Me about your disappointments. Ask Me to help you see your challenges in a new light.

Fix your thoughts on the promises in My Word. Even if the source of your discouragement is not immediately removed, I will be with you at all times. Develop the habit of trusting Me before you see the answer to your prayer. I'm offering you peace. Memorize this Scripture verse: "You will keep in perfect peace all who trust in you, all whose thoughts are fixed on you!" (Isaiah 26:3). Shift your focus from your problems to Me. Guard against attacks from the enemy by making a daily appointment with Me. This is the most important item on your to-do list. Free yourself from unnecessary tasks so you can meet with Me, and know that I will lift your spirit.

Do not be afraid or discouraged,
for the LORD will personally go ahead of you.
He will be with you; he will neither fail you nor abandon you.

DEUTERONOMY 31:8

July 31

BEAUTIFUL FEET

God isn't looking for people of great faith, but
for individuals ready to follow Him.

Hudson Taylor

My plan for enlarging My Kingdom is simple—one person telling another person what My Son did when He died on the cross. You sometimes explain away your reasons for not speaking up: You're too busy, too shy, too inadequate, too new in the faith, too imperfect, or too troubled. You've been concerned about what people might think if you're bold in talking about Me. The thought of rejection immobilizes you. It's uncomfortable when a direct question about faith is followed by awkward silence. You don't want to look pushy. You get tongue-tied. Every one of those reasons is an excuse.

Jesus modeled what I want you to do—"to proclaim good news to the poor" and "to proclaim liberty to the captives and recovering of sight to the blind, to set at liberty those who are oppressed" (Luke 4:18-19, ESV). As His beautiful feet and hands, focus on leading people to faith in Christ and help them with their physical needs, too. "You will be my witnesses, telling people about me everywhere" (Acts 1:8). The joy you'll have when you meet people in heaven whom you led to My truth will far outweigh any discomfort you had in boldly sharing the gospel.

How beautiful on the mountains are the feet of the messenger who brings good news, the good news of peace and salvation, the news that the God of Israel reigns!

ISAIAH 52:7

August 1

AMAZED

God wants to surprise you; He wants you to be amazed at the blessings He lays upon your life. When we begin to trust Him . . . our outlooks will begin to change, and our attitudes will begin to change as we begin to realize our Heavenly Father enjoys surprising us with His goodness.

Darrell Creswell

Keep your eyes open for My surprises. I want to bless you in unexpected ways. Sometimes you forget how powerful I am. Consider the way My Son's actions astonished onlookers. When He healed a twelve-year-old girl who had just died, she immediately stood up and started walking around. His disciples were "overwhelmed and totally amazed" (Mark 5:42). When Jesus cast a demon out of a man, the crowds were astonished. They said, "Nothing like this has ever happened in Israel!" (Matthew 9:33). When Jesus healed a paralyzed man, "everyone was gripped with great wonder and awe, and they praised God, exclaiming, 'We have seen amazing things today!'" (Luke 5:26).

Be aware of My presence in every part of your day. I may take your breath away with unexpected provision, a surprising word of encouragement, or an unanticipated encounter with a friend. You may discover a Scripture verse that speaks directly to your heart. Or you may have an opportunity to perform a random act of kindness, bringing a smile or much-needed hope to the recipient. Never lose your sense of amazement when you see My hand at work in your life, sometimes augmented through your actions.

The crowd was amazed! Those who hadn't been able to speak were talking, the crippled were made well, the lame were walking, and the blind could see again! And they praised the God of Israel.

MATTHEW 15:31

— *August 2* —

EMBERS

When God calls . . . he bids [us] come and burn—burn with a new love . . . that will take all the mixed and muddled desires and ambitions and burn till it has refined all that was God-given in them and purged out all that was going the other direction.

N. T. Wright

Spend extended time with Me today. You may feel that your once brightly burning faith-fire is turning into an ash heap. At one point your love for Me was so strong that the light of your passion was visible to everyone who crossed your path. But lately, I've noticed that you're listening to people who are pulling you away from Me. You're spending your time on projects that have no eternal value.

Make this the day you ask Me to stir up the embers of your faith so they can be dispersed across a larger area. I will help you use your setbacks and broken dreams as a testimony of how to grow a wildfire faith that can endure anything. By nurturing your faith-embers, you can spark fresh assurance and reliance upon Me in the hearts of those questioning My goodness. Teach them to let My Spirit fan the flickering flames in their hearts, and remind them to feed on My Word. Keep your own faith ablaze and spread it to others who need My hope.

You're blessed when you're at the end of your rope.
With less of you there is more of God and his rule.

MATTHEW 5:3, MSG

— *August 3* —

CHANGE

It is wonderful what miracles God works in wills that are utterly surrendered to Him. He turns hard things into easy, and bitter things into sweet. It is not that He puts easy things in the place of the hard, but He actually changes the hard thing into an easy one.

Hannah Whitall Smith

You cannot change your past, but you can embrace the miracle I want to do in your life right now. You've been stuck in a rut, ruminating on your imperfect choices, your lack of support, your meager resources, your dead-end situation.

The thing you *can* change is your attitude. I want you to change from the inside out and use your life for My eternal purposes. I want you to know you are loved deeply by Me and that I am a changeless God. I am "the same yesterday, today, and forever" (Hebrews 13:8). That means I'll be here for you today and tomorrow and for the rest of your life. Positive change begins in your mind—so fill your mind with My truth every day. Think on things that are excellent and praiseworthy (Philippians 4:8). Ask Me to redeem your past and to use what you have learned to help others turn their hearts toward Me. The enemy says, "You can't change." But I tell you that as I transform your thinking, you are already changing for the better.

Don't copy the behavior and customs of this world, but let God transform you into a new person by changing the way you think. Then you will learn to know God's will for you, which is good and pleasing and perfect.

ROMANS 12:2

August 4

SALT AND LIGHT

Jesus said that we are "the salt of the earth" and "the light of the world." Being salt and light is not optional. Jesus did not say *you can be . . . or you have the potential to be . . .* He said *you are.*

Michael Youssef

Salt is a highly effective preservative—and that's what I want you to be in this world. All around you are signs of moral decay and a culture that is falling away from honorable living. As My representative, you are an influence for good. Keep in mind that salt becomes useless when it is contaminated. Likewise, you must remain pure in your thoughts and actions to represent Me well. Let the salt-seasoning of your life flavor your daily activities. When others see the benefits of your vibrant faith, they will consider what I can do for them.

Become a lighthouse of hope for those who are floundering—people who need Jesus but don't know how to change their lives. Your positive attitude, your words, your compassion, and your genuine interest in them will open a door for conversation about the only way to eternal life with Me—faith in Jesus Christ. Your joy in the midst of suffering illuminates the difference My peace makes when life is hard. People will be curious, and they'll ask, "What is the source of your hope? How can I find the inner strength you have?" That's your opportunity to whet their appetites for a relationship with Me.

You are the salt of the earth. But what good is salt if it has lost its flavor? Can you make it salty again? . . . You are the light of the world—like a city on a hilltop that cannot be hidden.

MATTHEW 5:13-14

— *August 5* —

BITTERNESS

Forgiving does not erase the bitter past. A healed memory is not a deleted memory. Instead, forgiving what we cannot forget creates a new way to remember. We change the memory of our past into a hope for our future.

Lewis B. Smedes

Bitterness usually starts out small. Someone says something that stings, and the offense burns its way into your heart. You replay the offense—to yourself and out loud to others. Slowly, resentment builds, and layers of hurt harden into unforgiveness. Sometimes you try to hide your feelings, but bitterness slips into every part of your life, causing a rift in your relationship with the person who hurt you and with Me.

Meditate on Romans 12:18 and apply it to your situation: "If it is possible, as far as it depends on you, live at peace with everyone" (NIV). Bitterness is dispelled by forgiveness, but it's especially difficult when the offending person doesn't know how deeply you've been wounded, or when he or she simply doesn't care. Forgiveness doesn't negate the wrong done to you, but it frees you from anger, backbiting, harsh comments, and bitterness. It allows you to live unencumbered, with joy and confidence. Ask Me to heal your memories of hurtful words and offensive or abusive treatment. Focus on the future, not the past.

Get rid of all bitterness, rage, anger, harsh words, and slander, as well as all types of evil behavior.

EPHESIANS 4:31

— *August 6* —

SACRED MOMENTS

The sacred moments, the moments of miracle,
are often the everyday moments.

Frederick Buechner

Look for My fingerprints on your everyday activities. You find it easy to discover evidence of My presence when extraordinary things happen, but you find it more difficult to detect Me in the ordinary moments of life. Today, be aware of My involvement in your routine. Rather than looking for supernatural happenings, trust Me to reveal the divine opportunities in your life. "The LORD leads with unfailing love and faithfulness all who keep his covenant" (Psalm 25:10).

Your most sacred moments may be caring for your children; feeding a homeless person; offering a smile to a stranger; delivering a meal to a shut-in; volunteering at an assisted living facility; sharing your faith with a coworker; taking games, coloring books, and crayons to the visitation area at a prison; or talking to a lonely person. Sometimes you think you are only about My business when you are quoting Bible verses to others. But as you continue to follow Me, I want you to see how your everyday encounters are holy opportunities and divine appointments.

When you come looking for me, you'll find me.
Yes, when you get serious about finding me and want
it more than anything else, I'll make sure you won't be
disappointed. . . . I'll turn things around for you.

JEREMIAH 29:13-14, MSG

— *August 7* —

WORN OUT

By default, most of us have taken the dare to simply survive. Exist. Get through. For the most part, we live numb to life—we've grown weary and apathetic and jaded . . . and wounded.

Ann Voskamp

If you are tired, you are not alone. Exhaustion often accompanies the stress of carrying heavy burdens or experiencing great loss. At times you have neglected eating or you've eaten too much. You get little sleep, and it's tempting to become apathetic or even cynical. Your circumstances never seem to change, and you feel responsible for more than you can handle. You didn't ask for this heaviness, but it's been thrust upon you. The psalmist said, "I am worn out waiting for your rescue, but I have put my hope in your word" (Psalm 119:81). "My vision is blurred by grief; my eyes are worn out because of all my enemies" (Psalm 6:7).

When you feel overwhelmed, look to Me. Follow this advice from the writer of Hebrews: " Take a new grip with your tired hands and strengthen your weak knees. Mark out a straight path for your feet" (12:12-13). Get rest for your body and strength for your soul. Delegate what others can do and be humble enough to receive help from compassionate people. I did not create you to do everything on your own. You need assistance from family members, friends, and Me. Do what you can and then sleep. Everything else will wait for tomorrow.

He gives power to the weak and strength to the powerless.

ISAIAH 40:29

August 8

JUSTICE

Justice flows from God's heart and character. . . . As we experience the wholeness that Jesus offers, we are to carry his justice forward in the world.

Paul Louis Metzger

Take time to understand My righteousness and justice. The psalmist said of Me, "Righteousness and justice are the foundation of your throne. Unfailing love and truth walk before you as attendants" (Psalm 89:14). You choose righteousness when you do the right thing, based on what you know about My truth. When you practice justice on My behalf, you work to make wrong things right. "For the righteous LORD loves justice" (Psalm 11:7).

When you see injustice, don't think to yourself, *Someone should do something about this. You* be the one to take action and make things right. Sometimes you will share the need with others and get help to rectify a situation. You will see many injustices and sometimes feel conflicted about what to do first. Pick one problem and take positive action. Don't allow indifference to blind your eyes. Be assured that when you are standing up for righteousness and righting a wrong, you are following My will for your life.

But let justice roll on like a river,
righteousness like a never-failing stream!

AMOS 5:24, NIV

August 9

LIKE A TREE

Let us not be surprised when we have to face difficulties. When the wind blows hard on a tree, the roots stretch and grow the stronger. Let it be so with us. Let us not be weaklings, yielding to every wind that blows, but strong in spirit to resist.

Amy Carmichael

To flourish in your faith, you must be rooted, steadfast, mature, fruitful, and growing in your knowledge of Me. I will be your supernatural Stream of water when the heat is turned up on your struggles. When you find yourself battered by the wind of adversity, hold fast to My Word and grow your spiritual roots deeply into My truth. You've been planted in Christ by My grace, and I've given you My Spirit so you can thrive. Draw sustenance and strength from Me.

When trials come, resist the temptation to think I've forgotten you. Allow your hard times to produce even stronger roots that can withstand the storms of life. Your firm faith will bear witness to the fact that when you are grounded deeply in Me, courage and strength will be the fruit of your life. You will have some dry seasons and some rainy seasons, but be strong. As you look back on My faithfulness in the past, you'll have no worries. I will protect you and help you flourish as you fulfill My purpose for your life.

He will be like a tree firmly planted by streams of water,
which yields its fruit in its season and its leaf does not wither;
and in whatever he does, he prospers.

PSALM 1:3, NASB

August 10

TRIUMPH

No matter what problems we face, we already have the victory in Christ. . . . Let's give thanks to God and follow Christ who leads us in triumphal procession.

Warren Wiersbe

No matter what is happening in your life right now, live in victory. You may be facing problems with your work, your health, your marriage, your children or grandchildren, or your finances. Despite these struggles, I challenge you to lay hold of My promises. I will meet all your needs according to My glorious riches (Philippians 4:19). When people lie about you and spread hurtful rumors about your character or your actions, remember where your strength comes from. "The LORD is with me; he is my helper. I look in triumph on my enemies" (Psalm 118:7, NIV). Let Me be your Defender.

Imagine yourself in a triumphal procession with Me out in front as your Leader. Sometimes you forget that when you face battles in your Christian life, you are not alone. Here is the blueprint for walking in triumph: "We use God's mighty weapons, not worldly weapons, to knock down the strongholds of human reasoning and to destroy false arguments. We destroy every proud obstacle that keeps people from knowing God. We capture their rebellious thoughts and teach them to obey Christ" (2 Corinthians 10:4-5). Claim your victory in Christ every day and walk confidently in it.

But thanks be to God, who always leads us in triumph in Christ, and manifests through us the sweet aroma of the knowledge of Him in every place.

2 CORINTHIANS 2:14, NASB

August 11

HERE I AM

God did not direct His call to Isaiah—Isaiah overheard God saying, ". . . who will go for Us?" The call of God is not just for a select few but for everyone. Whether I hear God's call or not depends on the condition of my ears, and exactly what I hear depends upon my spiritual attitude.

Oswald Chambers

Look forward to the opportunities I place before you every day. Sometimes I want you to listen to someone who feels forgotten. At other times My Spirit will nudge you to perform a specific act of kindness for a person who needs encouragement. I may open a door for you to share your faith with a coworker. You might have an opportunity to advocate a cause I care about. Sometimes I will call you to an assignment that will take a longer block of time—something that will further My Kingdom agenda and require a sacrifice of time and resources from you.

You may be thinking, *I have problems myself. How can I possibly help someone else?* But remember, I will equip you with everything you need for the assigned mission. Your job is to answer the call and listen to My instructions. Sometimes you'll know what to do after reading My Word or listening to a fellow Christ-follower. Often, I will prod your inner spirit and reveal your next steps. When you say, "Here I am, Lord," I will use you in ways you might never have imagined.

Then I heard the Lord asking, "Whom should I send as a messenger to this people? Who will go for us?" I said, "Here I am. Send me."

ISAIAH 6:8

— *August 12* —

THANK YOU

I thank God for the way he made you, distinct, special and unique. You were not made from a common mold.

Erwin Lutzer

Focus your gratitude today on the people I've placed in your life who have blessed and encouraged you. Take time to list their exceptional and praiseworthy qualities. Consider how their walks with Me have inspired you to hold on to hope. How has their uniqueness provided creative ways for them to come alongside ministries and individuals to bring an increase in joy, faith, and love? Begin by thanking Me for the specific ways they have assisted you during a long and arduous journey.

Now read a letter the apostle Paul wrote to Philemon, and notice the way he thanks and challenges this friend. "I always thank my God when I pray for you . . . because I keep hearing about your faith in the Lord Jesus and your love for all of God's people. And I am praying that you will put into action the generosity that comes from your faith as you understand and experience all the good things we have in Christ. Your love has given me much joy and comfort, my brother, for your kindness has often refreshed the hearts of God's people" (1:4-7). Make a list of the ways a friend has supported you physically, emotionally, or spiritually and write a note of thanks. You will encourage that person, and your own heart will be refreshed by the memory of his or her kindness.

Every time I think of you, I give thanks to my God.

PHILIPPIANS 1:3

— *August 13* —

POSTURES IN PRAYER

God wills that men should pray everywhere, but the place of His Glory is in the solitudes, where He hides us in the cleft of the rock, and talks with man face to face as a man talketh with his friend.

Samuel Chadwick

Talk to Me, dear one—when you rise up, when you sit down, when you are glad, when you are sad, when you think I'm answering your prayers and when you think I haven't heard your requests. Keep talking to Me. Sometimes you have neglected prayer when you think your day isn't quiet enough and when the busyness of life keeps you from going to a secluded, private place. Because I'm your friend, I want you to converse with Me as you're walking, with your eyes wide open. Pray for the people you encounter, that they will get to know Me intimately, that their needs will be met.

Here's what I want you to do. Practice approaching Me with different postures—kneeling (Daniel 6:10), bowing down (Psalm 95:6), standing (2 Chronicles 20:5-6), lifting your hands (Psalm 134:2), and lying prostrate before Me (Joshua 5:14). There is a time and place for every posture—come close to Me in the way your heart directs today. Sometimes you will rejoice in My presence with hands lifted high. Or you might be flat on your face crying out your pain. Or you might kneel in humble submission, asking for guidance. However you come before Me, I'm listening. I will answer.

Come, let us worship and bow down. Let us kneel before the LORD our maker.

PSALM 95:6

— *August 14* —

NO MISTAKES

God can be trusted. He keeps His promises.
He doesn't make any mistakes.

Nancy DeMoss Wolgemuth

Your life is not an accident. When you wake up each day and breathe in fresh air, it's because I have a plan for your life. Before your parents knew you were conceived, I did. I knew the color of your eyes and hair. I knew your personality and the gifts you would have. I scheduled each day of your life before you took your first breath, and I knew the number of your days before you were born. Every day of your life was recorded in my book (Psalm 139:16).

Your birth was not a chance happening. Be confident that I will work out My plans for your life (Psalm 138:8). I've searched your heart, and I know you've sometimes wondered why I allowed you to be born and why you've had to endure disappointments, hurts, and hardships. When you're struggling, your focus tends to move away from My truth. Remember My promises: "I have cared for you since you were born. Yes, I carried you before you were born. I will be your God throughout your lifetime—until your hair is white with age. I made you, and I will care for you. I will carry you along and save you" (Isaiah 46:3-4). Trust Me to be your Protector. I will accomplish My purpose for your life.

God's way is perfect. All the LORD's promises prove true.
He is a shield for all who look to him for protection.

2 SAMUEL 22:31

— August 15 —

LIMITLESS

How completely satisfying to turn from our limitations to a God who has none. . . . Those who are in Christ share with Him all the riches of limitless time and endless years. God never hurries. There are no deadlines against which He must work.

A. W. Tozer

Think about your needs. Now consider My unlimited power and complete control. I never get tired, and I never run out of time to accomplish My work. I am never late. "Do you not know? . . . The LORD is the everlasting God, the Creator of the ends of the earth. He will not grow tired or weary, and his understanding no one can fathom" (Isaiah 40:28, NIV).

I am aware of your questions: "If You are all-powerful, why did You allow my child to be born with a disability? If You hold the world in Your hands, why didn't You keep that hurricane from making landfall? If You don't work against deadlines, why did the ambulance get to the scene too late to save my loved one? Why did my spouse get cancer? Why was I abused? Why do I struggle with infertility?" In the midst of your pain, take time to explore My character. I cannot sin. I came to save you from the evil in this world. "The LORD is righteous in all his ways and faithful in all he does" (Psalm 145:17, NIV). I will use My limitless resources to work on your behalf. Quiet your spirit and relax in My arms. One day you will understand how I was interceding for you and holding you by the hand, even on your most difficult days.

I pray that from his glorious, unlimited resources he will empower you with inner strength through his Spirit.

EPHESIANS 3:16

August 16

THE ADVOCATE

What does the Spirit do? Scripture says He comforts the saved. He convicts the lost. He conveys the truth. Have you ever been convicted? Ever sensed a stab of sorrow for your actions? Understood a new truth? Then you've been touched by the Holy Spirit.

Max Lucado

You are never without support. When you need wisdom, I will be your Teacher. When you are grieving, I will be your Comforter. When you don't know which direction to go because too many people are giving you advice, I will be your Guide. When you make wrong choices, I will bring conviction, pointing the way to confession and restored joy. When you can't find the words to represent your deepest needs, My Spirit will intercede on your behalf "with groanings that cannot be expressed in words" (Romans 8:26).

You can't escape My presence. I am never preoccupied with distractions. I am here as your Backer—providing everything you need to assure you of a future hope beyond this world. I will guide you to truth, keep you on course, reassure you during fear, and console you in loss. Hear Me whisper again and again, "I am with you. I am with you. I am with you."

But the Advocate, the Holy Spirit, whom the Father will send in my name, will teach you all things and will remind you of everything I have said to you.

JOHN 14:26, NIV

— August 17 —

HIS TOUCH

Have you felt His merciful touch? . . . Have you felt His strong hand lifting you out of darkness and failure and despair? Have you felt the pressure of His fingers shaping you into someone who will reflect His glory for all eternity?

Jennifer Rothschild

Today I ask you to let your senses be heightened by My presence. Become aware of My unseen touch in your everyday circumstances. Sometimes My touch is felt through unexpected encounters with My people. They encourage you and provide tangible assistance when you need advice or resources. At other times I move in your heart through music, and you shift into a posture of worship. Even when I don't immediately deliver you from harsh trials, I am walking beside you, giving you courage, holding your hand, and shaping your story into a powerful testimony of redemption.

There are days when you stubbornly try to do everything yourself. You don't ask Me for wisdom or guidance or support. Pain has clouded your thinking, and you wonder whether I can be trusted. Let My Word remind you of My faithfulness. I always provide deliverance for My people. Rest assured that in due time you will reflect My glory for the rest of eternity.

The works of his hands are faithful and just; all his precepts are trustworthy. They are established for ever and ever, enacted in faithfulness and uprightness.

PSALM 111:7-8, NIV

August 20

ALMIGHTY GOD

Circumstances may appear to wreck our lives and God's plans, but God is not helpless among the ruins. . . . He comes in and takes the calamity and uses it victoriously, working out his wonderful plan of love.

Eric Liddell

I am El-Shaddai, the One to whom nothing is impossible. I am all-powerful, and I am completely capable of taking your broken situation and turning it into something good. Right now you can't envision how that could be possible, but I can turn your tragedy into victory. "Is anything too hard for the LORD?" (Genesis 18:14).

Stop long enough to consider how your circumstances have created a pathway for good. Have you sensed My presence in the middle of your difficulty? Have your basic needs been met? Has your compassion for others increased? Have you recognized My intense love for you, and has it comforted you? I am great and mighty, and I will be with you to the end—with resources, support, encouragement, wisdom, strength, and love. Nothing escapes My notice—including your faithfulness amid adversity. Do not despair. I will continue to use My power for your good.

"I am the Alpha and the Omega—the beginning and the end," says the Lord God. "I am the one who is, who always was, and who is still to come—the Almighty One."

REVELATION 1:8

August 21

LOVE EACH OTHER

Love pays attention. Love listens to the fears and the doubts of others and treats them with respect. Love accepts others the way Jesus accepts you.

Rick Warren

Love Me with your whole heart. Talk to Me. Sing to Me. Listen to Me. Seek My advice for your questions about everyday living and about difficult, life-altering decisions. Tell Me about your anxieties, your fears, and your doubts. I enjoy communicating with you. Once you have established a relationship with Me, learn to love yourself. You've read this command in My Word: "*Love your neighbor as yourself.*" Celebrate the progress you've made personally and spiritually.

Now it's time to love others. Loving the people around you is a distinguishing characteristic of My followers. "The way we know we've been transferred from death to life is that we love our brothers and sisters" (1 John 3:14, MSG). Through your words and actions, demonstrate your love. Pay attention to the needs of others and be creative in the ways you show how much you care. When you love others in practical ways, not only will the love be returned to you, but you'll experience more joy, peace, and contentment. Make a daily habit of loving Me, loving yourself, and loving others.

Jesus replied, "The most important commandment is this: . . . 'And you must love the LORD your God will all your heart, all your soul, all your mind, and all your strength.' The second is equally important: 'Love your neighbor as yourself.'"

MARK 12:29-31

August 22

CONQUERED

If you are paralyzed by your past, if Satan is destroying your gifts and your calling by his incessant replaying of old tapes, you're actually being hit by a double whammy. The original damage in the past is one thing—but now you're letting yourself be hurt . . . again by the memory of what happened. . . . We should not be ignorant of Satan's devices.

Jim Cymbala

You've allowed the enemy to influence your life. He has tried to impede My plans for your future. He's been tempting you to give in to discouragement and even despair. He's been telling you there is no way you can overcome that bad habit. He's made you believe that you are to blame for all the wrong choices of the people closest to you. He's made you think you'll never surmount the missteps of your past. He's been whispering, "You're a loser! You'll never be a good Christian, so why don't you quit trying?" None of these accusations are true because they originate with the father of lies.

Here is the truth about what will happen to Satan: "Then the devil, who had deceived them, was thrown into the fiery lake of burning sulfur" (Revelation 20:10). Done. Finished. Conquered. Defeated. Vanquished. Crushed. So stop giving him any access to your mind and live in the confidence of knowing you belong to Me.

Submit yourselves, then, to God. Resist the devil, and he will flee from you.

JAMES 4:7, NIV

August 23

UNASHAMED

I am not going to apologize for speaking the name of Jesus. . . .
If I have to sacrifice everything, I will.

Rachel Scott

Think of someone you know who doesn't know Jesus. Have you ever shared the Good News with that person? Do you long to see that individual in the family of God, but you can't bring yourself to speak out loud about your faith in Christ? You may feel that you simply can't articulate the truth of the gospel or that you can't remember the Scripture references that explain My plan of redemption. At other times you feel afraid of what someone will think of your beliefs. Perhaps you'd be mocked or humiliated. Or maybe it's been so long since you became a Christian that you've lost your compassion for people who need hope. It could even be that your personal pain has distracted you from thinking about anyone but yourself.

Begin by praying for the spiritually lost people you know. Reacquaint yourself with Scriptures that explain how to help people recognize their need and accept Christ's sacrifice for them on the cross. Think of specific ways you can bring up your personal faith in Christ. Pray for yourself—to have boldness and confidence as you speak aloud about this important relationship. Trust Me to give you opportunities to talk about salvation through Christ. If the gospel is rejected, decide in your heart that you will not give up. Live unashamed of this important message!

I am not ashamed of the gospel, because it is the power of God that brings salvation to everyone who believes.

ROMANS 1:16, NIV

— *August 24* —

ENOUGH

The last and greatest lesson that the soul has to learn is the fact that God, and God alone, is enough for all its needs. . . . This is the crowning discovery of our whole Christian life. God is enough!

Hannah Whitall Smith

You are working hard to fix the difficulties in your life all by yourself. Your independence alienates you from people and tempts you to avoid asking for help. You are like someone who has money in the bank but lives like a pauper—never cashing in on the available resources. You're tired. You're out of ideas. You fear the future, and hopelessness is clouding your thinking.

Discover the wealth in front of you. I am a generous God. I am a God of abundance. I have blessed you with every spiritual blessing because you are united with Christ (Ephesians 1:3). I will be enough for all of your needs—not just a few, but *all* of your needs. Once you put your faith in Me, nothing can ever separate you from My love—not even the powers of hell can pull you away from Me! When you walk with Me, you can say with the psalmist, "Because the Lord is my Shepherd, I have everything I need!" (Psalm 23:1, TLB).

I am convinced that nothing can ever separate us from God's love. Neither life nor death, neither angels nor demons, neither our fears for today nor our worries about tomorrow—not even the powers of hell can separate us from God's love.

ROMANS 8:38

August 25

GIFTED

You have inside you the capacity to invest your mental, emotional, and spiritual gifts in a way that glorifies God, impacts the world, and satisfies your own soul.

David Jeremiah

I have gifted you in a unique and personal way. When you use your gifts—whether they include teaching, praying, helping, giving, administrating, exhorting, leading, serving, discerning, evangelizing, showing hospitality, or having great faith—you are bringing glory to My name. "There are different kinds of spiritual gifts, but the same Spirit is the source of them all" (1 Corinthians 12:4). What you may not expect is that when you use your gifts, you will experience great joy that satisfies your soul and brings fulfillment to your life.

Spiritual gifts are not meant to draw attention to you. Use them to bless and to build others up, and to further My work in this world. "God has given each of you a gift from his great variety of spiritual gifts. Use them well to serve one another" (1 Peter 4:10). In the process of using your gifts, expect moments when you want to cry out, "Eureka!" That's the joy you experience when your God-given gifts are perfectly matched with an opportunity to serve someone else, or to further My Kingdom. In that instant, you know beyond any doubt that you are living in the smile of My approval. I've designed you to experience My pleasure when we are working together in this way. Want joy? Use your gifts!

It is the one and only Spirit who distributes all these gifts.
He alone decides which gift each person should have.

1 CORINTHIANS 12:11

— *August 26* —

ENDURING LOVE

Though our feelings come and go, His love for us does not. It is not wearied by our sins, or our indifference; and, therefore, it is quite relentless in its determination.

C. S. Lewis

I want you to understand what enduring love is. King Darius published a proclamation about who I am: "He is the living God, world without end. His kingdom never falls. His rule continues eternally. He is a savior and rescuer. He performs astonishing miracles in heaven and on earth. He saved Daniel from the power of the lions" (Daniel 6:26-27, MSG). I am not wishy-washy in My character or in My actions. What I do is righteous. What I say, I mean. "I have loved you, my people, with an everlasting love. With unfailing love I have drawn you to myself" (Jeremiah 31:3).

Today I want you to say, "God's love endures forever." Then say, "God's love for *me* endures forever." There is no wrong choice you could ever make that would change that. My love for you endures forever. There is no outside force that can change this fact. My love for you endures forever. Even if you try to flee from My presence—My love for you endures forever. There is nothing in this world or in heaven that will distract Me from caring about you. My love for you will never end.

Give thanks to the LORD, for he is good!
His faithful love endures forever.

PSALM 136:1

— *August 27* —

ANTICIPATION

We are to wait for the coming of Christ with patience. We are to watch with anticipation. We are to work with zeal. We are to prepare with urgency. Scripture says Christ is coming when you're least expecting him.

Billy Graham

Look up! The coming of the Lord is near. Read the promise in My book: "He who testifies to all these things says it again: 'I'm on my way! I'll be there soon!'" (Revelation 22:20, MSG). If your body is in pain, if your mind is clouded with confusion, if your finances are falling apart, if your loved one is in prison, if your child is making bad choices, if your job is squeezing the joy out of you, if your circumstances seem insurmountable—don't give up!

There will be an end to all of this suffering and sadness. Even the mountains and the seas cry out for relief. "The creation looks forward to the day when it will join God's children in glorious freedom from death and decay" (Romans 8:21). My Son repeatedly promised to come again—and He will come for you in all His power and glory, accompanied by a host of angels. Let this bring new hope to your heart today: "Look! He comes with the clouds of heaven. And everyone will see him—even those who pierced him. . . . Yes! Amen!" (Revelation 1:7). Hold on. It won't be long.

For you who fear my name, the Sun of Righteousness will rise with healing in his wings. And you will go free, leaping with joy like calves let out to pasture.

MALACHI 4:2

— August 28 —

COME AND SEE

To those who have been hauling around a long list of rules. . . . To those who are weighed down with the fear and guilt of religion. To all the fans who are worn out on religion, Jesus invites you to follow him.

Kyle Idleman

Invite people to spend time with you before you ask them to accept My gift of eternal life. Many are burned out on religion and tired of reading a list of everything they shouldn't do. You've made attempts at verbalizing the story of how you came to know Me, but there are awkward silences and you aren't sure what to do next. Sometimes a heart is ready for the gospel, and faith comes quickly. But more often, skeptical people want to observe what they are considering before saying yes.

Invite those people to walk beside you. Study the example in John 1. When two curious disciples of John the Baptist asked where Jesus was staying, He said, *"Come and see."* They accepted the invitation and spent the rest of the day with Him. Allow people to be with you and to see your faith in action. When they observe your strength under the pressure of disappointment, pain, and loss, they will be curious about what gives you so much peace and joy. Point them to Jesus by the way you live your life. Answer their questions about the hope you have beyond this world. Let them hang out with you, and in due time they will respond to the invitation to follow Me.

"Come and see," [Jesus] said. It was about four o'clock in the afternoon when they went with him to the place where he was staying, and they remained with him the rest of the day.

JOHN 1:39

— *August 29* —

READY FOR ORDERS

The will of God is not something you add to your life. It's a course you choose. You either line yourself up with the Son of God . . . or you capitulate to the principle which governs the rest of the world.

Elisabeth Elliot

You are a soldier in My army. As your Commanding Officer, I've given you the code of conduct in My Word. Your enemy seeks to destroy you with discouragement, criticism, disappointment, and despair. Your weapons of warfare are not what you'd expect to find in most battles. But I know how effective the defenses of prayer, faith, courage, and Scripture are. I have personally instructed you in how to use them properly. You have been tested by the fire of adversity and have found Me trustworthy. Now you can confidently and boldly engage in defending My truth.

Have a spirit of humility and come before Me as Joshua did with this question: *"What do you want your servant to do?"* As a good soldier of Jesus Christ, "put on the whole armor of God" (Ephesians 6:11, ESV) and be alert (1 Peter 5:8). Stand up for righteousness. Defend the downtrodden. Speak up for those who have no voice. Proclaim victory in My name.

"I am at your command," Joshua said.
"What do you want your servant to do?"

JOSHUA 5:14

August 30

POWERFUL PRECEPTS

Only one thing validates a message or a messenger: the whole counsel of the Word of God.

Kay Arthur

My Word is true, and it is a shield to everyone who comes to Me for protection (Proverbs 30:5). One of the most important things you can do is to meditate on Scripture. "If your law had not been my delight, I would have perished in my affliction. I will never forget your precepts, for by them you have preserved my life" (Psalm 119:92-93, NIV).

I want you to be prepared to deal with life—and the more you understand and apply the teachings in My inspired Word, the more success you will have as you do the work I've assigned to you. The precepts in My Word are correct, and they give joy to your heart. My commands are radiant and give light to your eyes (Psalm 19:8, NIV). Consider this: My principles give you all the guidelines and instruction you need to live productively. My truth illuminates the issues you face in a complicated world and also brings the comfort of knowing you hold in your hand everything you need to make right choices. It will equip you to do every good work (2 Timothy 3:17).

The fear of the LORD is the beginning of wisdom; all who follow his precepts have good understanding. To him belongs eternal praise.

PSALM 111:10, NIV

— August 31 —

TEACHABLE

Who you become while you're waiting is as
important as what you're waiting for.

John Ortberg

Maintain a teachable spirit while you're waiting on answers to prayer. My Son found glory in His cross. He gave up His divine privileges and came to earth as a helpless baby. After going into public ministry, He was ridiculed, betrayed by one of His own followers, and despised by many in authority. He endured intense agony and died a criminal's death on the cross instead of using His power to escape His suffering. Jesus' example of humility amid great adversity can help you learn how to make it through each day.

Discover the value of thorny experiences. Allow your tears to make your heart tender. Seek wisdom from fellow Christ-followers who have learned important spiritual lessons as they persevered in the midst of trials. Your sorrow is never wasted when you nurture a teachable heart. The benefits include an awareness of My presence, insight for hard choices, and humility that allows you to receive direction for your next steps. If you wait on Me and listen for My instruction, I will teach you what you need to know.

Guide me in your truth and teach me, for you are God my Savior,
and my hope is in you all day long.

PSALM 25:5, NIV

September 1

LAVISH MERCY

When our God who is Mercy comes like a shout into your darkness, when the Father stoops down and tenderly picks up the pieces of your broken life, when Jesus steps in front of what you could have deserved, and when the Lord of heaven says, "I still want you," after you thought no one would, it is the most amazing truth of all.

Angela Thomas

I want you to experience My lavish mercy. It's the best kind of clemency—not earned, but freely given. Not because you've worked so hard or because you've been through so much—just because I love you. Enjoy My compassion, kindness, and love. Bask in the radiant sunshine of My company. Know that I am aware of the rejection and hurts of your past. When you are mistreated because of someone else's sin, it hurts Me deeply because you belong to Me. You are not responsible for the wrong choices of others. You are only responsible for your own relationship with Me.

I have heard your cry: "Lord, have mercy on me." Look to Me for your protection. Hide under the shadow of My wings until the danger that threatens you passes by (Psalm 57:1). Because of My tender mercy, the morning light from heaven is about to break upon you (Luke 1:78). Relax in the warmth of My compassion and kindness. I am with you. I am gently putting the pieces of your life back together. Your humble, tender heart brings Me great joy.

He shows mercy from generation to generation
to all who fear him.

LUKE 1:50

— September 2 —

IDENTITY

In your brokenness and imperfection,
God whispers three words: You are mine.

Margaret Feinberg

Do you know who you are? You've looked in the mirror and criticized the way I made you. You've evaluated your life and underscored all your failings. You've wished you were smarter, more talented, more energized, and more successful. You've listened to degrading words from someone else about your lack of accomplishments. Stop believing what other people say and quit accepting the labels they've placed on you. Resist the temptation to look at your broken places and then to feel unloved and unimportant.

Start believing what I've said about you—and let *that* define you. You are created in My image. I'm pleased with the way I made you. I've adopted you and given you the gift of My Holy Spirit. You're in My family. I've given you spiritual gifts that will bless the people around you. Don't allow the opinions of others to define you. Let your brokenness bring you to My arms and hear Me whisper, "You are mine. I love you. I will take care of you. I will never let go of you." Fix your heart on My promises and move forward in confidence. When you need answers, My Spirit will guide you. Your identity is this—you are My precious child.

He has identified us as his own by placing the Holy Spirit in our hearts as the first installment that guarantees everything he has promised us.

2 CORINTHIANS 1:22

— September 3 —

PRIDE

Pride builds walls between people; humility builds bridges.

Rick Warren

Pride distorts reality. It affects your ability to see yourself as you really are. Pride looks down on things and on other people—which keeps you from understanding My perception of you. You've wondered how you can have too much pride when you're in so much personal pain. The truth is that you've been so concerned about keeping up the image of handling everything yourself that you haven't been humble enough to admit your needs to others. Can a person without resources be prideful? *Yes.* Can someone without good health or ideal circumstances be filled with pride? *Yes.* Can an individual who has a relationship with Me be prideful? *Yes.*

Pride produces an "I can do it myself" attitude. Pride makes you more concerned with other people's perception of you than with being open and honest about your life. A prideful person is defensive and judgmental, and the result isn't pleasant. "Pride goes before destruction, a haughty spirit before a fall" (Proverbs 16:18, NIV). Develop humility by having a correct view of Me. Ask Me to reveal Myself to you more clearly. Confess your pride as sin and practice grace-filled humility. Remember these truths: "Anyone who becomes as humble as this little child is the greatest in the Kingdom of Heaven" (Matthew 18:4). "So humble yourselves under the mighty power of God, and at the right time he will lift you up in honor" (1 Peter 5:6). A spirit of humility always gets My attention.

I learned God-worship when my pride was shattered. Heart-shattered lives ready for love don't for a moment escape God's notice.

PSALM 51:17, MSG

— *September 4* —

UPWARD

As we gaze upon the wonders of creations, we look up towards the heights of a God who is merciful in His ways and magnificent in His deeds. The life of worship always points us upwards.

Matt Redman

Enjoy the world I made for you. Make some space in your day to focus on the beauty around you. Walk outside and look for the variety in My creation—the trees, the flowers, and the birds. Each one is unique. Take a deep breath. Feel the gentle breeze. When your life is complicated and you feel pulled in too many directions, consider these everyday wonders.

You may not be able to spend time in My creation due to harsh weather or desolate surroundings, but even then, you can look up. Take in the majesty of the sky. Trace the outline of the clouds. Ponder the landscape in front of you. Hear Me whisper, "I made these things for your enjoyment, and I designed a beautiful place for you to live." When life comes crashing in around you, practice the habit of concentrating on My handiwork in nature. Worship Me. Speak out loud about what you observe. Keep looking up, and your heart will be heaven-focused, not earthbound.

For ever since the world was created, people have seen the earth and sky. Through everything God made, they can clearly see his invisible qualities—his eternal power and divine nature.

ROMANS 1:20

September 5

ABBA FATHER

Our highest privilege and deepest need is to experience the holy God as our loving Father, to approach him without fear and to be assured of his fatherly care and concern.

Greg Ogden

My love for you is high and deep and wide. My promise to My followers is this: "I will be your Father, and you will be my sons and daughters" (2 Corinthians 6:18). You are My child, and I am your Father. Come to Me without hesitation or fear. I want you to experience My closeness, with the intimate security that is yours when you belong to Me. When you have questions, come to Me for answers. When you feel lonely, come to Me for companionship. When you are frightened, come to Me for comfort. When you are hopeless, find your way to My open arms and discover a fresh perspective.

I will not turn away from you. I am never too busy for you. I know your needs before you even ask for help. Don't be discouraged when you pass through deep waters; I will be with you and will not let you drown (Isaiah 43:2). My Son asked for My will to be done and paid the ultimate price for your redemption. During your toughest times, I hear your cries. I see the end from the beginning. One day you will understand why your journey has had detours and U-turns. Crawl into My lap, take a deep breath, and feel the warmth of My embrace. Let Me hear you say, "Lord, I know You love me, and I trust You."

"Abba, Father," he cried out, "everything is possible for you. Please take this cup of suffering away from me. Yet I want your will to be done, not mine."

MARK 14:36

— September 6 —

JOIN HIM

Watch to see where God is working and join Him in His work.

Henry Blackaby

You have asked Me for the entire blueprint of your life, but I want you to focus on following My leading *today.* Be careful not to get so caught up in long-range planning that your schedule keeps you on a rigid path that doesn't allow for flexibility. Often, on the way to the major work I have for you to do over your lifetime, I will send you on short-term assignments that accomplish My will and train you for what is ahead. As you go through your day, be alert. I have already been at work in people's hearts. Ask Me for the wisdom and discernment to know when it's time for you to enter a conversation and point someone to Christ.

In some cases, I want you to notice a worthy cause—feeding the hungry, caring for a sick family member, giving to a mission project, visiting a prisoner, teaching a class, or providing hospitality to someone involved in My work. These opportunities are not distractions. Sometimes they are inconvenient and wearisome, but they are important work—Kingdom work! Once engaged, you'll discover a new kind of fulfillment, and it will whet your appetite for joining Me.

I take joy in doing your will, my God, for your instructions are written on my heart.

PSALM 40:8

— *September 7* —

THE SECRET PLACE

In place of our exhaustion and spiritual fatigue, He will give us rest. All He asks is that we come to Him . . . meditating on Him, talking to Him, listening in silence, occupying ourselves with Him—totally and thoroughly lost in the hiding place of His presence.

Charles Swindoll

Come close to Me. I will be your Covering, your Shelter, and your Dwelling. When needed, I will conceal you in a secret hiding place. This haven is sometimes an actual physical location. More often, it is a condition of your heart in relationship with Me. It's a state of peace in the midst of physical, mental, or spiritual attacks. I long to commune with you as we walk together. When your hand is in Mine, you are always in a place of security and safety.

Instead of worrying, meditate on My Word, and I will protect you from trouble. Rather than giving in to defeat and fear, hide Scripture in your heart: "The one thing I ask of the LORD—the thing I seek most—is to live in the house of the LORD all the days of my life. . . . For he will conceal me there when troubles come; he will hide me in his sanctuary. He will place me out of reach on a high rock" (Psalm 27:4-5). When you take refuge in Me, you'll find a deep spiritual rest that overcomes debilitating circumstances.

You are my hiding place; you will protect me from trouble and surround me with songs of deliverance.

PSALM 32:7, NIV

— September 8 —

MY BANNER

No child of God needs to live in bondage to feelings of inferiority, insecurity, or inadequacy. No matter what battle you face, God is your victory. . . . So raise high the banner! Victory is yours.

Sharon Jaynes

Do not allow the difficult circumstances of your life to make you feel like a failure. You've looked around and made comparisons. Other Christians look strong and courageous—even daring. Satan wants you to cower and tremble, like someone who has arrived at a battlefield already feeling defeated.

Rehearse your strategy for battle by repeating Scripture that promises victory. My divine power has given you everything you need for a godly life (2 Peter 1:3, NIV). I have given you the mind of Christ (1 Corinthians 2:16). I have equipped you with the power of the Holy Spirit (Acts 1:8). I have provided never-failing promises (2 Peter 1:4). Get ready to hear even more great news. "Overwhelming victory is [yours] through Christ, who loved [you]" (Romans 8:37). Remember the story of Moses. Before he led My chosen people out of Egypt, he had trouble speaking, felt inadequate and unqualified, and made mistakes. But Moses trusted Me, and I gave him many victories during the subsequent wilderness journey. To commemorate the conquest of the Amalekite army, "Moses built an altar there and named it Yahweh-Nissi (which means 'the LORD is my banner')" (Exodus 17:15). Raise your banner high. I am your Victor!

Thanks be to God! He gives us the victory through our Lord Jesus Christ.

1 CORINTHIANS 15:57, NIV

— *September 9* —

ABUNDANCE

Do you want more abundance? More is always possible, but you'll have to do something opposite of what you're currently doing. You'll have to cooperate with God's ways and respond in obedience and trust.

Bruce Wilkinson

Think about what it means to have a life overflowing with abundance. You may have looked around at other people and wondered why they have so much when it feels like you have very little. Consider this: You've been thinking about abundance as monetary wealth and an accumulation of comfort-producing items. But genuine abundance is not about what you get or claim—it's about receiving blessings from My hand and being a good steward of My gifts.

You can be assured that your life will overflow with good things when you share what you have with others. Here's what I give you: "Mercy, peace and love be yours in abundance" (Jude 1:2, NIV). Living in abundance means you have a large quantity of My grace, wisdom, patience, hope, joy, love, and peace. Be creative about how you can share those gifts with the people around you. Sometimes you will pass on tangible items to people in need. More often, you will express the inexplicable joy and peace of walking with Me during difficult times and finding Me faithful. When you give these blessings to others, I keep giving you more and more—they will never run out.

From his abundance we have all received one gracious blessing after another.

JOHN 1:16

September 10

WHIRLWINDS

I believe that suffering is part of the narrative, and that nothing really good gets built when everything's easy. I believe that loss and emptiness and confusion often give way to new fullness and wisdom.

Shauna Niequist

Right now life feels like a hurricane that has lifted you off your feet and thrown you in an unexpected and uncomfortable direction. You can hardly breathe, much less stand up and start living in a productive way. Celebrate this moment. The time when you experience great loss and emptiness is when you hear My voice best. "You're blessed when you feel you've lost what is most dear to you. Only then can you be embraced by the One most dear to you" (Matthew 5:4, MSG). Sometimes your whirlwind isn't physical—it's emotional and spiritual due to people who have questioned your faith or verbally attacked you because of your relationship with Me. Remember this: "You're blessed when your commitment to God provokes persecution. The persecution drives you even deeper into God's kingdom" (Matthew 5:10, MSG).

When you are weak, I am strong. When your thoughts are swirling because of adversity, you depend upon Me more than when you believe you can handle everything yourself. Build your life on the firm foundation of faith in My Son, Jesus Christ, and you will withstand the storms of life triumphantly.

When the whirlwind passes by, the wicked is no more,
but the righteous has an everlasting foundation.

PROVERBS 10:25, NKJV

— *September 11* —

BONUS BENEFITS

All of a sudden it dawned on me that God was saying to me, "Why don't you take what you have and what you are—your being—and I will take what I have and what I am—my being—and we will share." I began to see . . . that I had stumbled on to the bargain of a lifetime.

Bob Benson

Tap into the benefits I've provided for you. You read in My Word that I've given you great and precious promises and that through them you can "participate in [My] divine nature" (2 Peter 1:4, NIV). Envision reaching up to Me with all your might. Picture My hand grasping yours, and hear Me speak these words over you: "You don't have enough strength, but I have plenty. You don't have enough unconditional love, but I can help you. You don't have enough endurance, but I do. You don't have enough patience, but I am long-suffering. You don't have enough grace, but I specialize in unmerited favor. You don't think you can make it through the day, but with Me, you can!"

Suddenly, you realize you've stumbled onto bonus benefits. Every time you run low on love, compassion, strength, wisdom, endurance, or perseverance, you can partner with Me. You will always have enough because you have entered a relationship where you have "come to share the very being of God" (2 Peter 1:4, NEB).

And because of his glory and excellence, he has given us great and precious promises. These are the promises that enable you to share his divine nature and escape the world's corruption caused by human desires.

2 PETER 1:4

September 12

PASS IT ON

Pass on godly legacies in your own home and in the community around you. What a joy it would be to have someone say to you down the road, "I learned about God through your love and belief in me!"

Twila Paris

You are a teacher to those in your home and in your sphere of influence. You teach with your words, but also by the way you live your life. The people closest to you listen to the Scripture that comes out of your mouth, and they observe your response to personal pain and struggles. They are watching to see if your life matches your words. As you live a life pleasing to Me and teach My precepts to others, they will be equipped to pass My truth on to the next generation.

In addition to teaching, love the people you are investing in unconditionally. They will make mistakes, and sometimes they won't follow your advice. That's when they need you the most. Pray with them, believe in them, and let them know you are coming alongside them for the long haul. My Spirit will guide you as you live out your faith in front of people who need an example of how to follow Me. When you see them internalizing what they believe and then passing it on to others, you will know you're accomplishing My purpose.

You have heard me teach things that have been confirmed by many reliable witnesses. Now teach these truths to other trustworthy people who will be able to pass them on to others.

2 TIMOTHY 2:2

September 13

GOD'S PLANS

God has plans for you and His plans are for good because God Himself is good. He can neither think nor do evil.

Elizabeth George

You have questioned how I could allow trouble to enter your life. It goes against every rational thought in your mind that a loving God would permit trials to challenge someone He loves. As you read these Scriptures, be aware of My faithfulness to you and My plans for you: "The LORD will work out his plans for my life—for your faithful love, O LORD, endures forever" (Psalm 138:8). I made you and I will not abandon you. "The LORD's plans stand firm forever; his intentions can never be shaken" (Psalm 33:11). Because you belong to Me, one day you will live in a world that cannot be shaken. That's My promise to you.

Spend time today thinking about these truths: *The intentions of God toward me are good. He cannot sin. He is incapable of doing evil. What He allows to happen in my life will work out for my good, even if I can't see that fact today.* Here is My encouragement and My commitment to you: My goodness and unfailing love will pursue you all the days of your life, and you will live in My house forever (Psalm 23:6). Be assured that everything I have designed for you is good.

O LORD my God, you have performed many wonders for us. Your plans for us are too numerous to list. You have no equal. If I tried to recite all your wonderful deeds, I would never come to the end of them.

PSALM 40:5

— *September 14* —

LOOK UP

Love Jesus with your heart and head and hands! Focus your heart's affections on him as your greatest Treasure. Focus your head's thoughts on the kingdom he will bring and the reason he is waiting. . . . [W]hen you love Jesus with your heart, head and hands, your life will become much simpler and fuller—and your desire for his return will grow.

John Piper

When you get up in the morning, anticipate the coming of the Son of Man. When the security you once enjoyed is crumbling, look up. When you wonder if you can bear the pain for one more hour, focus your thoughts on heaven. When you have lost your way, call out to Me for help. When you wonder why you have not yet been caught up to meet My Son in the air, be patient. The reasons for waiting are unclear to you now. Trust Me without knowing all the answers.

Concentrate on loving Me and loving the people around you. Simplify your day's activities and ask, "If Jesus returns today, what do I want to be doing? Do I have unfinished business? Is there anyone else I should speak to about his or her eternal destiny? What are the things that matter in my day? What can I let go of? Am I ready to meet my Maker? What will I say when I see Him face-to-face?" When you anticipate the coming return of the King of kings and Lord of lords, your life will be happier and fuller.

Everyone will see the Son of Man coming on a cloud with power and great glory. So when all these things begin to happen, stand and look up, for your salvation is near!

LUKE 21:27-28

September 15

CLENCHED FISTS

We come into this world with our fingers curled and only slowly, by repeated practice, do we learn to open our hands. It takes a great deal of dying to get us ready to live.

Virginia Stem Owens

I know it's hard for you to let go and trust Me with the complicated circumstances of your life. People have betrayed you in the past, and you've grown accustomed to controlling the outcome of every scenario in order to avoid being hurt in the future. You are in a battle every day, and you have a choice to make. Do you want to be in charge of your life, or do you want Me to be in control of your life? You can continue to hold tightly to everything and everybody around you, or you can let go. "Let go of your concerns! Then you will know that I am God. I rule the nations. I rule the earth" (Psalm 46:10, GW).

To begin positive change, physically open your fists before Me and say, "God, I'm giving up my control, and I'm asking You to be in charge of the things in my life that are out of control." You're experiencing stress and anxiety because you keep trying to maintain total management of the people closest to you. Sometimes your behavior crosses over into manipulation, which makes you and others miserable. As you open your fists of control and let Me take you by the hand, I will teach you what to say and help you navigate unfamiliar terrain. Learn to walk in step with Me and allow our relationship to grow in maturity.

Those who trust in the LORD are as secure as Mount Zion; they will not be defeated but will endure forever.

PSALM 125:1

September 16

DESTINY

There is no greater discovery
than seeing God as the author of your destiny.

Ravi Zacharias

You are My masterpiece, and I created you anew in Christ Jesus so you can do the good things I planned for you long ago (Ephesians 2:10). Consider this: I saw you before you were born, and every day of your life was recorded in My book. In fact, every moment was laid out before you were a day old (Psalm 139:16). You belong to Me, and you have a destiny. No matter what your life's work is, your ultimate calling remains the same—to bring glory to My name and to tell others about Jesus.

I have designed you with specific passions, gifts, creativity, ambitions, and desires that are unique to you. There is no one else like you anywhere in the world. But here's the challenge: You can miss My destiny for your life if you're running after momentary pleasures, or if you choose not to walk through doors I open for you due to fear, feelings of inadequacy, or anger toward Me because your life has been hard. I won't make you choose to follow My will—that's up to you. But I guarantee that if you say yes to an unknown future at My side, you will never cease to be amazed at where My purpose for your life takes you.

If you remain completely silent at this time, relief and deliverance will arise for the Jews from another place, but you and your father's house will perish. Yet who knows whether you have come to the kingdom for such a time as this?

ESTHER 4:14, NKJV

September 17

OUTCOMES

God never takes away something from your life without replacing it with something better.

Billy Graham

Your home is in heaven. You're only traveling through this world. The key to thriving amid personal crises and unwanted pressures is to live every day in step with Me. Today I will be your Teacher, your Guide, your Companion, and your Friend. As we walk together through unexplored territory, you're tempted to turn toward alluring pathways that offer access to an easier, more predictable way of living. But I'm asking you to stay the course and continue to walk beside Me. The road will not always be comfortable, and at times it might feel risky. But remember who is right beside you—I'm not leaving!

Beware of looking too far ahead, because that gives the enemy an opportunity to fill your mind with fearful ideas about what might happen to you or your loved ones. Close your eyes, hold My hand, and trust Me to lead you on a purposeful and meaningful adventure. Enjoy My presence and begin to plumb the depths of My unfailing love. Continue in this pattern, and you'll find that together we can make it past every roadblock, every pothole, every reversal, and every challenge. And don't be surprised when you experience great joy on this journey. We'll be home soon.

With your unfailing love you lead the people you have redeemed.
In your might, you guide them to your sacred home.

EXODUS 15:13

September 18

CHOOSE JOY

Joy is the settled assurance that God is in control of all the details of my life, the quiet confidence that ultimately everything is going to be all right, and the determined choice to praise God in all things.

Kay Warren

When life falls apart, choose joy. When people are abrasive, choose joy. When the bottom drops out of your finances, choose joy. When you're exhausted and feel like giving up, choose joy. When your prayers aren't answered in the way you wanted, choose joy. When people you trusted betray you, choose joy. When your body hurts all over, choose joy. When you feel forgotten, choose joy. Joy is not a vague sense of happiness that encompasses you in an ethereal cloud—it's an attitude you purposefully decide to embrace many times a day.

In this world you will have trouble (John 16:33, NIV). Joy, for you, means choosing to be hopeful because I am still in control. As surely as you know your own name, know that in the end, I will make everything all right. I am still all-powerful. I am still everywhere-present. I am still all-knowing. Discover the truth about joy. In a fallen world, there is a thread of sorrow even in the middle of exhilarating happiness. Likewise, even in the throes of the deepest grief, there is the light of Christ. Find your real joy there—in the person of My Son—and then start praising Me. Very soon your spirits will be lifted, your pain will decrease, your hope will return, and your confidence will be in Me.

He will once again fill your mouth with laughter
and your lips with shouts of joy.

JOB 8:21

September 19

THE REARVIEW MIRROR

God reveals Himself in rearview mirrors. And I've an inkling that there are times when we need to drive a long, long distance, before we can look back and see God's back in the rearview mirror. Maybe sometimes about as far as heaven—that kind of distance.

Ann Voskamp

My precious child, your journey through suffering has been long. I hear your questions: "Why doesn't God come to my rescue? What good can come out of this impossible situation? Why do other people have easy lives, but my family is falling apart? How long do I have to wait for answers to my prayers? Does God really love me if He allows me to struggle in the midst of so much pain?"

Please know that I hear you. I see you. I am aware of your misery. In this world you may not fully understand why some people are rescued from adversity and others continue to struggle. But relying on Me in the midst of your difficulty will strengthen the foundation of your faith. It will reveal My faithfulness to your children and grandchildren. When you still experience My supernatural peace in the middle of your trials, it is a testimony to the world that your faith is based on a secure relationship with Me. Remember this. One day you will look back and understand My plan. Your trust will be rewarded.

And these men of faith, though they trusted God and won his approval, none of them received all that God had promised them; for God wanted them to wait and share the even better rewards that were prepared for us.

HEBREWS 11:39-40, TLB

September 20

THE RELAY

The Christian life isn't a one-person race. It's a relay. You are not alone; you're part of a team assembled by our unstoppable God to achieve his eternal purposes.

Christine Caine

I never intended for you to go through life alone. You've been trying hard to be independent and to run your Christian race on your own, but that's not what My plan is for your life. I designed you to be part of a group of believers who trust each other, work together, and spur each other on to excellence. When you have the same objective—wanting to glorify Me with your attitudes, your choices, your work, and your goals—remarkable things happen. There is no stopping a team of people who are focused on My eternal purposes.

Here is what the apostle Paul said to the Philippian believers: "Make me truly happy by agreeing wholeheartedly with each other, loving one another, and working together with one mind and purpose" (Philippians 2:2). When you move in the direction of My purpose for your life, I will provide encouragers, wisdom givers, truth speakers, and comforting companions who are also in the race of this life. As you keep running toward the finish line, be ready to pass on the baton of My faithfulness to the next generation.

He makes the whole body fit together perfectly. As each part does its own special work, it helps the other parts grow, so that the whole body is healthy and growing and full of love.

EPHESIANS 4:16

— September 21 —

AMBASSADOR

You have no idea how many people there are in the world whose day could be made and their life changed for the better if someone would just look them in the eye, smile, and say, "Hello."

Stormie Omartian

Your current limitations have made you think there isn't much you can do to benefit My Kingdom. Dear one, that thought is far from the truth. Because of your personal relationship with Me, you bring My presence into every space you occupy. It's the influence of My Holy Spirit dwelling within you that lets others experience Christ through you. As My ambassador, you influence people to consider the difference I can make in their lives—not through physical force or formal authority, but by your character and wisdom. When people see you living for Me in the face of trials, you are My messenger of hope. You point people to a different kind of joy—a joy that can exist, and even thrive, amid pain, struggle, and hardship. I have given you the joy of My presence (Psalm 21:6).

As My faithful representative, you exemplify another way of life—life in Christ. Look for people who need a smile, a word of encouragement, a simple act of kindness, or a comforting hug. Practice hospitality, courtesy, and graciousness as you advance My Kingdom. Through your testimony, some people will discover Christ for the first time and others will come back to Him.

We are Christ's ambassadors; God is making his appeal through us. We speak for Christ when we plead, "Come back to God!"

2 CORINTHIANS 5:20

September 22

PERSISTENT PRAYER

Prayer lays hold of God's plan and becomes the link between His will and its accomplishment on earth. Amazing things happen, and we are given the privilege of being the channels of the Holy Spirit's prayer.

Elisabeth Elliot

Make a habit of persistently praying at all times. That doesn't mean you have to be alone in a quiet room every minute of each day. It means following the apostle Paul's advice: "Rejoice always, pray continually, give thanks in all circumstances; for this is God's will for you in Christ Jesus" (1 Thessalonians 5:16-18, NIV). Get up each day and talk to Me about your joys—what good things are happening in your life? Throughout the day, keep speaking with Me, sometimes with words and at other times with thoughts, lifting your own concerns and talking to Me about the needs in your home, your community, and your world. Ask Me to intervene in the hard tasks and impossible situations you are facing.

Then move to thanksgiving. The most challenging part of prayer is to express your gratitude for the difficulties that I've allowed to enter your life. Thank Me for the lessons learned, for the closeness we've experienced as you struggle to find meaning in the chaos. Don't give up. You matter to Me, and your persistent prayers move Me to action.

Keep on asking, and you will receive what you ask for. Keep on seeking, and you will find. Keep on knocking, and the door will be opened to you.

MATTHEW 7:7

September 23

UNSHAKEN

Sometimes God chooses to demonstrate his power by supernaturally changing our circumstances. And sometimes he chooses to leave us in hard, difficult places, but gives us his sustaining power.

Crawford W. Loritts Jr.

Your life feels like it's in upheaval. When you listen to the news, you worry about what the world will be like for your children and grandchildren. The uncertainty about the future is overwhelming. There are natural disasters and personal earthquakes, and you're not sure about how to move forward. On some days you feel hopeful, but at other times you are upended due to anxiety and fear. You are tempted to live in a constant state of insecurity. When trials come, you struggle to reconcile what you know to be true about Me with the seemingly insurmountable challenges of life.

Sometimes I bring immediate deliverance from adversity, but not always. The apostle Peter understood how to live with an unshaken faith in an uncertain world—he focused on eternal glory. "Don't be surprised at the fiery trials you are going through, as if something strange were happening to you. Instead, be very glad—for these trials make you partners with Christ in his suffering, so that you will have the wonderful joy of seeing his glory when it is revealed to all the world" (1 Peter 4:12-13). An unshaken, peaceful heart will only come when you trust in My unfailing love for you.

"Though the mountains be shaken and the hills be removed, yet my unfailing love for you will not be shaken nor my covenant of peace be removed," says the LORD, who has compassion on you.

ISAIAH 54:10, NIV

September 24

IRRITATING PEOPLE

People who say that small things don't bother them have never slept in a room with a mosquito.

Dennis Rainey

When you come face-to-face with an annoying person, it's usually a small comment, action, look, or attitude of theirs that brings out the worst in you. Just having that person breathe next to you gets on your nerves. You're expecting her to realize the hurt you're experiencing or the pain you're in, but she only seems to care about herself, which compounds your frustration.

In these situations, pray first and beware of judging too quickly. Often, the aggravating person is in a difficult situation not visible to you, and she's masking her grief with obnoxious behavior. Look for wisdom in My Word. Ask Me for self-control and for the wisdom to speak encouraging, considerate words. Listen more than you talk, and look for ways you can reach out in love. You don't know the difficult person's whole story yet—and you may be the first one to make a heart connection with this person who wants to change but doesn't know where to begin. She may be reeling from the sting of injustice or the ache of loneliness. Ask Me how you can be My agent of healing—and expect results.

If you have any encouragement from being united with Christ, if any comfort from his love, if any common sharing in the Spirit, if any tenderness and compassion, then make my joy complete by being like-minded, having the same love, being one in spirit and of one mind.

PHILIPPIANS 2:1-2, NIV

— *September 25* —

JUST FOR YOU

Next time a sunrise steals your breath or a meadow of flowers leaves you speechless, remain that way. Say nothing and listen as heaven whispers, *"Do you like it? I did it just for you."*

Max Lucado

Every day holds great potential for discovering My work on your behalf! I want you to be encouraged. You've been learning to be alert to the beauty in My creation. Now begin looking for Me in other places and in everyday activities—in the warm greetings people give, in an answered prayer, in the giggles of a small child, in the "God bless you" salutation from the sales clerk, in the unexpected text message from a friend, and in the "aha" moment you found in My Word.

Your past habit has been to ask Me for My presence during your major conflicts, heartaches, and physical upheavals. That's okay, but I want you to start a new habit—looking for Me in every part of your day. Consider these words from Solomon: "The flowers are springing up, the season of singing birds has come, and the cooing of turtle-doves fills the air" (Song of Songs 2:12). Begin by listing your daily God-finds—those unexpected moments and interactions. They make you smile, don't they? Then close your eyes and hear Me say, "I did it just for you."

Great is his faithfulness; his mercies begin afresh each morning. . . . The LORD is good to those who depend on him, to those who search for him.

LAMENTATIONS 3:23, 25

— *September 26* —

BRAND NEW

The same Jesus Who turned water into wine can transform your home, your life, your family, and your future. He is still in the miracle-working business, and His business is the business of transformation.

Adrian Rogers

You are not your past. You do not have to live in bondage to every bad decision you ever made, or to any wrong action done to you. You are not the names you were called or the criticisms spoken against you. When you belong to Me, you are not the last one chosen for the sports team, the person no one wants to sit with, or the unappreciated family member. You are not chained to a bad reputation or locked up in a prison of rejection. You are not what you used to be—you are brand new!

The day you said yes to following My Son as your Lord and Savior, it wasn't only your *day* that took a good turn—it was the rest of your life, for all eternity. You have literally been remade, like a newborn baby with a clean slate and a whole future of possibilities for living a good, happy, and productive life. Only now, your life is even better than a brand-new baby's, because your sins have been forgiven and I will remember them no more! Dwell on these thoughts: *I am related to the King of kings and Lord of lords. My sins are buried in the deepest sea. My future is filled with hope. My old life is gone, and I am brand new!*

Anyone who belongs to Christ has become a new person. The old life is gone; a new life has begun!

2 CORINTHIANS 5:17

September 27

POWERFUL SEED

I think faith is the small mustard seed of opportunities every day. For example, am I going to love this person? Am I going to share my faith with this person? Am I going to pray that little prayer? It really is a daily thing where you seize those little mustard seed opportunities and then see what God does.

Mark Batterson

You keep looking for big miracles and gigantic breakthroughs, but I want you to grab hold of mustard-seed faith. As you go through your day, believe that I will guide you to surprising opportunities to exercise your faith. Look for openings to speak out loud about your relationship with Jesus, or to pray with someone who is hurting, or to respond kindly to the person who is the most critical of you.

Your doubts about Me are the trigger points for your faith failures. They make you question My ability to work in your life and in the lives of those you love. Unbelief is a barrier between your prayer requests and your longed-for results. Mountain-moving faith doesn't develop overnight, but as you pray and find Me faithful—every time—you'll soon discover nothing is impossible for Me. Surround yourself with people of great faith, and you'll discover they've learned that when their faith is stretched by a delayed answer to prayer, I always have a reason.

"You don't have enough faith," Jesus told them. "I tell you the truth, if you had faith even as small as a mustard seed, you could say to this mountain, 'Move from here to there,' and it would move. Nothing would be impossible."

MATTHEW 17:20

— September 28 —

JUST ASK

Simply put, God favors those who ask. He holds back nothing from those who want and earnestly long for what He wants.

Bruce Wilkinson

One person who dared to call upon Me boldly, asking for My blessing and favor, was a man named Jabez. I saw his faithfulness and humility, and I granted his request. I want you to follow his example, praying with authority and confidence, believing that I will answer. Jabez recognized the importance of prayer, and he implored Me out loud, *"Oh, that you would bless me and enlarge my territory!"* As you pray in this way, I will expand your influence on the people around you. Whenever you encounter an open door for conversation about what I have done in your life, seize the opportunity as My blessing.

I also desire that you pray, *"Let your hand be with me."* When I take you by the hand or lead you in a certain direction, be sure you are remaining in My will for your life. Then pray, *"Keep me from harm so that I will be free from pain."* Never forget that I am your Shield and your Refuge. I want for you to be free from the things that have caused you pain. I take delight in granting your requests within My will and in My perfect timing. Just ask!

Jabez cried out to the God of Israel, "Oh, that you would bless me and enlarge my territory! Let your hand be with me, and keep me from harm so that I will be free from pain." And God granted his request.

1 CHRONICLES 4:10, NIV

— *September 29* —

ROOTS

A tree is nothing without its foundation; it has no nourishment and no anchor. Life may be wreaking havoc above the surface, as it often does, but our roots remain fed and secure in God's love.

Sandy Hamstra

I long for you to be deeply rooted in My Son, Jesus, and to know Him intimately. Only then will you bear spiritual fruit. Follow the instructions of the apostle Paul: "Let your roots grow down into him and draw up nourishment from him. See that you go on growing in the Lord, and become strong and vigorous in the truth you were taught. Let your lives overflow with joy and thanksgiving for all he has done" (Colossians 2:7, TLB). Your roots get deeply established in Christ when you stay in My Word, talk to Me through prayer, listen for My instructions, worship Me, and give thanks in all things.

When your roots grow deep, *[I] will empower you with inner strength through [My] Spirit.* Be grounded in love for Me and for others. Growth doesn't happen in one day—it happens over time, by My grace, as you become strong in your faith. I'm inviting you to an ever-deepening relationship with Me. Grow tall and robust as your roots continue to be fed with living water and the nutrients in My Word.

I pray that from his glorious, unlimited resources he will empower you with inner strength through his Spirit. Then Christ will make his home in your hearts as you trust in him. Your roots will grow down into God's love and keep you strong.

EPHESIANS 3:16-17

— *September 30* —

IDOLS

Idols aren't stone statues. They are thoughts, desires, and longings that we worship in the place of the true God.

Elyse Fitzpatrick

Watch out for little idols that consume your energy and time. An idol can be a person, an object, or an activity that has a higher priority in your life than your relationship with Me. Even suffering can become an idol when it defines the way you live and controls your attitude—toward Me and others.

Small distractions don't start as idols, but as they lure you away from reading Scripture and lessen our quality time together, they slowly begin to control the way you use the hours in your day. You don't think of your attention to these desires and longings as a problem, but you are gradually beginning to worship these things instead of holding Me in the highest place of honor. Ask yourself if there is an idol holding you back from loving, trusting, and serving Me with your whole heart. I am jealous of your affection. I long to hear you say, "There is nothing I desire more than You."

You must not have any other god but me.

EXODUS 20:3

— October 1 —

RELIANT TRUST

It's one thing to believe God can do something. It's quite another to put yourself in a position of reliant trust. This is the distinction between intellectual belief and wholehearted faith.

Linda Dillow

Develop the habit of trusting Me with your whole heart. You say you trust Me, but when you're faced with difficulties and stress-producing situations, you tend to rely on yourself first. You've become fatigued and discouraged with trying to manage the people and problems that surround you. Intellectually, you believe I'm trustworthy, but you still live as if everything depended upon you. You are wearing yourself out—mentally, physically, emotionally, and spiritually.

Begin a new way of living. Verbalize your trust in Me to handle the challenges you face. Say "Lord, You are my Strength and my Shield. You see how weary I am. I want You to help me with the details of everything I've been handling on my own. I am choosing to loosen my grip on them. Help me, Lord, because it's easy for me to slip back into old patterns. As I choose to trust You, fill my heart with joy. The thought of relinquishing my control and trusting You brings such peace that I want to burst out in a song of thanks." My precious one, keep practicing wholehearted faith, and leave the results to Me.

The LORD is my strength and shield. I trust him with all my heart. He helps me, and my heart is filled with joy. I burst out in songs of thanksgiving.

PSALM 28:7

October 2

PASSING THROUGH

If I find in myself desires which nothing in this world can satisfy, the only logical explanation is that I was made for another world.

C. S. Lewis

You've been longing for a more peaceful life, more ideal circumstances, and more comfortable living conditions. But in your pursuit of satisfaction, you've been disappointed. Nothing in the world offers what your heart desires. You've talked to Me about some of these wants. Your body hurts, and you've asked for a pain-free life. Your loved ones have run away from biblical teaching, and you've begged Me to bring them back into a relationship with Me. You have yearned for spiritual direction, but a pastor has made ungodly choices, tempting you to quit looking to church leaders for help. There's an ongoing restlessness within you, and you don't know how to handle it.

Here's the bottom line—you were never meant to be a permanent resident of earth. Because you know Me, you are already a citizen of heaven. As you eagerly await the return of the Savior, life will not be perfect. You will not be totally free of physical or emotional pain. You will experience disappointments, and people will continue to let you down. But the good news is this—this world is not your home. You are only passing through, on your way to your eternal home with Me. Don't expect perfection here—but keep a forward focus on the place of your eternal residency. You were made for another world!

We are citizens of heaven, where the Lord Jesus Christ lives. And we are eagerly waiting for him to return as our Savior.

PHILIPPIANS 3:20

October 3

HUNGRY

Hunger for God compels us to seek the Lord. At times our desire for God overcomes our physical desires, and the ache for God is palpable. . . . When we seek God with our whole hearts and souls, he promises to reveal himself to us.

Margaret Feinberg

I am drawn to you when you hunger for Me with your whole heart. I look down from heaven on the entire human race and look for people who are seeking Me (Psalm 53:2). There are times when you look for Me out of desperation and other times when you need guidance for living. I'm always available to you, and I love being your Helper during everyday activities. But when you come to Me out of hunger for My presence, I sense your desire to be close to Me. I feel the ache in your soul for the intimacy that brings deep connection, loving oneness, and abiding trust.

David captured similar thoughts in a psalm written to Me: "I thirst for you, my whole being longs for you" (Psalm 63:1, NIV). When you desire Me in that way, I love satisfying your deep spiritual hunger and thirst. The world offers substitutes for Me that look attractive, but they only bring passing enjoyment. Invite Me to be the Strength of your heart and your Portion forever (Psalm 73:26, NIV). Taste and see that I am good (Psalm 34:8). Passionately embrace the sweetness of our relationship as I fill you with contentment, security, love, and peace.

Blessed are those who hunger and thirst for righteousness, for they will be filled.

MATTHEW 5:6, NIV

— *October 4* —

REFUGE

Where does your security lie? Is God your refuge, your hiding place, your stronghold, your shepherd, your counselor, your friend, your redeemer, your saviour, your guide? If He is, you don't need to search any further for security.

Elisabeth Elliot

What do you face today? There may be obstacles, pressures, obligations, and hard decisions ahead of you. It's tempting to choose fear instead of faith. Invite Me to provide a haven for you. I will be your hiding place, and there you will find shelter from the chaos that surrounds you. Call out My name and take comfort in these words: "The name of the LORD is a strong fortress; the godly run to him and are safe" (Proverbs 18:10).

When you turn to Me for help and protection, you'll begin to know Me as your refuge. Don't be afraid of people or situations that threaten your physical or emotional well-being. Nothing you will ever face is out of My control. Stay close to Me, and you will always be safe. Remain in the center of My will, and you will have no cause for fear. When difficulties come, boldly say, "My victory and honor come from God alone. He is my refuge, a rock where no enemy can reach me" (Psalm 62:7). I am your *ever-present help* whenever you are dealing with stressful situations.

God is our refuge and strength, an ever-present help in trouble.

PSALM 46:1, NIV

October 5

ENDURANCE

Endurance is not just the ability to bear a hard thing,
but to turn it into glory.

William Barclay

Your life isn't a sprint—it's a marathon. Learn how to get your sustenance from Me when you're confronted with tiring tasks or unexpected hardship. As you cling to My promises, I will provide the stamina and resources needed to tolerate discomfort and keep moving forward. There will be temptations along the way that could slow you down or lead you down an appealing path. Don't give in, and and don't get sidetracked. Pay close attention to the map I've laid out for you in My Word.

Take care of yourself physically by eating healthy food and by pacing yourself. Never try to do more than one day requires. That, too, can trip you up and will eventually cause discouragement. Keep your eyes on My Son, Jesus, and remember how He endured suffering but stayed focused on the glory set before Him. You can make it! I'm right beside you—cheering you on and guiding you to the finish line.

Therefore, since we are surrounded by such a huge crowd of witnesses to the life of faith, let us strip off every weight that slows us down, especially the sin that so easily trips us up. And let us run with endurance the race God has set before us.

HEBREWS 12:1

October 6

A TRUE DISCIPLE

The relationship between the disciple and his teacher is not merely that of a student listening to a lecturer, or a passively interested listener. A disciple listens with attention and intention. He drinks in every word of his teacher, marking every inflection of voice with an intense desire to apply what has been learned.

Greg Laurie

You've been a follower of Mine for a while, but I want you to consider a deeper commitment as a disciple of My Son, Jesus. In My Word, He explained what this means: "You are truly my disciples if you remain faithful to my teachings" (John 8:31). Through a lifestyle of faith and obedience, you become more and more like Christ. It wasn't an easy path for the disciples of Jesus. They left their homes, gave up their security, took up their crosses, and followed Him.

Living as a disciple may look different for you than it did for Jesus' first followers—but it is still demanding and it still requires sacrifice. It means feeding the poor, caring for the weak, and knowing My Word and sharing it with others. It requires a life of prayer, and it includes walking in the fullness and power of My Holy Spirit and showing love to your enemies. If you agree to be a true disciple, you'll tell others about the transformation My Son has brought to your life and how He sustains you in the midst of pain and suffering. It's the costliest and most fulfilling choice you can make at this point in your journey. It's worth every ounce of sacrifice. You won't regret saying yes.

Calling the crowd to join his disciples, he said, "If any of you wants to be my follower, you must give up your own way, take up your cross, and follow me."

MARK 8:34

— October 7 —

BREVITY OF LIFE

"What is the greatest surprise you have found about life?" a university student asked me several years ago. "Its brevity," I replied. . . . Time moves so quickly, and no matter who we are or what we have done, the time will come when our lives will be over.

Billy Graham

When life is hard, time seems to move slowly, but in reality life is only a vapor. You see the mist of a fog for a short time, and then it's gone. Moses lamented the shortness of life when he wrote, "Seventy years are given to us! Some even live to eighty. But even the best years are filled with pain and trouble; soon they disappear, and we fly away" (Psalm 90:10). At any age, you don't know what will happen tomorrow. Pray like Moses prayed: "Teach us to realize the brevity of life, so that we may grow in wisdom" (Psalm 90:12).

Look at each day as a gift from Me. Seek My guidance about how to use your time. Follow My Son's instruction, "We must quickly carry out the tasks assigned us by the one who sent us. The night is coming, and then no one can work" (John 9:4). When personal challenges tempt you to get off course, remember that each day moves you closer to being with Me for eternity. For now, be strong and continue on the path I've charted for you. Live each day as it comes—redeeming the time!

Satisfy us each morning with your unfailing love,
so we may sing for joy to the end of our lives.

PSALM 90:14

— *October 8* —

COMPLAINING

What the Lord wants is that you shall go about the business to which He sets you, not asking for an easy post, nor grumbling at a hard one.

Catherine Booth

Examine your heart and consider your verbal responses to the challenges you face. When you feel overwhelmed with your problems, you are tempted to complain—to others, to yourself, and to Me. There is a righteous way and a faithless way to complain . My Word talks about both responses. Faithless complaining is grumbling, which drags you down, along with others. When you grumble your complaints, you're directly or indirectly suggesting that I'm not good, wise, loving, or competent. If it's easy for you to fall into this habit, apply the apostle Paul's advice to the believers in Philippi: "Do everything without grumbling or arguing" (Philippians 2:14, NIV).

The right kind of complaining is the honest expression of the groaning of your heart. That's when you come to Me in humility and pour out your pain, anguish, grief, and trouble. It's understanding that you live in a broken world. You're echoing the truth of Paul's words in Romans 8:23: "We believers also groan, even though we have the Holy Spirit within us as a foretaste of future glory, for we long for our bodies to be released from sin and suffering." I encourage this kind of complaining, and I understand your longing for the day when you will have your full rights as My adopted child, along with a new body. I hear your appeals for help.

I cry out to the LORD; I plead for the LORD's mercy. I pour out my complaints before him and tell him all my troubles.

PSALM 142:1-2

— October 9 —

THE DWELLING PLACE

A Christian is a tabernacle of the living God. He created me, he chose me, he came to dwell in me, because he wanted me. Now that you have known how much God is in love with you, it is but natural that you spend the rest of your life radiating that love.

Mother Teresa

Your life is full of uncertainty, and that gives your imagination room for speculation. You question—what if *this* happens, or what if *that* happens? At times you go through an entire day anxious and stressed, worrying about things that haven't taken place and may never happen. Change your thought process by fully embracing the fact that you are My dwelling place. My Holy Spirit lives within you.

The day you became a follower of Christ, you became the residence of the Most High God. When My Spirit dwells within you, no evil can penetrate you. Rest and be at peace knowing that you are safe in My arms. Experience the benefits of this close relationship. Strength and joy are in My dwelling place (1 Chronicles 16:27). Bask in the protection I offer. Feel My love pouring over you. Then confidently demonstrate My love to others, knowing the Source of that love will never leave you. You are My dwelling place, and I am your Dwelling Place. Abide in Me, and I will abide in you (John 15:4).

In him you too are being built together to become a dwelling in which God lives by his Spirit.

EPHESIANS 2:22, NIV

October 10

A REFLECTION

You were made to reflect God's glory.

Tony Evans

What do you see when you look at yourself in a mirror? I want you to look more and more like Me. Absorb My principles and meditate on My promises, then speak aloud about them to others. The most powerful way you can glorify Me is to show the radiance of My Son, Jesus Christ. When you reflect His light, you are bringing Me joy. The wonderful brightness of His presence is in the sparkle of your eyes, the curve of your smile, and your openhanded generosity to the people you meet.

When your head touches the pillow in the evening, do what the psalmist did: "I reflect at night on who you are, O LORD; therefore, I obey your instructions" (Psalm 119:55). Ask Me to so fill you with My love, compassion, comfort, and peace that when you awaken and face your day, everyone you encounter will see My glory reflected in your speech, your behavior, your choices, and your attitude. You are My image bearer, and I am celebrated when you identify with Me. Like a proud parent, I want to shout, "That's My kid—a spitting image of Me!" You are living out your purpose when you display My glory.

All of us who have had that veil removed can see and reflect the glory of the Lord. And the Lord—who is the Spirit—makes us more and more like him as we are changed into his glorious image.

2 CORINTHIANS 3:18

October 11

DIFFICULT DAYS

Snuggle in God's arms. When you are hurting, when you feel lonely, left out. Let Him cradle you, comfort you, reassure you of His all-sufficient power and love.

Kay Arthur

Learn to appreciate the tough days. When you and I face obstacles together, you can trust Me to give you guidance and wisdom for every decision. The more you worship Me as we walk hand in hand on the rocky terrain of life, the more you find unexpected joy, stronger faith, and growing confidence. You will discover that we can face anything together. The U-turns and detours help you learn the rhythm of facing difficult days with Me at your side.

When your problems seem insurmountable, take a break and rest without guilt. Everything doesn't need to be done today. It will wait for tomorrow. Curl up in My embrace and let Me comfort you. Let go of your "I can do it myself" attitude and hear Me whisper, "I love you and I am here for you. I'm all-powerful, and I see your hurting heart and your physical pain." Just as a parent comforts a child who is facing a hard day, I want to be your Comforter today. My everlasting arms are holding you.

The eternal God is your refuge, and his everlasting arms are under you.

DEUTERONOMY 33:27

— October 12 —

THE MAIN POINT

The point of your life is to point to Him. Whatever you are doing, God wants to be glorified, because this whole thing is His.

Francis Chan

You are always more content when you focus on the purpose of your life. You were created to glorify Me and to enjoy Me. Worship comes from your heart and overflows in praise. As you find delight in Me and verbalize your genuine joy through songs of praise and expressions of love, everything about your day improves. You concentrate on Me and not on your problems. Your focus is on what you can do for others instead of what they can do for you. Your disappointments turn into longings for a deeper relationship with Me, and your delight in My presence is evident to everyone who spends time with you.

When you understand the main point of your life, you are more settled and secure in your daily routine. Even ordinary activities take on eternal meaning because everything you do—small and large—has spiritual significance. As you acknowledge Me in the mundane activities of life, the works of your hands become an offering to Me and I am glorified by your humility and service. Your life exhibits an understanding of My precepts. The more you know Me and love Me, the more your heart change becomes a testimony that points people to Me.

Lord, we show our trust in you by obeying your laws;
our heart's desire is to glorify your name.

ISAIAH 26:8

— October 13 —

ENOUGH ALREADY

When the Lord makes it clear you're to follow Him in this new direction, focus fully on Him and refuse to be distracted.

Charles Swindoll

My child, I've been watching you walk around in circles. You feel stuck in a rut, and you're not sure how to move forward. Beware of holding too tightly to old habits and patterns from the past. I am doing a new thing in your life. It's time for you to admit that your repeated behaviors are holding you back from a much better future.

Begin by praying, "Lord, help me to recognize what isn't working in my life and to be willing to leave the comfort of predictable patterns that have gotten me nowhere. Give me eyes to see the new direction You have for me. I give my fears to You because change is hard. I give my pain to You because it keeps me from focusing on a better way to live. I give my will to You because I'm stubborn and opinionated, and I often think I know the best plan for my life. I give my fatigue to You because walking in circles has been exhausting." I am not asking you to walk this new path alone. I'll be with you the whole way—bringing companionship, comfort, and joy. It's time to move forward.

You have circled this mountain long enough. Now turn north.

DEUTERONOMY 2:3, NASB

October 14

INFINITE RESOURCES

Perhaps God brings us to the end of our resources so we can discover the vastness of His.

Neil T. Anderson

My child, you have looked at your emotional, physical, mental, and spiritual stamina, and it isn't enough. When you evaluate your own assets, there is no way the math works out for you to have anything extra to share with others. I want you to start looking at your available resources differently. Ask Me to show you the abundance that is yours.

Remember the story of My Son feeding five thousand people with five loaves and two fish? He bypassed human effort and did the impossible. He miraculously multiplied the loaves and fish, and after all the people were fed, there were twelve baskets of leftovers—it was more than enough! I want to do the same for you—only I'm not talking about preparing your dinner. Give Me what you have right now, even if it seems like a small offering. Give Me your worn-out body, your dashed hopes, and your broken dreams. Then let Me have your time, your health, your family, your money, and your potential. In My hands, all that you offer will be all that's needed to give you more than enough. Tap into My limitless resources and know that you will have a never-ending source of strength and provision.

Jesus took the five loaves and two fish, looked up toward heaven, and blessed them. Then, breaking the loaves into pieces, he kept giving the bread and fish to the disciples so they could distribute it to the people. They all ate as much as they wanted, and afterward, the disciples picked up twelve baskets of leftovers!

LUKE 9:16-17

October 15

HIGH STAKES

Seasons will come when He requires so much from you that you feel like you can't bear it. You do have a choice. You don't have to do it His way. . . . Or you can go for it. . . . You can experience the unmatched exhilaration of partnering in divine triumph. The stakes are high. The cost is steep. But I'll promise you this: there is no high like the Most High.

Beth Moore

There is a cadence to life. Some of your years have been easier and more encouraging than this one. You look back and remember good health, supportive friends, and peaceful family relationships. But things have changed. You've experienced unwanted interruptions, irritating people, and unexpected crises. You thought your personal relationship with Me would keep you from facing the harsh seasons of life, and you're disappointed. Your once rock-solid faith feels tenuous.

I am offering you a choice. You can pull away from Me, or you can step into this period of your life with a gusto that says, "Lord, I trust You to walk with me through the deepest valley. I'm clinging to You because You'll never let go of me. I want my faith to grow higher, deeper, and wider. I'm learning that You give me precious treasures in the midst of adversity. You lead me to still waters and prepare me for coming storms. You've made my once routine life a faith-journey that makes me stronger. I relish the opportunity to partner with You in unmatched adventures. Oh, Lord, I would never go back to an easier life."

I have set the LORD always before me; because He is at my right hand I shall not be moved.

PSALM 16:8, NKJV

— October 16 —

UNFAILING LOVE

The unfailing love that we desire comes from Him. His love runs toward me, even when I am unlovely. His love comes to find me when I am hiding. His love will not let me go. His love never ends. His love never fails.

Angela Thomas

I will pursue you even if you turn away from Me. You hide your face from Me when you know I'm not pleased with your mind-set or your behavior. Instinctively, you try to make yourself too small for Me to see, but you will never be invisible to Me. As you get to know My character, you'll understand that there is nothing you could ever do that would make Me love you less. There is no choice you could ever make that would banish you from My presence. There is no heart-rebellion that would make Me turn My back on you.

Plain and simple—I love you! I know your hiding places, and I will find you. Even when you try to run away, I will follow you. I will pull you close to Me, cup your face in My hands, look into your eyes, and tell you that My love for you is relentless. You are the one My heart desires. You are the one I long to hold. You are the one who makes My heart sing. When you make wrong choices, I will forgive you. When you get sidetracked, I'll help you get back on My path. When you feel unworthy of My love, look at Me and lean into My embrace. I am here for you. Stop resisting the best thing that ever happened to you—a personal relationship with Me. Say it out loud: "I am loved!"

Surely your goodness and unfailing love will pursue me all the days of my life, and I will live in the house of the LORD forever.

PSALM 23:6

October 17

SHAKY TIMES

The presence of fear does not mean you have no faith. Fear visits everyone. But make your fear a visitor and not a resident.

Max Lucado

Current news brings too much anxiety. You read of wars, rumors of wars, hurricanes, tsunamis, earthquakes, viruses, antibiotic-resistant bacteria, fluctuating financial markets, political turmoil, racial unrest and demonstrations. Humanly speaking, you have much to fear. But when you read My Word, you'll discover that the world has been on the brink of disaster on numerous occasions. Don't worry or lose hope because nothing can thwart My purposes.

When fear begins to make you uneasy, turn your worries into prayers. Speak to Me often about what's going on in your personal life and in the world. Review the words of the psalmist: "The angel of the LORD is a guard; he surrounds and defends all who fear him" (Psalm 34:7). "We will not fear when earthquakes come and the mountains crumble into the sea" (Psalm 46:2). "When I am afraid, I will put my trust in you" (Psalm 56:3). As My Son's return to earth draws near, there will be turmoil in the world. You can choose fear or faith. If you choose faith, you will remind everyone around you that all these signs point to Christ's coming. Let that news make you excited. It won't be long.

People will be terrified at what they see coming upon the earth. . . . Then everyone will see the Son of Man coming on a cloud with power and great glory. So when all these things begin to happen, stand and look up, for your salvation is near!

LUKE 21:26-28

— October 18 —

NO UNFINISHED BUSINESS

I want to live in such a way that, if it is only twenty-nine more days or twenty-nine more weeks, or if it is twenty-nine more years or more, I want to be faithful with each one of those—that I could go and meet the Lord without regrets, without unfinished business.

Nancy DeMoss Wolgemuth

Beloved, as each new day dawns, I have a purpose and a plan for you. Instead of looking at the past, regretfully pointing out everything you did wrong, look at today with all of its opportunities and promises. If you ask for guidance, *I will teach you wisdom's ways and lead you in straight paths*. As you live and move within My will, you'll discover a fulfillment that brings spontaneous joy and renewed hope to your own heart. When you see someone in need, ask yourself, How can I represent Jesus to this person? What are the resources I have that can help this individual? How can I be a vehicle of encouragement and healing in this situation?

When you stay close to Me, My Holy Spirit will give you creative ideas to keep doing My will. You'll have fresh energy, and you'll begin looking for the next opportunity I have for you. As you keep developing the mind of Christ, ask Me to open doors in front of you. *You won't be held back*. As you run in the direction of My leading, *you won't stumble*. If you live each day with this frame of mind, your life's work will be filled with meaning and at the end of your journey you'll hear Me say, "Well done, my good and faithful servant" (Matthew 25:21).

I will teach you wisdom's ways and lead you in straight paths. When you walk, you won't be held back; when you run, you won't stumble.

PROVERBS 4:11-12

— *October 19* —

HIS SMILE

The Bible says, *"Noah was a pleasure to the Lord."* God said, "This guy brings me pleasure. He makes me smile. I will start over with his family." . . . God smiles when we love him supremely.

Rick Warren

I created you with the ability to smile. Your smile can brighten a day, give hope to a stranger, and change the mood in a room from despair to hope. It can also bring joy to Me. You may wonder what it takes to make *Me* smile. The psalmist wrote, "Smile on me, your servant; teach me the right way to live" (Psalm 119:135, MSG). You bring a smile to Me when you live a blameless life, when you think and act in such a way that no one can justifiably point a finger at you.

Review the life of Noah. He brought pleasure to Me as he lived a life of obedience. "Noah did everything exactly as God had commanded him" (Genesis 6:22). Like Noah, when you trust Me completely even when you don't understand why I've asked you to do something, you bring Me joy. I'm not asking you to build a big boat, but I *am* asking you to believe that I know what is best for you. When you know what I want you to do but choose not to do it right away, your delayed obedience is actually disobedience. But when you choose to follow My instructions—even without knowing why I'm asking you to do something—you are living in the smile of My approval.

May the LORD bless you and protect you. May the LORD smile on you and be gracious to you. May the LORD show you his favor and give you his peace.

NUMBERS 6:24-26

October 20

HARVEST

God has willed that his miraculous work of harvesting be preceded by prayer. He loves to bless the world. But even more, he loves to bless the world in answer to prayer.

John Piper

Jesus often looked out at the crowds and had compassion on them. They appeared confused and helpless. I know you often feel the same way, not understanding which way to turn or what to do next. You will learn the secret of climbing out of despair and into a place of hope if you follow this practice: Look around and find someone who is struggling more than you are. He or she might be dealing with a spiritual issue, a physical need, or a mental challenge. Ask Me what you can do for that person. Check your existing resources and then do something to help.

Continue to pray about your role in sowing seeds of hope into that person. Does she need to hear the gospel message? Does he need to be reminded that I love him and care about meeting his needs? Does she need someone to listen to her story? Does he need a hot meal or clothing? As you continue to sow healing and hope into other people's lives, look for the harvest. It may not come immediately, but it *will* come. And as you pray that I send more workers to meet the needs of the people you see, don't be surprised when I ask *you* to be My representative! Keep sowing good seed and then rejoice in the harvest that will follow.

He said to his disciples, "The harvest is great, but the workers are few. So pray to the Lord who is in charge of the harvest; ask him to send more workers into his fields."

MATTHEW 9:37-38

— October 21 —

SUFFERING

We can do one of two things with suffering: we can absorb it and let it change us, or we can let it crush us. Suffering will change you, or it will crush you.

Jennie Allen

Suffering is a battleground for your soul. The book of Job is a reminder that when My people are hard pressed, they make a choice. Some curse Me, while others praise Me in the middle of their suffering. Job's wife wanted him to curse Me and die, but Job responded, " 'Should we accept only good things from the hand of God and never anything bad?' So in all this, Job said nothing wrong" (Job 2:9-10). When you're suffering, you face difficult questions: "Why would a good God allow this horrible thing to happen? If God loves me, why wouldn't He come and rescue me out of my pain?"

Your suffering can come in many ways—mentally, physically, emotionally, or spiritually. It throbs. It captures your thoughts. It wears you down and attacks your faith. When suffering comes, remember that you were never meant to bear the pain alone. "Share each other's burdens, and in this way obey the law of Christ" (Galatians 6:2). If you turn to Me, I will comfort you in all of your troubles so that you can comfort others. As your friends go through troubled times, you will be able to give them the same comfort I gave you (2 Corinthians 1:4). Allow suffering to change you for the better.

We are hard pressed on every side, but not crushed;
perplexed, but not in despair; persecuted,
but not abandoned; struck down, but not destroyed.

2 CORINTHIANS 4:8-9, NIV

— October 22 —

EVER-PRESENT GOD

The most holy and necessary practice in our spiritual life is the presence of God. That means finding constant pleasure in His divine company, speaking humbly and lovingly with Him in all seasons, at every moment, without limiting the conversation in any way.

Brother Lawrence

I am here, always available to you, listening to your voice and desiring your company. You will become more and more aware of My presence by talking to Me often. Ask for My advice throughout the day. Let My presence infuse every moment—your rising in the morning, your activities during the day, and when you lay your head on your pillow at night. When you need wise counsel, I am here. When you are lonely, I am close to you. When you are afraid, I am protecting you. There is never a time when I am away from you.

There are times when you become so engaged in the temporary trials of life that you no longer feel My presence and you question where I am. Consider Jacob, the man who ran away from his angry brother, Esau. He slept on a stone pillow in a desolate land, and he had a dream. In his dream he saw a ladder that went from earth to heaven, and angels were going up and down the steps. Jacob suddenly awakened, aware that there was so much more going on in the invisible world than he realized. At that point Jacob knew that even when I seem the most absent, I am indeed ever-present.

Jacob awoke from his sleep and said, "Surely the LORD is in this place, and I wasn't even aware of it!"

GENESIS 28:16

— October 23 —

CHILDLIKE FAITH

Childlike faith is for ordinary people. People like you and me who know our flaws only too well. Are you willing to be ordinary for God? Are you willing to admit your flaws and shortcomings and assume that God can do the extraordinary things through you?

Michael Yaconelli

Come to Me like a child. Tell Me what you are genuinely thinking, without stopping to make sure that what comes out of your mouth is "fixed up" and "grown up." Talk to Me honestly and without reservation. Children know that prayers are important, and they're eager to voice their concerns and requests. They don't worry about fancy speech and appropriate decorum. They don't like to wait for responses, and they are not embarrassed by tears.

Make a run for Me and let Me swoop you up in My arms. Let Me hear you laugh out loud. Let Me see you jump up and down. Let Me see the look in your eyes as you ask Me for God-sized miracles and fully believe that I will supply everything you're asking for. Childlike faith is for desperate people who are sick and tired of being pretentious know-it-alls. It's for someone like you who is coming to Me with giant needs, like a child to a father, asking for help or wanting to spend time together. I simply can't resist you. Come!

Jesus said, "Let the children come to me. Don't stop them! For the Kingdom of Heaven belongs to those who are like these children."

MATTHEW 19:14

October 24

RADICAL OBEDIENCE

Obedience becomes radical when we say, "Yes, God, whatever You want," and mean it. We release our grip on all that we love and offer it back to Him, who loves us more. And it is into these upturned hands that God will pour out His blessings—His abundant, unexpected, radical blessings.

Lysa TerKeurst

I want you to experience the joy and blessing of partnering with Me in all your decisions and actions. Sometimes you waver, spending too much time wondering what to say yes to and what to say no to. Begin by asking Me to make your thoughts holy. Holy thinking focuses on what is pure, good, godly, and righteous. Then ask Me for wisdom and discernment as you embark on everyday activities. Expect that some of the nudges you receive from My Spirit will seem unusual and way out of your comfort zone.

When you begin a life of radical obedience, I may ask you to give up something precious to you. I may ask you to sacrifice financial comfort. I might even ask you to take strangers into your home or to visit a prisoner or to adopt a child from a foreign country. I might ask you to endure suffering without complaining because I have a purpose in your pain that you will one day understand. Never forget—radical obedience brings radical blessing!

So you must live as God's obedient children. Don't slip back into your old ways of living to satisfy your own desires. You didn't know any better then. But now you must be holy in everything you do, just as God who chose you is holy.

1 PETER 1:14-15

October 25

THE SWEETEST LESSON

Spread out your petition before God, and then say, "Thy will, not mine, be done." The sweetest lesson I have learned in God's school is to let the Lord choose for me.

D. L. Moody

As you and I walk hand in hand, your trust in Me increases. You know I want what is best for you, reflecting the goodness of My heart. I know the way I designed you and long for you to fulfill My purpose in your day-to-day living. You've encountered obstacles in your path that seem unnecessary, and you have begged Me to remove these cumbersome, time-consuming interruptions.

I want you to pray in a different way—the way My Son taught His disciples to pray: *Your will be done*. When you pray this way, you are beginning to understand My power over every aspect of your daily life. You're acknowledging that I know the end from the beginning and that you trust Me with the outcome of your situation. You're aligning your will with Mine, and you understand that even in your most difficult trials, I will work things out for your good. Praying "Your will be done" will free you from having to figure out and fix everything yourself. You are learning the sweetest lesson—that you will not be spared from all sorrow in this world, but that you can have peace in My presence, knowing I manage all the details of your life.

May your Kingdom come soon.
May your will be done on earth, as it is in heaven.

MATTHEW 6:10

— *October 26* —

JEWELS

We can't shine on the outside unless God's power is at work on the inside. No matter how much work we put into the outside, it will be worthless unless we are plugged into the true power source.

Priscilla Shirer

The day you put your faith in Me, I wrote your name in the Book of Life. Remember that you belong to Me. "'They shall be Mine,' says the LORD of hosts, 'on the day that I make them My jewels'" (Malachi 3:17, NKJV). I see your exceptional hidden characteristics and all the potential I've placed within you. You've been buffeted during times of suffering, but I am shaping and polishing you into a gem of magnificent quality. When you are in My hands, even in the midst of adversity, you shine like a precious jewel.

The refining process is just that—a *process*—and it doesn't happen overnight. It's the daily routine of allowing Me to transform you by renewing your mind as you dwell in My presence. Jewels are precious things, costly treasures. As you and I spend more and more time together, I'm watching you start to sparkle, like a star in the sky (Philippians 2:15, NIV). I've noticed your humble submission to My will for your life, even though your journey has not been easy. Jewels like you are scarce, and as a proud Father, I can't help but brag on you. "The LORD will hold you in his hand for all to see—a splendid crown in the hand of God" (Isaiah 62:3).

On that day the LORD their God will rescue his people, just as a shepherd rescues his sheep. They will sparkle in his land like jewels in a crown.

ZECHARIAH 9:16

October 27

HIS NAME

A tower that's stronger than any man-made fortress and large enough to see from a distance, even if we've lost our way. . . . His Name will never fall. His Name will never be defeated. His Name will never be reduced to rubble.

Liz Curtis Higgs

There is power in the name of My Son, Jesus. Pause for a moment and say His name over and over: "Jesus, Jesus, Jesus, Jesus." When you face obstacles today, let His name echo in your heart and be exhaled through your breath—*Jesus*. There is no temptation that He doesn't understand. There is no pain that is worse than what He experienced. There is no loss of comfort or reputation that He doesn't fully comprehend. There is no one who knows the anguish of your broken heart the way He does. The enemy trembles at the name of Jesus.

When the spirit of fear comes upon you, threatening to consume you, concentrate on this truth: "The name of the LORD is a strong fortress; the godly run to him and are safe" (Proverbs 18:10). Envision putting on running shoes and making a beeline for My strong tower. All the way to safety, speak His name again and again: "Jesus, Jesus, Jesus. Satan can't touch me. I live by the power of the name of Jesus."

God elevated him to the place of highest honor and gave him the name above all other names, that at the name of Jesus every knee should bow, in heaven and on earth and under the earth, and every tongue declare that Jesus Christ is Lord, to the glory of God the Father.

PHILIPPIANS 2:9-11

October 28

LIFE-CHANGING BOOK

As you read, pause frequently to meditate on the meaning of what you are reading. Absorb the Word into your system by dwelling on it, pondering it, going over it again and again in your mind, considering it from many different angles, until it becomes part of you.

Nancy DeMoss Wolgemuth

I've noticed a refreshing change in our relationship. You used to seek advice in My Word mostly when you were hurting—either physically or emotionally. When you weren't involved in time-consuming distractions, you would sometimes open up My book. You got better at looking for specific answers in the Bible when you were meeting with a group of other Christ-followers in a weekly study. I saw your face light up when you discovered a new truth or when a verse spoke directly to a need you were experiencing.

Now that we've walked together for a while and our relationship is sweeter, more intimate, more trusting, and more personal than ever before, you spend more time meditating on Scripture. That practice has transformed your thinking. You've been sharing My precepts with others who are looking for answers. You've delighted Me by memorizing verses that help you navigate the tough days. There's a satisfying tempo in our friendship as I see you first seeking wisdom from Me before asking others for help. You're learning the secret of inner peace—dwelling on, pondering, memorizing, and soaking in My holy Word. As our relationship continues to deepen, it brings Me joy.

I will meditate on your precepts and fix my eyes on your ways.
I will delight in your statutes; I will not forget your word.

PSALM 119:15-16, ESV

— *October 29* —

LABELED

It is incomprehensible grace to be a prodigal who is held by God again.

Angela Thomas

It's been hard for you to look in My direction recently. You've made some bad choices that have brought Me sorrow. You've labeled yourself a total failure, and you feel unworthy of My love. The problem started with small decisions, but the temptation to seek an easier, more exhilarating life was like a magnet, tugging harder and harder until you made a mad dash for what looked like a more enjoyable and far less restricted pathway.

Now you know it was a devastating mistake, and you want to come back. But every time you see your reflection in the mirror, there are words covering your face: *Loser. Failure. Unfaithful. Unworthy. Too Far Gone. Unwanted. Unloved.* Those labels are self-inflicted, not God-imposed. If you confess your sin, turn away from it, and come back to Me, I'll give you new labels: *Forgiven. Loved. Wanted. Worthy. Desired.* It's up to you to decide. You can keep hurrying away, or you can come back to Me. I'm already at the door, arms open wide, waiting to welcome you home. A gift of grace awaits you there.

His son said to him, "Father, I have sinned against both heaven and you, and I am no longer worthy of being called your son." But his father said to the servants, "Quick! Bring the finest robe in the house and put it on him. Get a ring for his finger and sandals for his feet. And kill the calf we have been fattening. We must celebrate with a feast, for this son of mine was dead and has now returned to life. He was lost, but now he is found." So the party began.

LUKE 15:21-24

October 30

TENDERNESS

Our identity rests in God's relentless tenderness
for us revealed in Jesus Christ.

Brennan Manning

Live every day dependent upon Me. Since you've been hurt and rejected by people you trusted to show you kindness, you've allowed an invisible wall to come between you and others. Getting close to people feels risky, and you don't want to look vulnerable and unprotected. Your personal pain hurts enough—and you don't know whom to confide in. Sometimes you put distance between you and Me because of this habit. You automatically shy away from Me, afraid of being dismissed.

Beloved, learn a new way to respond. I have tender affection for you. In My presence, you'll find warmth, mercy, love, and protection. I'm not here to criticize you. I'm here to comfort you and to gently reveal a better way to live. Dare to experience My tender mercies, compassion, and love. Allow Me to take you by the hand and lead you to a safe place. I am always aware of your hurts, your suffering, and your fears. Your endurance in this fallen world has gotten My attention, and as I did for My servant Job, I will bring you to a place of peace and blessing—beyond anything you could ever imagine. Keep your hand in Mine, and we'll walk this road together.

We give great honor to those who endure under suffering.
For instance, you know about Job, a man of great endurance.
You can see how the Lord was kind to him at the end,
for the Lord is full of tenderness and mercy.

JAMES 5:11

October 31

COMPARISON

Comparison will be the number one thing that will keep you from doing what God's calling you to do. He's put a gift and a call and a desire in your heart that is different than anyone else's. And you're wired that way for a reason.

Kari Jobe

Accept yourself the way I made you. Discontent and envy creep into your life when you look around and ask yourself, "Am I as attractive as that person? Are my gifts as important as his? Is my family as perfect as that family? Does God love other people more than He loves me? Why is her life free of suffering while I live in pain every day?" Envy will take away your happiness. It will eat away at your contentment. Anytime you compare yourself with others and feel like you don't measure up, your satisfaction in life diminishes and you end up questioning your worth.

Instead of looking at others, consider why I created *you*. Contentment in life comes from doing the best you can with the gifts I've given you. Follow the passion I've placed within you and pour your energy, time, and resources into the people and projects that allow you to follow the calling I've given you. Strive to be the person I made you to be, and you'll find fulfillment, satisfaction, and abiding joy. You are unique. There is no one like you. Do the work I've assigned to you and seek your approval from Me. I'm already delighted by your giftedness.

Pay careful attention to your own work,
for then you will get the satisfaction of a job well done,
and you won't need to compare yourself to anyone else.

GALATIANS 6:4

November 1

LET GO

I had struggled so hard and so long that I had simply exhausted myself, only to find that God had all the time in the world to wait for me to allow Him to free me.

Michelle McKinney Hammond

My plan for your life is unfolding differently from the picture you envisioned. For a while, your life felt unencumbered and stress-free. But as the years have gone by, there have been times when you fell down and ran away from Me due to wrong choices. When trials came, you begged Me for miracles—and sometimes clenched your fists in defiance against what I allowed to happen. You've built walls of isolation because you've been too busy or indifferent to listen to wise counsel from Me or others. You've been making demands of the people around you, and they are pushing back or even avoiding you. Every day seems more complicated and disruptive than the last. You're not enjoying life; you're just trying to make it through another cycle of rushing around until you fall into bed exhausted.

Today I want you to take a deep breath and consider a better way to live. My Word will give you the answers you need. When you spend time with Me, the fruit you will reap is peace. Instead of staying crazy-busy with activities, pause long enough to see the real needs of others. Seek My advice about how to comfort them. Realize that a spirit of quietness and confidence only comes when you stop and focus on Me. After sufficient rest, you will get more done. Let Me free you from your frenzy. Breathe in. Experience My peace.

The fruit of that righteousness will be peace; its effect will be quietness and confidence forever.

ISAIAH 32:17, NIV

November 2

HOMESICK

We need to be homesick for heaven. Though we have never been there, we still have something God has built within us that gives us a certain homesickness, a desire to be there.

Greg Laurie

Beloved, as you have kept your hand in Mine through many trials and hardships, I've seen a change in your perspective. In earlier years you were focused on getting rid of problems, making things easier and less stressful. But as you've read My Word, talked to Me, and sought to live within My will, you have become more aware of the brevity of your life, and you're focusing more on where you're headed, rather than trying to be totally free of pain.

You've learned that I'm preparing a spectacular home for you in heaven—and the longer you live in the far-from-satisfying place called Earth, the more you long for the home I've promised you. Allow your aches, pains, disappointments, and discouragements to make you homesick for the place I'm getting ready for you. On your hardest days, time moves slowly, but it won't be long. My entire creation is groaning under the weight of sin. I won't withhold your heart's desire from you much longer. The longing you feel is from Me. Wait with anticipation. You'll be home soon.

Yes, we are fully confident, and we would rather be away from these earthly bodies, for then we will be at home with the Lord.

2 CORINTHIANS 5:8

— *November 3* —

CHASING GOD'S BEST

Your greatest regret at the end of your life will be the lions you didn't chase. You will look back longingly on risks not taken, opportunities not seized, and dreams not pursued. Stop running away from what scares you most and start chasing the God-ordained opportunities that cross your path.

Mark Batterson

Each day you have a choice—to seize the opportunities I have for you or to live with hesitancy and indecision. You've held back, hoping your impossible situation would be resolved, or that your family would straighten up, or that your sorrow would disappear. I've asked you to welcome My embrace and to find safety and protection in My arms during these trying times. I've watched you grow in spiritual maturity as you seek to live in My presence day and night.

Now I want you to consider a big step. Instead of waiting to serve in your church, or to go on a missions trip, or to get involved in a service organization, or to start teaching a Bible study, or to mentor someone younger, I am asking you to make yourself available right now—in the middle of your adversity, without every detail of this hard place worked out and resolved. I'm inviting you to give Me everything you are and everything you have—from the depths of your greatest weakness. Chase the dream I've placed in your heart. Pursue My leading without making excuses. Don't settle for anything less than the highest and best calling I have for you. I am with you, and I promise you will lack for nothing.

I cry out to God Most High, to God who will fulfill his purpose for me.

PSALM 57:2

November 4

WOUNDS

Wounds do heal, but there are times to allow the Great Physician to perform surgery so they heal right.

Nancie Carmichael

Bring your brokenness to Me. I will heal your childhood wounds of neglect, abuse, and abandonment. I will heal your guilt-infested sores that came from bad decisions and ungodly choices. I will heal your emotional bruises that were inflicted by the hurtful comments of someone you trusted. I will heal the heart-wrenching ache you felt when someone who promised to love you walked away. I will heal your physical wounds that have brought severe pain or depleted your energy. I will heal your spiritual wounds that have triggered cynicism and mistrust of Christian leaders.

Begin by placing your wounds in My hands. Tell Me what happened that caused your hurt. You can pour out your grief and sorrow to Me. I will listen. Then pray, "Search me, O God, and know my heart; test me and know my anxious thoughts. Point out anything in me that offends you, and lead me along the path of everlasting life" (Psalm 139:23-24). Sometimes before a wound can heal, a scab has to be removed—maybe sin needs to be confessed, or you need to forgive someone who wronged you. Ask Me if there is any action you need to take. Respond in obedience and then begin living in the confidence that I will provide balm for your wounds. This is never an easy process, but it's worth it in the end. My child, I long to see you restored and whole.

He heals the brokenhearted and bandages their wounds.

PSALM 147:3

— November 5 —

LIVING RIGHT

Jesus demonstrated perfectly what it means to rejoice always, pray without ceasing, and give thanks in all things.

David Jeremiah

If you want to have a happy life, follow the example of My Son. No matter how many times He was criticized, rejected, wrongfully accused, sneered at, or ridiculed, He never paid back evil for evil. If someone is treating you unfairly, instead of retaliating, do something good for that person and allow Me to handle the outcome. People often act out of their own insecurities or hurts, and you are an easy target. Find your affirmation in My approval, not in the attitudes and responses of others.

Always be joyful. Make this the motto of your life. Today, list everything you have to be joyful about—life itself, your daily provision, your family, your home, and your faith. Now write down the difficult circumstance you're in. Think of everything you've learned and the ways you've grown during this hard time. Will you thank Me for that, too? Instead of grumbling about your situation, practice turning your complaints into words of thanksgiving: "Lord, thank You that You trusted me to carry this burden. I'm grateful that You have helped me become more compassionate toward others who have hurt me. I praise You for holding me in my pain." The key to living right is to rejoice, pray, and give thanks.

See that no one pays back evil for evil, but always try to do good to each other and to all people. Always be joyful. Never stop praying. Be thankful in all circumstances.

1 THESSALONIANS 5:15-18

— *November 6* —

DEPENDENCE

God uses chronic pain and weakness, along with other afflictions, as his chisel for sculpting our lives. Felt weakness deepens dependence on Christ for strength each day. The weaker we feel, the harder we lean. And the harder we lean, the stronger we grow spiritually, even while our bodies waste away.

J. I. Packer

There are things you will learn about Me only through your suffering. You're already learning that when you're in anguish, you don't have time or energy for frivolous prayers. In the midst of your hard place, you cry out to Me with your honest frustration, even your anger, and I hear you. On your darkest days when you feel completely out of options, you turn to Me and ask for assistance.

When things are going well, I see you becoming more independent and self-sufficient. But life is filled with problems, and I want you to be prepared when the bottom drops out. Learn the relief of putting your total reliance on Me. Speak these words aloud today: "The LORD is my rock, my fortress, and my savior; my God is my rock, in whom I find protection. He is my shield, the power that saves me, and my place of safety" (Psalm 18:2). When you learn to depend on Me as your Deliverer, you'll have more joy; you'll sleep better; you'll live unafraid; you'll be bolder in your faith. The benefit you didn't expect is that your pain will drive you deeper into the safety of My arms.

We felt we were doomed to die and saw how powerless we were to help ourselves; but that was good, for then we put everything into the hands of God, who alone could save us, for he can even raise the dead.

2 CORINTHIANS 1:9, TLB

— November 7 —

GOD'S GRAND STORY

When we submit our lives to what we read in Scripture, we find that we are not being led to see God in our stories but our stories in God's. God is the larger context and plot in which our stories find themselves.

Eugene Peterson

Your story is woven into the fabric of My grand story. Sometimes you feel forgotten, insignificant, or unimportant—but that is another lie the enemy is tempting you to believe. Review the history of the beginning of time. I created the heavens and the earth. Then I created man and woman. The people I made in My image sinned, but after the Fall, I gave them a path to redemption.

When suffering clouds the vision you have of My purpose for your life, remember that I chose you to become like My Son (Romans 8:29). Jesus endured suffering on earth, and it will be part of your journey too as you are conformed to His image. Don't be shocked by these things. Come to Me for comfort. When you come to something in your story that makes no sense, remember to look back at *My* story in My Word. You don't know what's going to happen tomorrow. You *do* know what's happened in the past and what will take place in the future. I am the Author of this story—and your final chapter will bring overflowing joy, perfect peace, freedom from pain, and a stunning new home. It's all because you're a part of My grand story. Trust Me. The ending of your story here on earth is the beginning of the best part of your journey.

Everyone will share the story of your wonderful goodness;
they will sing with joy about your righteousness.

PSALM 145:7

November 8

NO FISHING

The Bible says, "As far as the east is from the west, so far hath he removed our transgressions from us." He throws them into the depths of the sea, forgiven and forgotten, and to warn the accuser He puts a sign saying NO FISHING ALLOWED.

Corrie ten Boom

Oh, My child, there are days when I see you looking back at your past and picking up the heavy weight of your ungodly behavior, your bad habits, and your negative attitudes. There are times when you say to yourself, "I'll never completely forgive myself for my sinful choices." I want you to understand that these are whispers from the devil, who revels in accusations and lies.

When reminders of your past mistakes come into your mind, immediately turn them over to the Holy Spirit. Allow His floodlight to illuminate every hidden place in your heart. If you've already confessed those sins, you're forgiven! Those are the very things for which My precious Son died. It's a done deal! If you've been nurturing a favorite sin, confess it now and be completely clean. The next time you're tempted to cast a line into the waters of your past, stop and say aloud, "I am forgiven. I am clean. I am faultless and blameless because of what Jesus did for me."

Yet now he has reconciled you to himself through the death of Christ in his physical body. As a result, he has brought you into his own presence, and you are holy and blameless as you stand before him without a single fault.

COLOSSIANS 1:22

— November 9 —

THE RIPPLE EFFECT

The long series of disappointments you accumulate in a lifetime can stop you from moving forward into all the goodness God has planned for you—and that means they'll be stopping not only you, but also all those God has destined you to reach along your life journey.

Christine Caine

You are a person of great influence. Your family and the people closest to you are observing the way you respond to life's disappointments. If you allow multiple frustrations, dissatisfactions, regrets, and disillusionments to make you despair, the enemy counts that as a victory. Satan *prowls around like a roaring lion, looking for someone to devour.* He studies your vulnerabilities and your weaknesses, and he sees what trigger points stop you in your tracks and keep you from telling others about My goodness. He knows that if he can keep you from speaking up about truth, peace, hope, and faith to the people I want you to reach, you won't fulfill your destiny.

Be watchful and attentive! When you feel discouragement pulling you down, issue this warning loudly: "Satan, you are a total loser! You have already been defeated. My mind, my heart, and my future belong to the Most High God, and you have no place in my thoughts. Leave now, in the name of Jesus Christ! Go away! I will not be a victim of your lies anymore! I belong to Jesus!" The ripple effect of this mind-set brings victory, joy, and opportunities to represent Me everywhere you go. You're a victor!

Stay alert! Watch out for your great enemy, the devil. He prowls around like a roaring lion, looking for someone to devour.

1 PETER 5:8

November 10

IGNITING HOPE

Take seriously the story that God has given you to live. It's time to read your own life, because your story is the one that could set us all ablaze.

Dan B. Allender

I am guiding you along a path that has, at times, seemed uncertain. Your unique journey has brought you through deep waters and rivers of difficulty. But I have heard your cries for help. I've seen your abiding faith and unwavering commitment to My will. You have experienced the truth of Psalm 34:15: "The eyes of the LORD watch over those who do right; his ears are open to their cries for help." You have walked through the fire of oppression while declaring that I am a good and trustworthy God.

You've learned to totally rely on Me, and your confident assurance that these experiences have a purpose beyond the pain has led you to a solid, mature faith. You are turning your story into a testimony. By the way you've responded to your challenges, you've ignited hope in others who are struggling to find meaning in the chaos of life. I love you with an unfailing love. I kept you from drowning in your trials. I walked with you through the fire of adversity. As you lean on Me, keep telling your story to everyone you meet. Let others know that I will empower them with My Holy Spirit, setting their hearts ablaze with an everlasting love.

When you go through deep waters, I will be with you. When you go through rivers of difficulty, you will not drown. When you walk through the fire of oppression, you will not be burned up; the flames will not consume you.

ISAIAH 43:2

November 11

HEART SACRIFICES

A heart sacrifice is not a formula that can be mastered. It is a decision that is intrinsically tied to the personal relationship between us and our God. It is born out of a trust that is developed in spending time communicating with an Abba Father.

Carol Kent

Consider this question: Will you continue to honor and trust Me in the middle of unthinkable circumstances, or will you try to direct an outcome that is way beyond your control? Are you ready to offer Me a heart sacrifice? Will you give Me that person, that loss, that situation, that pain, that disappointment, that anger—whatever is eating you up inside?

Here's what I'm asking you to do. Identify the source of your anguish. Come to Me in prayer, open your hands, and say, "Lord, I'm letting go of my control. This is my act of worship." Envision Me picking up your sacrifice and carrying it for you. Embrace My love for you during this process. Now pray, "Father, I will rest in whatever outcome You give me, even if in this lifetime I'm not allowed to understand the reason for the sacrifice and pain involved." I will never demand a heart sacrifice from you. It must be your decision. You need to choose fear or faith, anxiety or peace, control or release, sadness or joy, pain or comfort. Brokenness is never easy, but it leads to repentance, reconciliation, and hope. Take the risk. It's worth it.

The sacrifice you desire is a broken spirit. You will not reject a broken and repentant heart, O God.

PSALM 51:17

November 12

FIRST LOVE

God is calling you to a passionate love relationship with Himself. Because the answer to religious complacency isn't working harder at a list of do's and don'ts—it's falling in love with God.

Francis Chan

Remaining close to Me requires making Me your first love. Am I your highest priority, or are your urgent daily tasks pulling you away from My presence? Stop long enough each morning to hear My voice and seek My will. Remember when you first said yes to Me? You were madly in love, and you felt lighter because I took the weight of your sin. You sang a new song, and you sought out the closeness of nestling in My arms. You lingered in My embrace and waited for affirmation and instruction. There was a sparkle in your eyes every time you told someone about our relationship.

I miss those times. You've grown lukewarm in your affection for Me as you've focused more on the distractions and confusion in your life and in the world at large. Do you miss our closeness as much as I do? To return to your first love, you must put Me first in all things—above your job, above your family, and above your problems. Seek My presence above all else and allow Me to hold you, help you, console you, and meet your needs. Experience the incomparable joy we once knew. Come back, My love.

I have this complaint against you. You don't love me or each other as you did at first!

REVELATION 2:4

— *November 13* —

RENEWED

Renewing the mind . . . involves taking off the old and replacing it with the new. The old is the lies you have learned to tell or were taught by those around you. . . . The new is the truth. To renew your mind is to involve yourself in the process of allowing God to bring to the surface the lies you have mistakenly accepted and replace them with truth.

Charles Stanley

Today is a brand-new day. Instead of focusing on past mistakes or your current limitations, look at Me and say, "I can do everything through Christ, who gives me strength" (Philippians 4:13). Walk in that truth. The enemy flashes statements in front of you: *You're too weak to stay away from that old habit. You're too hurt to forgive that person. You're too unimportant to matter to God. You're too damaged to be loved unconditionally.* When you allow Me to renew your mind, you actively replace those lies with My truth.

The key to renewing your mind is to study and meditate on My Word. Read a verse and then think about it intently. Memorize Scripture that replaces the enemy's taunts with My promises. The more you know My Word, the more you will have strength to stand up to the oppressor and the more you will become like Christ. "Let the message about Christ, in all its richness, fill your lives" (Colossians 3:16). As you stand in His likeness, the enemy flees.

Put on your new nature, and be renewed as you learn to know your Creator and become like him.

COLOSSIANS 3:10

November 14

SECURITY

If the Lord be with us, we have no cause of fear. His eye is upon us, His arm over us, His ear open to our prayer—His grace sufficient, His promises unchangeable.

John Newton

I am your Protector. When fear and anxiety stalk you, come to Me. I am your Hiding Place. You are never safer than when you are in the center of My will. You have nothing to be afraid of when you find your security in Me. The psalmist said, "In peace I will lie down and sleep, for you alone, LORD, make me dwell in safety" (Psalm 4:8, NIV). Sometimes your insecurity comes from not knowing what to do in the face of adversity. Remember that I'm your Guide, your Counselor, and your Friend. Ask Me for advice, and look for My response in Scripture, through the wise counsel of people who know Me, and through the inner voice of My Holy Spirit.

Pray like my prophet Jeremiah did: "LORD, you are my strength and fortress, my refuge in the day of trouble!" (Jeremiah 16:19). Practice coming to Me first when you feel threatened or vulnerable, and you will discover that I am always available to be your safe place. The only time you need to fear is when you are running away from My loving arms.

Fear of the LORD leads to life,
bringing security and protection from harm.

PROVERBS 19:23

November 15

PRACTICE

Do you want to know what God's will is for you? It is for you to become more and more like Christ. This is spiritual maturity, and if you make this your goal, it will change your life.

Billy Graham

Determine to live each day practicing My principles and following My will for your life. Study the example of My Son, Jesus Christ, and you'll know how to live out your faith. He esteemed others above Himself. He responded to interruptions as if they were the most important appointments in His day. He taught spiritual truth by telling parables—stories people could identify with. He didn't allow criticism and derision to divert Him from His goal. He made time for children. He cared for the needs of the sick with compassion. He offered them healing and hope. He showed unconditional love to people who hadn't earned any special treatment, and He cast a vision for those who needed direction.

My Son also practiced this important habit: "Before daybreak the next morning, Jesus got up and went out to an isolated place to pray" (Mark 1:35). He spent time alone with Me on a regular basis. He made it a priority to seek My advice before charging into His busy days. If you follow His example and focus on living for things that will outlast your life, you will have joy and peace—more than you ever could have imagined. Daily practice produces life-changing results.

Keep putting into practice all you learned and received from me—everything you heard from me and saw me doing. Then the God of peace will be with you.

PHILIPPIANS 4:9

November 16

CARRY ME

There is only one secure foundation: a genuine, deep relationship with Jesus Christ, which will carry you through any and all turmoil. No matter what storms are raging all around, you'll stand firm if you stand on His love.

Charles Stanley

Rest in the guarantee that when you are too overwhelmed, too exhausted, too sick, too sad, too disappointed, or too frustrated, I will carry you. My Son has already carried your sins on the cross—that crushing load is gone. Let Me take your anxieties. Peter wrote, "Give all your worries and cares to God, for he cares about you" (1 Peter 5:7). Sometimes you think your little concerns aren't important enough to give to Me, and that means you're missing out on the peace of mind I long for you to experience. Give Me your apprehensions about your livelihood, your family, your decisions, and your afflictions. In return, you'll receive peace, comfort, joy, and hope.

You've felt the pressure of holding things together during a difficult year that's been filled with more detours, stressors, and hardships than you ever anticipated. You have carried these burdens on your own far too long. I am your Abba Father. Come to Me. Let Me pick you up, hold you close, and carry you.

I will be glad and rejoice in your unfailing love, for you have seen my troubles, and you care about the anguish of my soul.

PSALM 31:7

November 17

BELOVED

Self-rejection is the greatest enemy of the spiritual life because it contradicts the sacred voice that calls us the "Beloved." Being the Beloved constitutes the core truth of our existence.

Henri Nouwen

I want you to wake up every day and know how much you're loved. Say it right now: "I am loved by God. I am His beloved." There is nothing you could ever do to stop My unconditional love for you. There is no good deed you could accomplish that could make Me love you more. I'm crazy about you. Stop concentrating on your imperfections and inadequacies, avoiding My presence until you've cleaned up or feel good enough. Come the way you are right now. Embrace Me without embarrassment or insecurity.

You are the object of My love. Do you remember what I said at the time of My Son's baptism? "This is My beloved Son, in whom I am well pleased" (Matthew 3:17, NKJV). Because of His sacrifice, I feel the same way about you. I treasure you, and you have My approval. Look into My face and see My delight for you. Live today confident that you are My beloved child.

I am my beloved's and my beloved is mine.

SONG OF SONGS 6:3, NIV

November 18

THE WAY UP

We want gain without pain; we want the resurrection without going through the grave; we want life without experiencing death; we want a crown without going by way of the Cross. But in God's economy, the way up is down.

Nancy DeMoss Wolgemuth

You have grown up in a culture that demands instant gratification. Waiting, especially when persevering through adversity, feels unfair. Your unformed prayers have turned into questions: "God, why would You permit me to suffer when You are all-powerful? Why are You allowing me to agonize without resolution in the middle of this family conflict? Since heaven is my final destination, why can't I escape my problems and make the trip right now?"

It's hard for you to understand, but I'm conforming you to the image of My Son. You are growing in spiritual maturity and endurance. Look at His example to learn how to present your body as a living sacrifice. Offer Me your goals, hopes, and dreams, as well as your hurts. Place them in My hands and say, like Job did, "Though he slay me, yet will I hope in him" (Job 13:15, NIV). Jesus went to the grave and was resurrected three days later. Don't quit and don't be discouraged. The way up is down. You have suffered much. Now look up. Your deliverance will come soon.

Through suffering, our bodies continue to share in the death of Jesus so that the life of Jesus may also be seen in our bodies.

2 CORINTHIANS 4:10

November 19

SHOUT FOR JOY

When we fight back with joy, we embrace a reality that is more real than what we're enduring and we awaken to the deepest reality of our identity as beloved, joyful children of God.

Margaret Feinberg

My child, you will find joy if you hold on to Me. Remember—there is fullness of joy in My presence (Psalm 16:11, NKJV). You are one of my dear family members, and I want to hear the delight you feel when you are close to Me. Sometimes you withhold your audible happiness when we're together because you think someone might think you're too odd, too expressive, or too loud. Try saying what you're thinking about Me out loud—I want you to literally *shout for joy*!

Entrust yourself more fully to Me. Declare that your hope does not rest in a benign diagnosis, perfect children, a problem-free marriage, or a stress-free life. I have set you free from the weight of your sin. I have protected you. I have chosen you. I have loved you—and I will continue to love you for all eternity. Sing My praises. Shout out your reasons for loving Me. Let gladness be an automatic response of your heart every day as you reflect on who I am. Express your joy in My presence. Play. Delight. Rejoice. Sing. Dance. Cheer. Smile. Brighten. Bless Me. Be blessed. *Shout for joy!*

I will shout for joy and sing your praises, for you have ransomed me.

PSALM 71:23

— *November 20* —

RESTLESSNESS

God surpasses our dreams when we . . . walk the path He has chosen for us. He is obligated to keep us dissatisfied until we come to Him and His plan for complete satisfaction.

Beth Moore

There's a stirring in your soul, and it's made you feel unsettled. Ask My Spirit to reveal the meaning of this creative restlessness. It doesn't always mean I'm trying to convict you of sin or that you're going in the wrong direction. I often stir your spirit when I am about to do something new. Allow this heightened awareness of My presence to make you alert to the opportunities I'm placing before you.

You've often thought you need to resolve your own painful issues before you can do the work I've prepared for you. But this is a lie from the enemy to keep you from being productive and fruitful right now. Try praying in this way: "Lord, I feel like an imperfect vessel for doing Your Kingdom work. I've often waited to accept an leadership position, or to assist those who need help, because I've been so aware of my personal shortcomings and limitations. I've been self-focused instead of focused on You. Thank You for unsettling my spirit. I accept Your will for my next steps. Show me how to use my abilities for Your glory. I want my restlessness to lead me to complete fulfillment in Your plan for my future."

Commit your works to the LORD [submit and trust them to Him], and your plans will succeed [if you respond to His will and guidance].

PROVERBS 16:3, AMP

— November 21 —

THE CLASSROOM

There is no circumstance, no trouble, no testing, that can ever touch me until, first of all, it has gone past God and past Christ, right through to me. If it has come that far, it has come with a great purpose.

Alan Redpath

Accept each day as it comes to you. Look around to see what I have placed in your life to help you grow. You'll see beauty, even in the midst of sadness and pain, if you keep your eyes and ears open. Your emotions are tender when you're walking through a trial. Notice the people in your pathway. I'm sending them to brighten your life with physical and spiritual encouragement. These are not random occurrences. I want you to study how My followers show compassion and what they do to offer tangible help. Right now *you* need this blessing, but there will be a day when you'll have the opportunity to perform these acts of kindness for others.

I am teaching you how to persevere under pressure, and I've seen your progress. In this classroom of life, you're learning that the hard times you experience are only temporary. You're developing the habit of coming to Me first when you're struggling, and that action always leads to peace. I'm developing in you a tender, soft heart toward others—and you're pointing them to Me. When you face obstacles, your heart's response is, "Lord, what do You want me to learn?" Your attitude of submission pleases Me.

Teach me your ways, O LORD, that I may live according to your truth! Grant me purity of heart, so that I may honor you.

PSALM 86:11

— November 22 —

A NEW HABIT

Praise teaches us to be joyful and thankful regardless of our circumstances. It prepares us for God's service and helps us to see beyond our present circumstances to the immense possibilities that are ours through faith in Jesus Christ.

Michael Youssef

Your life will change for the better if you develop the moment-by-moment habit of praising Me. When good things are happening, it's easy for you to voice your thanks. But when you're hurting, you pull back as if I'm punishing you. Learn to voice your gratitude in the good times and in the difficult ones. Worship Me without first thinking about whether or not life seems fair. When you are in pain, hand your cares over to Me. Every single moment, have words of praise on your lips.

You love to be thanked, and so do I. Open your mouth and tell Me what your heart rejoices in. Praise Me for walking with you through your dark valleys. Give thanks for the glimmers of joy you experienced when you thought all hope was lost. Let My name be on your tongue as often in times of need as in times of plenty. Watch how that decision adjusts your attitude and brings peace to your heart.

Through Jesus, therefore, let us continually offer to God a sacrifice of praise—the fruit of lips that openly profess his name.

HEBREWS 13:15, NIV

— *November 23* —

OVERFLOWING

I'm just thankful for everything, all the blessings in my life, trying to stay that way. I think that's the best way to start your day and finish your day. It keeps everything in perspective.

Tim Tebow

What are you thankful for today? What blessings have surprised you, cheered you, and made your heart overflow with gratefulness? Consider these things. I will continue to provide your daily bread. I have given you the greatest Gift of all—my Son, Jesus Christ, who died on the cross and rose from the grave so you can know Him personally and spend eternity with Him in heaven. In the middle of trials and even persecution, I will not leave you. I am here every day to provide My power and presence in your life. "I am with you always, even to the end of the age" (Matthew 28:20).

Sit quietly in My presence and allow Me to fill your heart and mind with thankfulness. As you go through this day, look for specific ways I'm blessing you. When you discover these unexpected treasures, collect them—one by one—until you have a beautiful bouquet. When nightfall comes, lay them at My feet. Your display of overflowing thanksgiving brings Me pleasure, and in My presence you will find abiding joy.

You prepare a feast for me in the presence of my enemies.
You honor me by anointing my head with oil.
My cup overflows with blessings.

PSALM 23:5

— *November 24* —

APPRECIATION

Gratitude is at the center of a life of faith. It sounds too simple to be true, but isn't that the sign of all deep truth: so simple we're tempted to dismiss it, and so hard, it is exactly what God uses to change our hard lives.

Ann Voskamp

An attitude of thanks puts everything into perspective. Take a moment and think about the people who have encouraged you. What did they say that gave you fresh hope and a new perspective? What specific things did they do to meet your needs and demonstrate their love? How did they help carry your burden? How did they support you and remind you to keep going in the midst of adversity? How did they bring light to the dark despair you'd been experiencing?

You have been comforted by My people. Now ask Me to reveal ways you can show your gratitude for what they have done. Speak to them about the value of what they provided at the very time you needed encouragement. Let them see the joy-filled results of their kindness and the blessing they brought to your life. As they have needs of their own, reach out to them. Find thoughtful, personal ways to demonstrate the kind of love you received from them. Even if your own pain is weighing you down, find someone who needs a word of hope. I'll give you the strength to bless that person, and in that process, you'll discover that your own hardship is easier to bear.

They have been a wonderful encouragement to me, as they have been to you. You must show your appreciation to all who serve so well.

1 CORINTHIANS 16:18

— *November 25* —

EXPECTATIONS

Lower your expectations of earth.
This isn't Heaven, so don't expect it to be.

Max Lucado

Live each day with expectation because I have boundless resources. While you maintain high anticipation, be sure to place your hope in the right place. Right now you're earthbound. You would like your suffering to end, and you've been hoping to find heaven on earth. But that won't happen while this sin-cursed planet is plagued by the enemy of your soul. When you seek My help in your time of need, you can expect Me to listen, to advocate on your behalf, and to answer your prayers. Remember that My answers don't always match your desires. But while you await My Son's return, I'm working on a bigger plan, a purpose far beyond what you can visualize today.

Anticipate comfort in My presence, peace in the middle of chaos, hope that defies human understanding, joy in unlikely circumstances, and patience to wait for My timing in resolving your difficult issue. I see your pain. I hear your voice. Wait with patience.

In the morning, LORD, you hear my voice; in the morning
I lay my requests before you and wait expectantly.

PSALM 5:3, NIV

November 26

THE LONG HAUL

To endure the cross is not tragedy; it is the suffering which is the fruit of an exclusive allegiance to Jesus Christ.

Dietrich Bonhoeffer

My fondness for you is great. I've watched the way you've turned "gritting-your-teeth" endurance into "glory-strength" staying power. You've discovered the secret to hanging on to hope for the long haul—spending time in My Word. Like the psalmist, you can say, "You're my place of quiet retreat; I wait for your Word to renew me" (Psalm 119:114, MSG). The more you meditate on My truth, the more you understand that your setbacks are only temporary and your reward will last for all eternity.

No longer do you waver in your faith, allowing your circumstances and your feelings to dictate how much you trust Me. You're developing the kind of endurance that finds stability when life seems to be falling apart. As you face obstacles, your well-developed confidence in Me triggers a sense of expectation that I will use these momentary setbacks as springboards for growth. The maturity of your faith brings Me delight.

We pray that you'll have the strength to stick it out over the long haul—not the grim strength of gritting your teeth but the glory-strength God gives. It is strength that endures the unendurable and spills over into joy, thanking the Father who makes us strong enough to take part in everything bright and beautiful that he has for us.

COLOSSIANS 1:11-12, MSG

November 27

PERSPECTIVE

In Heaven . . . [t]o look into God's eyes will be to see what we've always longed to see: the person who made us for his own good pleasure. Seeing God will be like seeing everything else for the first time.

Randy Alcorn

I want you to see things from My point of view. This is difficult for you because right now your vision is clouded by the sin and pain in this world. I can see the end from the beginning—so I already know you will be just fine in the end, but that's hard for you to envision. You develop perspective when you grow in spiritual wisdom and discernment; you begin to understand why I have allowed certain things to happen.

Try looking at life from My vantage point and it will help you resist temptation. You'll realize the short-term enjoyment that sin offers is not worth the long-term consequences of wrongdoing. Perspective also helps you to endure hardship. My Son, Jesus, looked past the pain of the Cross to the joy that was set before Him. Follow His example when your load seems unbearable. Now your vision is limited, but one day it will all become clear—when you are with Me in heaven and understand what I have known all along. Stay close to Me and allow a maturing perspective to reveal how wide, how deep, and how high My love for you is (Ephesians 3:18).

"My thoughts are nothing like your thoughts," says the LORD. *"And my ways are far beyond anything you could imagine. For just as the heavens are higher than the earth, so my ways are higher than your ways and my thoughts higher than your thoughts."*

ISAIAH 55:8-9

November 28

THE RELIABLE GUIDE

You have a God who hears you, the power of love behind you, the Holy Spirit within you, and all of heaven ahead of you. If you have the Shepherd, you have grace for every sin, direction for every turn, a candle for every corner, and an anchor for every storm. You have everything you need.

Max Lucado

There's a beautiful rhythm in the way we walk together. As I hold your hand on the uneven path that each day brings, I find you leaning closer, depending upon the direction I provide regarding which way to turn. You've learned an important principle: to seek My will about your use of time—in daily activities and in the major commitments that involve a long-term investment of your energy. Sometimes you ask Me for specific guidance, and you find answers in My Word or through the wisdom of My people.

I'm watching your passion for making wise choices increase. I'm also pleased to see you applying what you've learned from Scripture in your day-to-day decisions. Your focal point is moving away from the comforts of this world and toward Christ. You are developing a purposeful, determined mind-set that desires to accomplish My mission. You're talking to Me often, seeking My leadership, and aligning your goals with Mine. The road is narrow, and some people don't understand your choices, but that's okay. *My presence will go with you.* Your final destination is heaven, and My Spirit is a reliable guide.

GOD said, "My presence will go with you. I'll see the journey to the end."

EXODUS 33:14, MSG

November 29

OUR HANDS IN HIS

God takes our hands in His. He lifts us up gently. He holds us up. . . . He is leading us on a smooth path, keeping us from blundering off into the wilderness. Will we still stumble and lose our balance at times? Yes, but Scripture assures us that if we're clinging to His hand, our stumbling will not result in devastating falls.

Ron Mehl

Be willing to lean on Me. You don't have to do all the work yourself. Sometimes your independent spirit keeps you from experiencing all the benefits My protection and provision offer. I know your life has been filled with unexpected challenges that make choices hard. Will you give Me your hands, your heart, and your impossible situation? My precious one, you were never meant to carry these difficult circumstances alone. I am here for you.

Cling to Me and allow Me to make the road ahead smooth. I am able to keep you from falling. Immerse yourself in this promise from My Word: "The Lord is my rock, my fortress, and my savior; my God is my rock, in whom I find protection. He is my shield, the power that saves me, and my place of safety" (Psalm 18:2). Do you want more security? Do you hope to avoid pitfalls? Are you looking for assurances? Think of yourself as a lump of clay in the hands of the Master Potter. I am gently holding you and carefully shaping you. Trust Me to create something beautiful; allow Me to do My work.

As the clay is in the potter's hand, so are you in my hand.

JEREMIAH 18:6

November 30

HIS HOME

The Lord showed me, so that I did see clearly, that he did not dwell in these temples which men had commanded and set up, but in people's hearts . . . his people were his temple, and he dwelt in them.

George Fox

You are My temple—the place I call "home." The day you said yes to Jesus was the day My Spirit took up residence within you. Think about what it means to house the Lord of glory. When you have questions, My Spirit will be your Counselor. When you are sad, My Spirit will be your Comforter. When you are lost, My Spirit will be your Guide. When you need assistance, My Spirit will be your Helper. Don't let this truth overwhelm you. When the disciples first heard about the role of the Holy Spirit, they didn't understand, but now you have My Word to teach you about this deeply personal relationship that you and I enjoy.

Bask in the knowledge of My daily, constant, all-consuming presence within you. Honor Me with your body. It's My home. You've been bought with a high price—the death of My Son on the cross. Be aware of My presence on the good days and on the hard days. Before you speak to Me about your needs, I know what's in your mind and heart. This decaying world has brought you sorrow, but I have overcome the world—and until that day when you live with Me in heaven, I will make your heart My dwelling place. I am fiercely loyal to you. You are mine and I am yours. Always.

Don't you realize that your body is the temple of the Holy Spirit, who lives in you and was given to you by God? You do not belong to yourself, for God bought you with a high price.

1 CORINTHIANS 6:19-20

December 1

MY LORD

Will you keep going when you don't know why? When you can't get any answers that would make the pain go away, will you still say, "My Lord," even though his ways are not clear to you? Will you keep going—with all the grace and grit and faith you can muster—and live in hope that one day God will set everything right.

John Ortberg

Centering your thoughts on the lives of other people often leads you to make comparisons. Their journeys seem easier, less complicated, and more hope filled. Your life feels painful, less promising, and more difficult. At times you've wondered whether I love you as much as I love them. Doubts swirl and uncertainty robs you of joy.

My Son's disciple Thomas often saw life through a skeptical lens. The evening after Jesus was raised from the dead, He stood in front of His disciples bringing words of reassurance. But Thomas missed the meeting. When he arrived later, the other disciples told him, "We have seen the Lord!" (John 20:25), but Thomas blurted out that he wouldn't believe it without proof. When Thomas actually saw Jesus and touched Him, he believed. Jesus said, "You believe because you have seen me. Blessed are those who believe without seeing me" (John 20:29). My child, will you call Me "Lord" without having all your questions answered right now? The choice is yours.

Then [Jesus] said to Thomas, "Put your finger here, and look at my hands. Put your hand into the wound in my side. Don't be faithless any longer. Believe!" "My Lord and my God!" Thomas exclaimed.

JOHN 20:27-28

December 2

EXTRAVAGANT GIVING

The more you give, the more comes back to you, because God is the greatest giver in the universe, and He won't let you outgive Him. Go ahead and try.

Randy Alcorn

I love to surprise you with jaw-dropping blessings. What have I provided that takes your breath away? A newborn baby. A sunset. Snow-capped mountains. Ocean waves splashing on the sand. A big answer to prayer. Extravagant kindness. Likewise, I want you to be a lavish gift giver. Be overgenerous. Offer to do something that can't be repaid. Be creative. Your gift might be monetary, or it might be a gift of time or a service rendered that meets a need.

Remember the words of the apostle Paul to Timothy, the young man he mentored. Timothy was to tell people who had resources "to do good, to be rich in helping others, to be extravagantly generous" (1 Timothy 6:18, MSG). Why? "If they do that, they'll build a treasury that will last, gaining life that is truly life" (1 Timothy 6:19). I know there are times when you feel too depleted to think of what you can do for others—but that is the very time I want you to give extravagantly. The joy that bounces back will bring healing to your heart and soul.

Just then [Jesus] looked up and saw the rich people dropping offerings in the collection plate. Then he saw a poor widow put in two pennies. He said, "The plain truth is that this widow has given by far the largest offering today. All these others made offerings that they'll never miss; she gave extravagantly what she couldn't afford—she gave her all!"

LUKE 21:1-4, MSG

December 3

THE BEST DEFENSE

The reason we must put on the whole armor of God is to withstand evil. We don't war against people, but against a spiritual hierarchy of invisible power.

Stormie Omartian

I will provide all the protection you need. You can count on Me to be your Defender and your Guard. When you hear bad news or when unexpected setbacks occur, your natural tendency is to withdraw and shrink back from your normal routine. That gives fear an open door. Instead, practice the daily habit of putting on My armor. It is your best defense against the cunning attacks of the enemy.

First, stand your ground—Satan is already defeated because you belong to Me. Rely on My power to make you strong. Here are the additional steps I want you to take: Put on the belt of truth and the body armor of My righteousness. Slip into the shoes of My peace, well balanced to combat evil. Confidently hold the shield of faith—the fiery arrows of the devil cannot penetrate it. Remember that the devil is deceitful and will try to hit you in your most vulnerable place. Don the helmet of salvation and grasp the sword of My Word in your hands. Be persistent in prayer for yourself and for others. Stay alert! (Ephesians 6:14-18). If you follow My instructions, you will win this battle—today and every day!

Be strong in the Lord and in his mighty power.
Put on all of God's armor so that you will be able
to stand firm against all strategies of the devil.

EPHESIANS 6:10-11

December 4

HOLDERS

Holders are people who stand beside us even when things are unpleasant; they have a capacity to stay unshaken for the long haul. . . . Holders are not afraid to speak the truth. . . . I've come to realize that the people who help me the most are the ones who have the questions, not the ones who have the answers.

Karen Burton Mains

Dear one, there are certain seasons of the year that are more difficult than others. People around you seem to have normal lives. They're surrounded by thoughtful family members and friends. It seems they never have to maneuver complicated circumstances. The sharp contrast to your situation is hard to comprehend, since you've asked Me for a more comfortable life. Instead of telling Me how to answer your prayer, look around and seek the companionship of the people I've placed in your path. They are My "holders," the ones who listen even when you're upset. They aren't intimidated by your mood swings or by your displeasure with everything that's happening. They hold you with their prayers and their presence, and they remain unshaken no matter how long you need support.

Listen to their words. They remind you that I am always here, offering you My hand. They tell you not to be afraid, because I'm going to help you. They speak My truth—even if it's not what you want to hear. If you allow them to bring you assurance and encouragement, you will be comforted. They are part of My plan for restoring your hope and joy.

For I am the LORD your God who takes hold of your right hand and says to you, Do not fear; I will help you.

ISAIAH 41:13, NIV

December 5

A TIMELY WORD

When you're fully aware that the words you speak are God working through you to bless another person, that's definitely a cause for joy. Shared joy at that.

Liz Curtis Higgs

We've been walking together for quite a while, and our conversations bring blessing to both of us. When you talk to Me, voicing your worship, speaking your praise, asking for My direction, or seeking a deeper relationship, I am pleased. When you hear My responses—through Scripture or when My Spirit brings insight, wisdom, or relief—you are blessed. Our communication is a cause for mutual joy!

Be aware of how your words can encourage, instruct, or cheer someone today. Go out of your way to deliver the gift of a timely word to someone who isn't expecting to hear from you. "Kind words are like honey—sweet to the soul and healthy for the body" (Proverbs 16:24). As you see the way your spoken blessing brings a smile, answers a question, or makes a heavy load lighter, be delighted. You are acting on My behalf. Your kind words bring triple joy—to the recipient, to you, and to Me!

A person finds joy in giving an apt reply—
and how good is a timely word!

PROVERBS 15:23, NIV

— December 6 —

WHAT TO DO

Often the very things that you think have disqualified you are the ones that qualify you to do what God has called you to do.

Christine Caine

Fear has been stalking you—the fear that your past has disqualified you from doing My work in this world. You've observed others who appear to lead perfect, Christlike lives. Their faith seems stronger than yours. They can quote Bible verses and remember the references. They are able to balance their personal lives, their work lives, and their ministries without showing fatigue. If they've made bad choices in their personal or spiritual lives, there is no visible sign of it now. The more you compare your qualifications with theirs, the more inadequate you feel. When these thoughts loom in your mind, recognize that they don't come from Me. Remember My imperfect servant David and start saying this Scripture out loud: "My heart is confident in you, O God; no wonder I can sing your praises with all my heart!" (Psalm 108:1).

Declare that because of Jesus and His shed blood for you on the cross, the past does not dictate your future. Say aloud, "I am forgiven. I am equipped with God's truth. I am empowered by the Spirit of the Most High God. My foundation rests on the truth of God's Word. My highest privilege is to offer my weaknesses, my failings, and my lack of faith to God my Father. I am confident and surefooted because I am His."

The Sovereign LORD is my strength! He makes me as surefooted as a deer, able to tread upon the heights.

HABAKKUK 3:19

HE IS HERE

When we practice the presence of God,
we train ourselves to *desire* His presence.

Mark Buchanan

*M*y precious child, you are still trying to figure out what it means to have Me with you every moment. Sometimes that thought is comforting. At other times, you'd like to escape My presence because you want to hide a favorite sin or an unhealthy habit. No matter where you run, I will pursue you. Sometimes you don't want Me to hear your tirades in the middle of disappointment and unresolved conflict. But even when you try to keep those things from Me, I know every last detail. Instead of feeling smothered by My presence, embrace it. Ask Me to give you victory in the areas of your life that drag you down and prevent you from spending time with Me.

Begin thinking in a new way: *God's Spirit is in me. I am His home, and I want it to be clean, comfortable, and holy for Him.* Now enjoy My presence. Ask Me for self-control, wisdom, and ever-growing spiritual maturity. Talk to Me as a child would speak to a father. Tell me about your fears, your failings, your temptations, and your desires. Invite Me to lead you to a deeper, more fulfilling, and richer faith than you've ever known before. My hand will guide you.

I can never escape from your Spirit! I can never get away from your presence! If I go up to heaven, you are there; if I go down to the grave, you are there. If I ride the wings of the morning, if I dwell by the farthest oceans, even there your hand will guide me, and your strength will support me.

PSALM 139:7-10

December 8

PURITY

Purity doesn't mean perfection. . . . None of us fit that description. God expects purity of motives, not perfection of action. It means when you do something wrong, you want to make it right. You can't have God's blessing on your family, your business, or any other area of your life unless you seriously pursue that kind of purity.

Rick Warren

Thinking about Me the moment you begin each day whets your appetite for becoming more and more like Me. When you ask Me to search your heart, I reveal the thoughts, actions, and habits you need to let go of so you can be a pure container for carrying the Good News of Jesus to others. This practice eliminates guilt over secret sins and brings the relief of an unencumbered conscience. I am pleased when you come to Me with a repentant heart. When you ask for My forgiveness, I flood you with mercy and make you brand new.

I've watched you endure pain and adversity without blaming Me or others for these hardships. Your pure motives allow Me to use the testimony of your life to dramatically impact the people who are watching you. They see your transparency, and they know your journey has been difficult—but they also see your face reflecting My joy, which inspires you to keep going. They want that joy for themselves. The purity of your heart has drawn others to consider the claims of Christ. My beloved, how precious you are to Me!

Be an example to all believers in what you say, in the way you live, in your love, your faith, and your purity.

1 TIMOTHY 4:12

December 9

BUILDING MATERIAL

I lay down my straining to fix what is broken around me, my hunger for something more perfect than I can produce. I sit with the shards of my very imperfect life, surer than ever that the pieces simply cannot be put back together again—at least not in the same way as before.

Elisa Morgan

Learn to appreciate your journey, even though the route isn't exactly what you would have mapped. You've wanted happy endings—and fewer problems, so the puzzle pieces of your life would snap together flawlessly—but that's not My plan at this time. I take the things that look broken and wrecked and arrange them in a pattern that is much more exquisite than the predictable, more "perfect" picture you had in mind. My masterpiece exudes individuality, creativity, and transformation.

As you review your imperfect life, ask Me to reveal a different kind of beauty—the kind in which uniqueness and redemption are refreshing and invigorating. The story of your life inspires others not because it is unblemished, but because it radiates the authenticity of pain, struggle, forgiveness, and unexpected joy. When you accepted the invitation to join Me on this journey, you didn't know where the path would lead—but you said yes. I'm taking the pieces of your life and building a work of art.

This is the kind of life you've been invited into, the kind of life Christ lived. He suffered everything that came his way so you would know that it could be done, and also know how to do it, step-by-step.

1 PETER 2:21, MSG

— December 10 —

FRIENDSHIP

A friend accepts us as we are and is patient with our faults. A friend points out our strengths and rejoices at our successes. A friend's presence and listening ear fill a void in us and give our lives a sense of validation and greater depth.

Charles Swindoll

You became My friend when you said yes to Jesus. True friendship always involves a relationship. At times you're disappointed when you reach out to other people, hoping for a meaningful connection, but find rejection. Friendship must be based on trust. The mutual sharing of thoughts, feelings, frustrations, heartaches, and dreams with someone trustworthy creates a bond that is not easily broken. Allow your relationship with Me to develop over time as you grow in wisdom and spiritual maturity. Unconditional love results when a friendship grows deep and there is uncommon support given during times of uncertainty and struggle.

When trust is broken, the cost is great. "An offended friend is harder to win back than a fortified city. Arguments separate friends like a gate locked with bars" (Proverbs 18:19). However, true friendship has pure motives—not "What can you do for me?" but "How can I sacrificially show my love to you?" There is no greater example than My only Son giving His life on the cross for you so that your friendship with Me could be restored. I am your Friend, and "I will never fail you. I will never abandon you" (Hebrews 13:5).

One who has unreliable friends soon comes to ruin,
but there is a friend who sticks closer than a brother.

PROVERBS 18:24, NIV

— December 11 —

HIDE ME

He uses our problems as building materials for His miracles. . . . [T]his was my first lesson in learning to trust Him completely.

Corrie ten Boom

The enemy is cunning and lurks in unexpected places, threatening you with fear of the unknown and tempting you to feel unstable and intimidated. In addition to those stressful challenges, there are times when people come against you with criticism or unfounded accusations. In these circumstances, look to Me for protection. Place your trust in Me, and I will be your Refuge. When you need a safe place, come to Me. I will hide you *beneath the shadow of [My] wings until the danger passes by.*

I am your Defender, and I am always available to you. Pick up My Word and speak this Scripture aloud: "You are my hiding place from every storm of life; you even keep me from getting into trouble! You surround me with songs of victory" (Psalm 32:7, TLB). When you feel exposed or helpless, try singing songs of triumph that lift your spirit and focus your mind on truth. Allow Me to turn your anxiety into peace as you find comfort in the hollow of My hand.

Have mercy on me, O God, have mercy! I look to you for protection. I will hide beneath the shadow of your wings until the danger passes by.

PSALM 57:1

— *December 12* —

HEAR MY CRY

God will sometimes allow things to get bad enough that we will be forced to look up. Victory always begins with a cry for help. When we come to the end of ourselves and cry out for help, amazing things happen.

Beth Moore

When tragedy hits your life, cry out to Me. You may be thinking, *There is no way I will ever get through this. I see no way that God could bring good out of a situation this devastating. How can I find hope and cling to my faith at a time like this?* I know there are times when you battle feelings of despair, confusion, and even anger because of the suffering you're experiencing. I see your desperation. I understand your longing for relief. What should you do in these tough moments? Cry out to Me for help. Acknowledge that you need My intervention, that you can't fix things yourself.

Here's My promise to you: "Call on me when you are in trouble, and I will rescue you" (Psalm 50:15). "Call to me and I will answer you and tell you great and unsearchable things you do not know" (Jeremiah 33:3, NIV). When righteous people cry out, I hear them and deliver them from their troubles (Psalm 34:17, NIV). Don't hold back. Your cry will bring rescue, answers, and deliverance—but these things will take place in My timing. When you reach the end of your rope, look up and have faith in My power to bring release and resolution. As you wait for relief, find respite in My presence. My love for you is great.

In my distress I cried out to the LORD; yes, I cried to my God for help. He heard me from his sanctuary; my cry reached his ears.

2 SAMUEL 22:7

December 13

GLORIFY HIS NAME

His perfect holiness, by definition, assures us that our words can't contain Him. Isn't it a comfort to worship a God we cannot exaggerate?

Francis Chan

There is nothing sweeter to My ears than the sound of your voice lifted in worship. Occupy yourself with *Me*—not just what I can do for you. When you glorify My name with a community of believers, you're expressing praise based on what you know to be true about My character and My Word. The habit of worshiping Me with others is an important practice to develop in your pursuit of joy. Your fear will dissipate, and your troubles will feel much lighter.

David expressed a significant result of worship: "I will be filled with joy because of you. I will sing praises to your name, O Most High. My enemies retreated" (Psalm 9:2-3). When you are under the enemy's attack, speak My name, lift your voice in praise, glorify Me in worship—and the enemy will flee. You will compound your joy and defeat your foes when you speak and sing of My goodness. Glorifying My name draws you close to Me; it floods you with an intimate sense of My presence, and it empowers you to move forward with strength.

Glorify the LORD with me; let us exalt his name together.

PSALM 34:3, NIV

— December 14 —

BOLD PRAYERS

Bold prayers honor God, and God honors bold prayers. . . . The greatest moments in life are the miraculous moments when human impotence and divine omnipotence intersect—and they intersect when we draw a circle around the impossible situations in our lives and invite God to intervene.

Mark Batterson

What is the most impossible situation you are facing in your life right now? Bring that need to Me with confidence that I will hear your request. You are My child, and I want you to know that you can look to Me for help. "I wait confidently for God to save me, and my God will certainly hear me" (Micah 7:7). Enjoy the relationship we have. You don't have to wait for permission to enter My presence. You don't have to be concerned that I will dismiss your prayers as unnecessary or unimportant. I hear everything you say to Me. Be assured that when you pray bold prayers within My will, you can expect answers.

On this very day, come to Me with your difficult situation, which seems to hold no hope for a positive resolution. Ask for My limitless power to intersect with your great need—and confidently ask for help. I hear the prayers of the righteous (Proverbs 15:29). I have noticed your passion to live an upright, blameless, and honorable life by following the instructions in My Word. I am not offended when you come to Me with unflinching prayers. Don't give up on praying before your miracle happens.

And we are confident that he hears us whenever we ask for anything that pleases him. And since we know he hears us when we make our requests, we also know that he will give us what we ask for.

1 JOHN 5:14-15

December 15

ADORATION

Adoration is the spontaneous yearning of the heart to worship, honor, magnify, and bless God. . . . We ask for nothing but to cherish him. We seek nothing but his exaltation. We focus on nothing but his goodness.

Richard J. Foster

Come, My child, and remember what My Son came to the earth to do—to be the Savior of the world. Instead of focusing on all you are anxious about, replace your worrisome thoughts with adoration. Thank Jesus for His willingness to leave heaven's glory to become a man, to be born in a lowly stable, subject to the limitations of earthly life. When He began His ministry, Jesus faced cruel people, hurtful criticism, strong temptations, and a poor, itinerant life rather than the grandeur of heaven. But He remained faithful to My will and followed it to the Cross.

Stop to think about all Jesus did for you. In whatever way you want, pause to adore Him. You can stand and look up; you can kneel with your head bowed; you can lie facedown; you can sing, speak aloud, or allow your thoughts to be turned into prayers of adoration: "Lord, thank You for coming to earth to save me. I worship You. I love You. I trust You. I desire Your sweet presence in my life." Let the meditation of your heart and the words of your mouth give praise and honor to the One who gave up everything for you. Come and adore Him.

Yours, O LORD, is the greatness, the power, the glory, the victory, and the majesty. Everything in the heavens and on earth is yours, O LORD, and this is your kingdom. We adore you as the one who is over all things.

1 CHRONICLES 29:11

December 16

A MASTERPIECE

Whether we are poets or parents or teachers or artists or gardeners, we must start where we are and use what we have. In the process of creation and relationship, what seems mundane and trivial may show itself to be a holy, precious part of a pattern.

Luci Shaw

You are My handiwork—created with purpose, gifted for service, and energized by My Spirit. You sometimes feel unimportant and believe the job you do doesn't have much meaning. You fight boredom and monotony and long for more excitement and fulfillment. In the middle of what feels like a mundane life, look for My unexpected surprises.

As you live by My principles and hide My Word in your heart, you'll discover holy moments in unforeseen, everyday places. It might be in the thanks you receive when you help someone in need, in preparing a meal for your loved ones, in the spectacular beauty of a sunrise, or in the laughter of a child at play. I made you new in My Son, Christ Jesus, and I want you to celebrate the masterpiece you are—no more complaining about what you look like, or pointing out your lack of achievements, or grumbling about your inability to get more done in a day. Breathe deeply and say, "I was made by God for His pleasure. I am His workmanship, and every day I am doing the things He planned for me to do." If you look for My hand at work in your daily activities, I will reveal holy moments of priceless value that will give meaning and joy to your life.

We are God's masterpiece. He has created us anew in Christ Jesus, so we can do the good things he planned for us long ago.

EPHESIANS 2:10

December 17

THE DECISION

As a matter of fact, God isn't asking you to *be* thankful. He's asking you to *give* thanks. There's a big difference. One response involves emotions, the other your choices, your decisions about a situation, your intent, your "step of faith."

Joni Eareckson Tada

My dear one, what will you do with your burdens today? You can choose dissatisfaction, bitterness, anger, or cynicism. Or you can look to Me and begin saying, "Thank you." Your emotions tempt you to enter into doubt, fear, or even despair—but your day will be better if you voice your gratefulness to Me. Begin listing everything you have to be thankful for—your daily bread, the air you breathe, the encouragement of friends, and the message of hope from My Word.

With your eyes wide open, express your appreciation for those things and many more. Now make the decision to thank Me for your pain, your challenges, your place of suffering, and the energy-depleting people in your life. Tell Me how these things have drawn you closer to Me. What have you learned? How have you applied My principles to these experiences? How have delayed answers to prayer drawn you deeper into My Word? How are you identifying with people who are walking a difficult path? Is your empathy greater? Do you weep with those who weep? How has the decision to be thankful in all circumstances changed your life for the better? These trials will soon be over. Give thanks!

I will give thanks to the LORD because of his righteousness;
I will sing the praises of the name of the LORD Most High.

PSALM 7:17, NIV

December 18

RELATIONSHIPS

I hope you will say YES to being uncomfortable. Say YES to that redeemable, uncomfortable person sitting in front of you.

Brooklyn Lindsey

Sometimes your most impossible situation is when a person you love is making wrong choices. As you repeatedly witness the negative results of his immoral thinking, bad behavior, disrespect of guidelines, and running away from Christian principles, you're very discouraged and incensed. At times you've called him out on his repeated disregard for everything that's important to you. You've even been unhappy with Me because you've asked Me to stop him in his tracks, turn him in the right direction, and force him to fall in line. Sometimes you've even tried to *be* Me in his life—but it hasn't worked.

You'll never be able to push him into changing for the better. It's your job to represent Me by exhibiting My love, My peace, and My perseverance. Instead of agonizing over what he's doing to himself and to your family, cover him with prayer. Be humble, gentle, and patient—especially when he makes you uncomfortable. There has never been a person who was not redeemable. Turn your churning emotions into songs of deliverance. Ask My Holy Spirit to give you a quiet heart, and then keep on loving that person. Unconditional love is hard to resist.

Always be humble and gentle. Be patient with each other, making allowance for each other's faults because of your love. Make every effort to keep yourselves united in the Spirit, binding yourselves together with peace.

EPHESIANS 4:2-3

— December 19 —

UNLIKELY CHANNELS

God wants us to relieve suffering, pursue justice, facilitate reconciliation, and free the heart to love, but He desires for us to do so in a way that reveals His Character. . . . We must do well in our unique way in order to reveal the vast creativity of a God who loves to bring change through the most unlikely channels.

Dan B. Allender

My heart is filled with tender love and compassion toward you. I know your journey has not been easy. You've compared your circumstances with those of others who have better health, supportive relationships, financial abundance, and unwavering belief, and your life appears to come up short. Your path has been tougher, more draining, and filled with unwanted obstacles. At times you've questioned why I've allowed you to struggle, but you've remained faithful to Me.

Precious one, you're learning the secret: I generously provide all you need—enough that you have "plenty left over to share with others" (2 Corinthians 9:8). As people receive your openhanded compassion, unconditional love, tangible support, and faith-infused words of comfort, direction, and encouragement, they see Me through your actions. Your weakness has become a platform for displaying My extravagant mercy to those recipients. Because you are an unlikely channel for My power, the world takes notice. Like the apostle Paul, your greatest weaknesses have produced profound results.

That's why I take pleasure in my weaknesses, and in the insults, hardships, persecutions, and troubles that I suffer for Christ. For when I am weak, then I am strong.

2 CORINTHIANS 12:10

December 20

A MARY HEART

[The] Mary-miracle approach to growth and victory isn't painless or problem-free—having babies never is. But it is alive and aglow, filled with joy. . . . God's surprise ways are superior to our best efforts at anything—even trying to live for Him.

Jack Hayford

I want you to have a heart like Mary's. When the angel Gabriel first announced to her that she was favored by Me and that she would give birth to a son and call Him Jesus, she was confused and frightened. This news was overwhelming to the young virgin Mary. Gabriel said, "The Holy Spirit will come upon you, and the power of the Most High will overshadow you. So the baby to be born will be holy, and he will be called the Son of God" (Luke 1:35).

Mary's response is the example I want you to follow. Without understanding all the details about what I was asking of her, she immediately said, "Let it be to me according to your word" (Luke 1:38, NKJV). There are often times when I ask you to do something way out of your comfort zone, or when I give you an assignment that feels formidable and beyond your experience or capabilities. As you put your complete trust in Me, I will continue to supply all the wisdom, provision, and stamina you need to accomplish My will. The birthing of new dreams, new ministries, and new spiritual adventures often begins with simple obedience—without seeing the end result. Sometimes it's painful, but it's always worth it. Nurture a Mary heart!

Mary responded, "I am the Lord's servant. May everything you have said about me come true." And then the angel left her.

LUKE 1:38

December 21

REJOICE

Rejoice? Why? you may ask. Because it's the only real way out. "This is the day the Lord has made," the psalmist tells us. "We will rejoice and be glad in it." This day? This messy, painful, frustrating day deserves a chance? Yes.

Max Lucado

You have struggled to find joy—always looking for a reason to change your outlook from gloom to happiness. Try something new. Start rejoicing exactly where you are right now—in your undesirable circumstances, in your far-from-perfect relationships, in your less-than-ideal job, and in your wavering faith-walk. It's hard to rejoice when you're hurting and everyone around you looks genuinely happy—even strangers expect to be greeted with a nod and a smile during this season of the year.

Remember what Paul said: *Always be full of joy in the Lord. I say it again—rejoice!* Let go of anxiety. Worry will not help your situation in any way. Start naming your blessings. Make thankfulness your default mind-set. You will soon discover that your list of blessings is longer than your list of worries. Allow your frustrations to be turned into prayers—and then leave them with Me. Anticipate celebrating the birth of My Son, Jesus, and prepare your heart for joy that will bubble up and overflow into the life of every person you'll spend time with this week. It pleases Me when you take great delight in remembering My Son's reason for coming to this earth. Rejoice!

Always be full of joy in the Lord. I say it again—rejoice!
Let everyone see that you are considerate in all you do.
Remember, the Lord is coming soon.

PHILIPPIANS 4:4–5

December 22

THE SHEPHERDS

Glory to God in the highest of heavens! And peace to the people with whom he is pleased! And who are these people? With whom does the good Lord choose to take his pleasure? The shepherds. The plain and nameless—whose every name the Lord knows very well. You. And me.

Walter Wangerin Jr.

Dear one, do you know how special you are to Me? Sometimes you pull away because you feel unworthy or unaccepted—but those feelings do not come from Me. The enemy wants you to feel unimportant and unqualified to give others the news of My Son's birth, death, and resurrection. If he succeeds, you withdraw from conversations that lead people to seriously consider the Good News of the gospel.

Think about those who tended the flocks on the night of Jesus' birth. These shepherds were not high-society people; they were not held in high esteem. They slept among the sheep and were regarded as lowly men, excluded from Temple worship because they were considered unclean. Their culture deemed them unworthy, but I chose them to be among the first to hear about the birth of Jesus. They are significant to Me—and so are you.

That night there were shepherds staying in the fields nearby, guarding their flocks of sheep. Suddenly, an angel of the Lord appeared among them, and the radiance of the Lord's glory surrounded them. They were terrified, but the angel reassured them. "Don't be afraid!" he said. "I bring you good news that will bring great joy to all people."

LUKE 2:8–10

— *December 25* —

THE BEST BIRTHDAY

Who can add to Christmas? The perfect motive is that God so loved the world. The perfect gift is that He gave His only Son. The only requirement is to believe in Him. The reward of faith is that you shall have everlasting life.

Attributed to Corrie ten Boom

Instead of letting yourself become frazzled and worn out with Christmas preparations, take time to contemplate what My Son, Jesus, did. He left the divine privileges of heaven to come to earth in a human form. He grew to manhood, and in complete obedience to Me willingly died a criminal's death on the cross for you. His birthday is cause for great celebration! My prophet Isaiah said it well: "For a child is born to us, a son is given to us. The government will rest on his shoulders. And he will be called: Wonderful Counselor, Mighty God, Everlasting Father, Prince of Peace" (Isaiah 9:6).

Today you will have many opportunities to celebrate—gathered with family and friends, eating together and exchanging gifts. Will you take time to thank Me for your best gift—Jesus? Will you remind everyone you see that it's Jesus' birthday? Will you spend time in My presence and consider what Jesus' coming means? Because He came, you have a glorious life awaiting you in a place with no pain, no fear, and no end. It's all because He came.

The Savior—yes, the Messiah, the Lord—
has been born today in Bethlehem, the city of David!

LUKE 2:11

My family has been a major support as I worked on the book. Thanks to my husband, Gene, for his help with household and ministry tasks while I wrote, for supplying me with lots of coffee, and for providing humorous breaks. Thanks too to my son, Jason, for his prayers and affirming words as this project became a reality. My mother, Pauline Afman, prayed for me every day, and my sisters and brother have been an ongoing source of joy.

Thank you to my friends, Lucinda Secrest McDowell, Jennifer Kennedy Dean, Wendy Lawton, and Cynthia Ruchti for praying over me and prayerfully lifting up this project when I first shared it with them. Thanks, too, to Sandi Banks, Kathy Blume, and countless friends for their ongoing prayers for Gene, Jason, and me. Your friendship and hands-on compassion bless us every day!

Most of all, thank You, Lord Jesus Christ, for holding my hand through these difficult years. You have comforted me with Your Word and given me fresh energy to speak and write, a renewed hope for each day, and a peace that endures.

SCRIPTURE INDEX

GENESIS 1:27
February 7

GENESIS 2:18
May 9

GENESIS 6:22
October 19

GENESIS 18:14
August 20

GENESIS 22:16-17
January 18

GENESIS 28:16
January 27
October 22

GENESIS 32:26-28
June 30

GENESIS 39:4-5
February 6

EXODUS 3:5
January 3

EXODUS 14:13
July 25

EXODUS 15:13
September 17

EXODUS 17:15
September 8

EXODUS 20:3
September 30

EXODUS 33:14
November 28

EXODUS 34:6-7
June 24

NUMBERS 6:24-26
October 19

NUMBERS 23:19
June 22

DEUTERONOMY 2:3
October 13

DEUTERONOMY 6:6-7
May 27

DEUTERONOMY 31:6
June 17

DEUTERONOMY 31:8
July 25
July 30

DEUTERONOMY 32:3
March 1

DEUTERONOMY 33:27
October 11

JOSHUA 1:9
June 17

JOSHUA 4:6-7
July 16

JOSHUA 5:14
August 29

JOSHUA 14:8
April 20

1 SAMUEL 2:2
April 2

2 SAMUEL 11:27
July 4

2 SAMUEL 22:7
December 12

2 SAMUEL 22:31
August 14

1 CHRONICLES 4:10
September 28

1 CHRONICLES 29:11
December 15

2 CHRONICLES 7:14
May 10

2 CHRONICLES 20:6
July 14

2 CHRONICLES 20:17
July 14

2 CHRONICLES 20:21
July 14

ESTHER 4:14
September 16

JOB 2:9-10
October 21

JOB 8:21
September 18

JOB 13:15
November 18

JOB 17:11
March 15

PSALM 1:3
August 9

PSALM 4:8
November 14

PSALM 5:3
November 25

PSALM 5:11
January 26

PSALM 6:7
August 7

PSALM 7:17
December 17

PSALM 9:2-3
December 13

PSALM 10:1
June 15

PSALM 11:7
August 8

PSALM 16:8
October 15

PSALM 16:11
January 27

PSALM 18:2
April 2
June 4
November 6
November 29

PSALM 18:30
April 23

PSALM 18:35
December 29

PSALM 19:1
July 17

PSALM 23:1
August 24

PSALM 23:1, 4
March 4

PSALM 23:2
February 28

PSALM 23:3
May 22

PSALM 23:5
November 23

PSALM 23:6
October 16

PSALM 25:5
August 31

PSALM 25:10
August 6

PSALM 27:1
January 13
June 17

PSALM 27:4-5
September 7

PSALM 27:5
May 14

PSALM 28:2
May 23

PSALM 28:7
October 1

PSALM 30:5
January 26
March 23

PSALM 30:10
May 12

PSALM 31:7
November 16

PSALM 31:15
March 18

PSALM 31:19
July 1

PSALM 31:24
January 29

PSALM 32:7
September 7
December 11

PSALM 32:8
January 11

PSALM 33:1
April 8

PSALM 33:9
June 26

PSALM 33:11
September 13

PSALM 34:3
December 13

PSALM 34:7
October 17

PSALM 34:15
November 10

PSALM 34:18
March 15

PSALM 37:3-7
April 27

PSALM 37:4
March 30
April 27

PSALM 37:23
March 22
May 24
July 9

PSALM 37:23-24
May 16

PSALM 38:9
January 16

PSALM 40:2
June 21

PSALM 40:3
March 9

PSALM 40:5
April 19
September 13

PSALM 40:8
September 6

PSALM 40:10
December 31

PSALM 42:9
April 11

PSALM 42:11
April 11

PSALM 46:1
October 4

PSALM 46:2
October 17

PSALM 46:10
January 17
September 15

PSALM 50:10
January 23

PSALM 50:15
December 12

PSALM 51:6
February 27

PSALM 51:7
June 27

PSALM 51:10
January 1

PSALM 51:12
May 22

PSALM 51:17
March 15
September 3
November 11

PSALM 54:4
May 12

PSALM 56:3
October 17

PSALM 56:8
March 23

PSALM 57:1
December 11

PSALM 57:2
November 3

PSALM 61:2
April 2

PSALM 62:7
October 4

PSALM 63:1
June 1
June 28
October 3

PSALM 63:3-4
May 15

PSALM 63:6
December 28

PSALM 63:8
February 17

PSALM 65:5
May 23

PSALM 68:4-5
May 4

PSALM 71:23
November 19

PSALM 73:23-24
March 18

PSALM 73:25
August 18

PSALM 78:4
May 8

PSALM 81:6
January 24

PSALM 86:11
November 21

PSALM 89:14
August 8

PSALM 90:10
October 7

PSALM 90:12
October 7

PSALM 90:14
October 7

PSALM 91:1-2
March 12

PSALM 91:11
February 1

PSALM 92:1-2
February 3

PSALM 95:6
August 13

PSALM 96:1
March 9

PSALM 97:1
July 19

PSALM 100:1-2, 4
April 8

PSALM 100:1-3
January 19

PSALM 103:11
June 6

PSALM 103:19
July 13

PSALM 108:1
December 6

PSALM 111:7-8
August 17

PSALM 111:10
August 30

PSALM 112:1
July 18

PSALM 118:7
August 10

PSALM 118:24
July 3

PSALM 119:11
March 16

PSALM 119:15
May 20

PSALM 119:15-16
October 28

PSALM 119:16
June 11

PSALM 119:35
June 10

PSALM 119:55
October 10

PSALM 119:68
July 1

PSALM 119:81
April 6
August 7

PSALM 119:92-93
August 30

PSALM 119:114
November 26

PSALM 119:135
October 19

PSALM 125:1
September 15

PSALM 136:1
August 26

PSALM 138:8
January 11
September 13

PSALM 139:7-10
December 7

PSALM 139:9-10
April 17

PSALM 139:13-14, 17-18
February 12

PSALM 139:14
April 4
June 18

PSALM 139:23
June 1

PSALM 139:23-24
February 22
November 4

PSALM 141:8, 10
May 14

PSALM 142:1-2
October 8

PSALM 145:5
March 1

PSALM 145:6-7
March 1

PSALM 145:7
November 7

PSALM 145:17
August 15

PSALM 145:21
March 1

PSALM 147:3
November 4

PSALM 150:1-2, 6
May 15

PROVERBS 2:7-8
June 5

PROVERBS 2:10-11
May 25

PROVERBS 3:5-6
March 14

PROVERBS 4:10-13
June 16

PROVERBS 4:11-12
October 18

PROVERBS 4:23
February 25

PROVERBS 8:11
January 21

PROVERBS 10:25
April 15
September 10

PROVERBS 11:13
July 8

PROVERBS 11:25
March 27

PROVERBS 13:12
January 4

PROVERBS 15:15
June 10

PROVERBS 15:23
December 5

PROVERBS 16:3
November 20

PROVERBS 16:18
September 3

PROVERBS 16:24
February 24
December 5

PROVERBS 16:28
July 8

PROVERBS 17:22
March 29

PROVERBS 18:10
October 4
October 27

PROVERBS 18:19
December 10

PROVERBS 18:21
February 24

PROVERBS 18:24
December 10

PROVERBS 19:11
February 19
May 7

PROVERBS 19:23
November 14

PROVERBS 22:4
May 10

PROVERBS 23:7
April 22
May 20

MATTHEW 6:33
February 2
April 18

MATTHEW 7:7
September 22

MATTHEW 7:7-8
January 2

MATTHEW 9:20-21
July 29

MATTHEW 9:33
August 1

MATTHEW 9:36
January 10

MATTHEW 9:37-38
October 20

MATTHEW 11:28
January 23
February 28

MATTHEW 11:28-29
April 6

MATTHEW 15:31
August 1

MATTHEW 16:24
March 2

MATTHEW 17:20
September 27

MATTHEW 18:4
September 3

MATTHEW 18:21-22
July 11

MATTHEW 19:14
October 23

MATTHEW 19:26
August 19

MATTHEW 20:26
May 31

MATTHEW 25:21
October 18

MATTHEW 25:35-36
April 14

MATTHEW 27:46
March 31
April 11

MATTHEW 28:20
November 23

MARK 1:35
April 6
November 15

MARK 4:2
April 21

MARK 4:35-41
April 15

MARK 5:42
August 1

MARK 8:34
October 6

MARK 9:41
June 19

MARK 10:27
December 27

MARK 12:29-31
August 21

MARK 13:33
December 28

MARK 14:36
September 5

MARK 14:38
March 16

LUKE 1:35
December 20

LUKE 1:37
June 23

LUKE 1:38
December 20

LUKE 1:50
September 1

LUKE 1:78
May 26

LUKE 2:7
December 24

LUKE 2:8-10
December 22

LUKE 2:11
December 25

LUKE 2:13-14
December 23

LUKE 4:18-19
July 31

LUKE 5:26
August 1

LUKE 9:16-17
October 14

LUKE 9:23-24
May 30

LUKE 10:27
July 18

LUKE 10:42
January 30

LUKE 12:34
May 13

LUKE 15:10
June 21

LUKE 15:21-24
October 29

LUKE 16:10
June 19

LUKE 21:1-4
December 2

LUKE 21:19
March 24

LUKE 21:26-28
October 17

LUKE 21:27-28
September 14

JOHN 1:16
September 9

JOHN 1:39
August 28

JOHN 3:16
May 28

JOHN 3:30
May 3

JOHN 4:9-10
June 14

JOHN 4:14
April 30

JOHN 7:37
April 30

JOHN 7:38
April 30

JOHN 8:31
October 6

JOHN 9:4
October 7

JOHN 10:27
March 7
June 28

JOHN 10:28-29
March 18

JOHN 11:25
April 16

JOHN 13:34-35
January 22

JOHN 13:35
February 14

JOHN 14:1
March 5

JOHN 14:2-3
May 19

JOHN 14:6
February 27
May 6

JOHN 14:26
August 16

JOHN 14:27
March 5

JOHN 15:2
April 25

JOHN 15:4
January 25
June 25

JOHN 15:11
March 29

JOHN 15:16
June 7

JOHN 16:33
April 9
May 11
June 13

JOHN 20:25
December 1

JOHN 20:27
July 24

JOHN 20:27-28
December 1

JOHN 20:29
December 1

ACTS 1:8
July 31

ACTS 3:20
March 27

ACTS 4:12
May 6

ACTS 4:13
February 18

ACTS 26:17-18
February 4

ROMANS 1:16
August 23

ROMANS 1:20
September 4

ROMANS 3:24
June 24

ROMANS 5:3-4
July 10

ROMANS 5:17
February 11

ROMANS 8:5-6
April 22

ROMANS 8:21
August 27

ROMANS 8:23
October 8

ROMANS 8:26
August 16

ROMANS 8:28
June 9

ROMANS 8:29
June 9

ROMANS 8:37
September 8

ROMANS 8:38
August 24

ROMANS 10:17
January 15

ROMANS 12:2
August 3

ROMANS 12:5
April 3

ROMANS 12:10
June 29

ROMANS 12:11-12
April 24

ROMANS 12:13
March 26

ROMANS 12:18
August 5

ROMANS 13:12
February 23

ROMANS 15:13
January 14

I CORINTHIANS 1:18
April 9

I CORINTHIANS 2:9
March 6
May 19

I CORINTHIANS 6:19-20
November 30

I CORINTHIANS 9:25
April 26

I CORINTHIANS 10:13
March 16
April 13

I CORINTHIANS 11:23-25
May 18

I CORINTHIANS 12:4
August 25

I CORINTHIANS 12:11
August 25

I CORINTHIANS 13:8
May 28

I CORINTHIANS 13:12
April 16
June 15

1 CORINTHIANS 13:13
April 16

1 CORINTHIANS 15:10
March 11

1 CORINTHIANS 15:14, 17
May 6

1 CORINTHIANS 15:57
September 8

1 CORINTHIANS 16:13
March 24

1 CORINTHIANS 16:18
November 24

2 CORINTHIANS 1:4
April 28

2 CORINTHIANS 1:9
November 6

2 CORINTHIANS 1:20
March 10

2 CORINTHIANS 1:22
September 2

2 CORINTHIANS 2:14
May 17
August 10

2 CORINTHIANS 3:3
April 5

2 CORINTHIANS 3:17
February 10

2 CORINTHIANS 3:18
October 10

2 CORINTHIANS 4:5
May 31

2 CORINTHIANS 4:7
July 28

2 CORINTHIANS 4:8-9
October 21

2 CORINTHIANS 4:10
November 18

2 CORINTHIANS 4:15
July 26

2 CORINTHIANS 4:16
July 21

2 CORINTHIANS 4:16-18
March 8

2 CORINTHIANS 4:17
July 15

2 CORINTHIANS 5:8
November 2

2 CORINTHIANS 5:17
September 26

2 CORINTHIANS 5:20
September 21

2 CORINTHIANS 6:10
January 31

2 CORINTHIANS 6:18
September 5

2 CORINTHIANS 8:9
June 25

2 CORINTHIANS 9:7
May 13

2 CORINTHIANS 9:8
December 19

2 CORINTHIANS 10:4-5
August 10

2 CORINTHIANS 10:5
January 29

2 CORINTHIANS 12:7
July 21

2 CORINTHIANS 12:9
March 28

2 CORINTHIANS 12:10
March 28
December 19

GALATIANS 5:1
February 10

GALATIANS 5:22-23
May 21

GALATIANS 6:2
April 10
October 21

GALATIANS 6:4
October 31

GALATIANS 6:17
July 24

EPHESIANS 1:4
June 7

HEBREWS 12:1-2
April 9

HEBREWS 12:2
March 6

HEBREWS 12:3
March 20

HEBREWS 12:12-13
June 8
August 7

HEBREWS 13:2
February 1

HEBREWS 13:5
May 9
December 10

HEBREWS 13:6
May 12

HEBREWS 13:8
August 3

HEBREWS 13:15
January 6
November 22

HEBREWS 13:21
February 13

JAMES 1:3-4
May 1

JAMES 1:5
January 21

JAMES 1:5-6
January 9

JAMES 1:12
March 24

JAMES 1:13
March 16

JAMES 1:17
July 1

JAMES 3:13
May 10

JAMES 3:17
March 17

JAMES 4:7
August 22

JAMES 4:7-10
May 5

JAMES 4:8
March 31
May 29

JAMES 5:11
October 30

JAMES 5:16
March 21
May 23
December 27

I PETER 1:3
March 17

I PETER 1:3-5
March 8

I PETER 1:4
April 5

I PETER 1:6-7
May 1

I PETER 1:9
June 26

I PETER 1:13
February 19

I PETER 1:14-15
October 24

I PETER 2:9
April 29
May 15

I PETER 2:9-10
July 2

I PETER 2:12
June 5

I PETER 2:21
December 9

I PETER 2:24
July 24

I PETER 4:9
March 26

I PETER 4:10
August 25

I PETER 4:12-13
September 23

I PETER 4:13
July 15

I PETER 5:6
September 3

1 PETER 5:7
November 16

1 PETER 5:8
November 9

1 PETER 5:10
May 22

2 PETER 1:4
September 11

2 PETER 1:5-6
July 23

1 JOHN 1:7
March 13

1 JOHN 1:9
June 20

1 JOHN 3:14
August 21

1 JOHN 4:18
February 8

1 JOHN 5:14
February 16

1 JOHN 5:14-15
December 14

2 JOHN 1:6
February 9
February 14

JUDE 1:2
September 9

REVELATION 1:5
May 28

REVELATION 1:7
August 27

REVELATION 1:8
August 20

REVELATION 2:4
November 12

REVELATION 15:4
July 26

REVELATION 17:14
June 7

REVELATION 20:10
August 22

REVELATION 21:1-2, 5
July 17

REVELATION 21:4-5
March 23

REVELATION 22:20
August 27